THE PALESTINIAN EXODUS

1948–1998

EDITED BY

GHADA KARMI

AND

EUGENE COTRAN

THE PALESTINIAN EXODUS
1948–1998

Ithaca Press is an imprint of Garnet Publishing Limited

Published by
Garnet Publishing Limited
8 Southern Court
South Street
Reading
RG1 4QS
UK

First Edition

ISBN 0 86372 244 X

British Library Cataloguing-in-Publication Data
A catalogue record for this book is available from the British Library

Jacket design by David Rose
Typeset by Samantha Abley

Printed in Lebanon

THE
PALESTINIAN
EXODUS

1948–1998

Contents

List of Maps, Tables, Aerial Photographs and Figures   vii

List of Contributors   ix

Foreword *Ian Gilmour*   xi

Preface *Ghada Karmi*   xix

Acknowledgements   xxiii

Introduction *Eugene Cotran*   1

PART I
HISTORY OF THE EXODUS 1948–1998

1 Palestinians in Exile: Legal, Geographical and Statistical Aspects
Marie-Louise Weighill   7

2 Were They Expelled?: The History, Historiography and Relevance of the Palestinian Refugee Problem
Ilan Pappe   37

3 The 1967 Palestinian Exodus
Nur Masalha   63

4 The Continuing Exodus – the Ongoing Expulsion of Palestinians from Jerusalem
Leah Tsemel   111

Part II
Solutions:
The Right of Return, Compensation
and Reconciliation

5   The Right of Return in International Law   123
     Anis Al-Qasem

6   The Right of Displaced Palestinians to Return to   151
     Home Areas in Israel
     John Quigley

7   The Feasibility of the Right of Return   171
     Salman Abu-Sitta

8   The Question of Compensation and Reparations   197
     Ghada Karmi

9   Truth, Justice and Reconciliation: Elements of a   221
     Solution to the Palestinian Refugee Issue
     Rashid Khalidi

     Concluding Vision: A Return to Israel/Palestine?   243
     Ghada Karmi

     Select Bibliography   253
     Index   257

Maps, Tables,
Aerial Photographs and Figures

MAP

7.1   Population Concentration in the Proposed Return Plan   182

TABLES

1.1   Jordan: UNRWA Camps and Registered Refugees   17
       (with distribution map)
1.2   Lebanon: UNRWA Camps and Registered Refugees   19
       (with distribution map)
1.3   Syria: UNRWA Camps and Registered Refugees   22
       (with distribution map)
1.4   West Bank: UNRWA Camps and Registered Refugees   23
       (with distribution map)
1.5   Gaza: UNRWA Camps and Registered Refugees   25
       (with distribution map)
7.1   Summary of the Return Plan   184
7.2   New Water Requirement with and without the   188
       Return Plan

AERIAL PHOTOGRAPHS

7.1   Ramleh   175
7.2   Bureir   176
7.3   Al Ma'in   177
7.4   Deir Yassin   178
7.5   Emmaus   179

FIGURES

1.1   Distribution of Palestinians   15

Contributors

Eugene Cotran is a circuit judge in England and Chairman of the Centre of Islamic and Middle Eastern Law at the School of Oriental and African Studies, University of London.

Marie-Louise Weighill is a researcher at The Refugee Studies Programme, Queen Elizabeth House, Oxford.

Ilan Pappe is Professor of Political Science at the Department of Political Science, University of Haifa, Israel.

Nur Masalha is Lecturer in Middle East Politics at Richmond College, The American International University in London, and Honorary Fellow at the Centre of Middle Eastern and Islamic Studies, University of Durham, England.

Leah Tsemel is a civil rights lawyer in Jerusalem.

Anis Al-Qasem is an international lawyer based in London.

John Quigley is Professor of Law at Ohio State University, USA.

Salman Abu-Sitta is a civil engineer based in Kuwait. He is also a member of the Palestine National Council.

Ghada Karmi is Research Associate at the Centre of Near and Middle Eastern Studies at the School of Oriental and African Studies, University of London.

Rashid Khalidi is Professor of Middle Eastern History and Director of the Centre for International Studies at the University of Chicago, USA.

Foreword

The State of Israel was founded in 1948 on force and violence. That was not particularly remarkable. What was highly unusual, though, was that Israel was also founded on a crime and a lie, or rather on two crimes and a lie. The first crime was the expulsion from their homes of some 750,000 Palestinians – 90 per cent of the Arabs living in the territory that became the Jewish state, or 50 per cent of the entire Arab population of mandatory Palestine. The second crime was the Israeli refusal to allow them to return. The lie was the denial of the first crime, coupled with the pretence that the refugees had not been evicted by the Israelis but had left of their own accord, having allegedly been encouraged to do so by Arab broadcasts telling them to leave. In reality no such Arab broadcasts were made. Instead, Arab leaders continually told the Palestinians to stay where they were; and the departure of only ten per cent of the refugees was in any sense voluntary.

The first President of Israel, Chaim Weizmann, called the Arab exodus "a miraculous clearing of the land". There was, of course, nothing miraculous about it. The exodus was the result of ruthless "ethnic cleansing", much more extensive though less bloody than that recently carried out in Yugoslavia. Weizmann himself had long hoped to make Palestine "as Jewish as England is English", and the two crimes of 1948–9 and the lie – a continuing lie, as the distinguished Israeli historian Ilan Pappe shows here in his remarkable essay – were the fulfilment of a long-held Zionist ambition. "Transfer", the Zionist euphemism for the expulsion of the Arab population of Palestine, was integral to Zionism from the start because the movement's most popular and persuasive slogan – Israel Zangwill's "a people without a land to a land without a people" – was an earlier lie. Palestine was a land with a people who had lived there for centuries; Zangwill later admitted that parts of Palestine were "already twice as thickly populated as the US". Yet the crucial fact that Palestine already belonged to another people was no deterrent to Zangwill or other Zionists trying to take it for themselves. Zangwill evolved what Nur Masalha, who by his persistent and illuminating research has done more than anybody to reveal the pervasive continuity of "transfer" in Zionist thought and action, calls in this book "the racist notion of an empty territory". There was, Zangwill wrote, "no Arab people living in intimate fusion with the country . . . there is at best an Arab encampment". In other words, the Arabs were an inferior people who did not deserve to live in Palestine and who could be treated in whichever way best suited Zionist convenience.

Arab possession of Palestine precluded the Zionist project from being the attempted colonisation of a deserted country; the project was therefore the conversion – or transfer – of Arab land to Jewish land and the substitution, locally, of a Jewish population for an Arab one. "We came here to this country which was settled by Arabs, and we are building a Jewish State", Moshe Dayan famously said in 1969; "there is not one single place built in this country that did not have a former Arab population." And the culmination of all those local "transfers" of Arabs from their land was the national "transfer" of most of them from their country in 1948–9. Since Palestine was not a deserted country, the Zionists had to force the Arabs to desert it.

Zionism differed from most other modern European imperialisms. These, which, however fitfully, had as one of their ambitions the improvement of the living conditions of the original inhabitants, usually involved merely the insertion of a ruling class or regime into the conquered country. In contrast, the Zionists aimed to insert an entirely new population of their own people and had little consideration for the rightful inhabitants of Palestine. Of course there always were some humane and exceptional Jewish immigrants, beginning with Ahad Ha'am who in the 1890s denounced the Zionist settlers' cruelty to the Arab peasants. Today Leah Tsemel is a notable representative of that noble tradition, but such people have always been a small minority. According to George Steiner, "Zionism was created by Jewish nationalists who drew their inspiration from Bismarck and followed a Prussian model." Later Zionists have come closer, though, to following an American model: the US treatment of the Red Indians. (As the United States was in no way to blame for the Holocaust and was solely responsible for the persecution of the Red Indians, the efficiency of which was much admired by Adolf Hitler, Washington had a far greater need of a museum for the Red Indians than one for the Holocaust).

If a colonist's ultimate objective is to remove the native inhabitants from their country, he has little incentive to treat them well before he does so. On the contrary, ill-treatment may well encourage them to depart. In any case, 1948–9 proved to be only the first and worst of the expulsions.

After 1948, however, the Israeli authorities initially concentrated on removing land from the few Arabs who had remained rather than removing the Arabs themselves from the country. This process was described by an Israeli journalist in *Haaretz* as "wholesale robbery in legal guise"; between 1948 and 1990 Israeli Arabs were despoiled of almost one million acres of their land. 1956 nearly saw a second wave of refugees. The massacre of 49 Arab civilians, including 16 women and children, at Kfar Qassim in October 1956 was linked to a plan to expel over 40,000 Israeli Arab citizens from the Little Triangle. The plan was abandoned when Israel decided to attack Egypt, not Jordan. Even so, Yitzhak Rabin then expelled between three and five thousand Arab villagers to Syria.

1967 brought another war, started by Israel, and the next big wave of expulsions. After the war, some 430,000 Palestinians were removed from the West Bank and Gaza Strip. Once again, the bogus claim was made that they had left of their own accord. (In 1967 I saw some of the refugees trudging across the Allenby Bridge with what they could carry of their possessions on their backs. Their departure was plainly not voluntary.) After 1967 deportations continued, but on a much less spectacular scale and usually of local leaders. In general, Israel relied on a cruel, discriminatory and illegal occupation to keep the Palestinians in submission and encourage them to leave. Hence, virtually nothing was done to improve economic conditions. Indeed Sara Roy, herself the daughter of Holocaust survivors, has written of the "de-development" of Gaza by the Israelis, and Israeli journalists have expressed shame that relatively impoverished Jordan treated its Palestinians so much better than did Israel, inundated with American dollars. Not surprisingly, probably some 300,000 people, or about 20 per cent of the population of the West Bank and the Gaza Strip, emigrated between 1967 and 1990.

Nevertheless, the ambition of many Israelis to achieve a forcible and more spectacular "transfer" of the remaining Palestinians was not concealed. In 1980 the Israeli journalist, Ammon Kapeliouk, described as "horrific" the "final solution" to the Palestinian problem being entertained by many high-ranking Israeli officials, while a Labour Member of the Knesset thought the idea of "transferring" the Palestinians to Arab countries was comparable to the expulsion of the Jews from Spain by the Spanish Inquisition in the fifteenth century. Israel is often called the only democracy in the Middle East, but its treatment of the Palestinians has seldom been remotely democratic. In any other genuinely democratic country the Likud and some of its allies would not be considered democratic parties. "Transfer" is therefore still far from unthinkable to many Israelis. In 1989, Binyamin Netanyahu publicly regretted that the Israeli government had not used the diversion of the Chinese massacre in Tiananmen Square to carry out "large-scale" expulsions of Palestinians.

All the same, as Leah Tsemel shows in her brief and compelling essay, Israeli governments have done much to displace Palestinians from Jerusalem, using methods from which even the former apartheid government of South Africa might have recoiled. At the same time, governments of both Israel's main parties have continued to steal more and more Palestinian land to erect their illegal and unsightly settlements.

Yet, even more remarkable than the depths to which so many Israeli politicians have sunk and are still prepared to sink is their ability to get away with behaviour which, in any other country, would have attracted almost universal censure and reprisals. Their ruthlessness has continued, virtually unimpeded by the Arab states, the international community, America or Europe. In his eloquent essay, Rashid Khalidi touches on the reasons for Israeli success and Palestinian failure, and for the Palestinians' both losing most of their country, and being reduced to becoming refugees. As he says, Palestinian leaders had a record of "massive political failures in the decades preceding 1948". And, since 1948, the leaders of other Arab countries have notched up many further failures. The record of the Palestinian leadership has been little better. Professor Pappe delicately refers to "the mis-policy of Arafat in the Gulf crisis", by which he means the PLO's senseless and disgraceful support of Saddam Hussein's invasion of Kuwait. That was an inexcusable and costly blunder, while the Oslo Agreement was negotiated by the Palestinian side with astonishing ineptitude.

Of the outsiders, Britain was, of course, the original culprit. It can be given to few Foreign Secretaries to be the cause of five wars (with probably more to come), countless massacres and a tragic diaspora. Arthur Balfour had had intimate experience of the trouble caused by the clash of nationalisms in Ireland; yet, though warned by Curzon of the likely consequences of imposing heavy Jewish immigration on a country already populated by Arabs, Balfour, with frivolous insouciance, introduced a similar conflict into Palestine. His Declaration, which was the outcome of assiduous lobbying by Chaim Weizmann, was disastrous not only for the indigenous Palestinian population but for British interests too.

During the last 50 years, the chief culprit has been the United States. America's Middle East policy has been corrupted by Zionism, or by what Gore Vidal calls "the serene corruption of American politics". Yet while that corruption is serene enough for both the corrupter and the corrupted, for the victims, as Vidal well realises, it is far from serene; it is squalid and disastrous. Corruption in this context means, of course, that US policy has been determined not by sober considerations of America's national interests, justice or human rights, but by the strength of the pro-Israeli pressure groups and by the Republican and Democratic parties' pursuit of votes and money. Hence, Congress has long been Israeli-occupied territory and, under Clinton, so has the White House. To make matters worse, the American press and the literary establishment are similarly influenced. Much of what leading US columnists write about the Middle East should not appear in the editorial pages; it would be more appropriately placed as advertisements for and by the government of Israel. A number of American Presidents and Secretaries of State have complained at one time or another (usually, but not always, in their memoirs) of the strength of the Israel lobby. Such complainants include Truman, Dulles, Nixon and Reagan, yet the first and last President consistently to stand up to Israel was Eisenhower.

So strong is the lobby and so weak are US politicians that for the last 30 years Israel has effectively controlled American policy in the Middle East. It has not, of course, controlled every move of American policy. Some – but not all – administrations have tried to escape Israeli dominance or become exasperated with it. But in the end their attempts to escape fail and their exasperation comes to nothing. Hence, the hypocrisy of US policy has been unbounded: strong condemnation of apartheid in South Africa, while bankrolling it in Palestine.

There is, of course, no doubt that Israel is an apartheid state. Ninety-two per cent of the land of Israel proper and 70 per cent of the West Bank are officially designated for the benefit of Jews alone, while Palestinians are prohibited from benefiting from those lands. Jews are given financial inducements to settle on land stolen from the Palestinians – Israel Shahak, the noted Israeli defender of human rights, has wondered "what would be the reaction of the US Jews if plans for the Christianisation of New York, or even only of Brooklyn" were proposed for their country. By this wholesale robbery, the West Bank has been effectively dismembered and Palestinians forced into ever-diminishing and disconnected areas.

Inability to understand the extent of Israel's control over US policy has led to expensive mistakes by Arab leaders. Thus Anwar Sadat, with his fatuous talk of "my friend Henry [Kissinger]", misguidedly thought that the US would intervene to help him. Less excusably, Yasser Arafat seems to have made the same mistake with President Clinton – less excusably because, of all the pro-Israeli US administrations during the period covered by this book, the Clinton–Gore administration has been even more craven and corrupt than its predecessors and the one most ignominiously in thrall to Israel. In consequence, even though according to Martin Indyk, as quoted by Rashid Khalidi, the US provides Israel with $13 billion annually in "US loans, grants and loan guarantees", and though Netanyahu is distrusted by nearly all his cabinet and is disbelieved in most other countries, the American government has allowed him to do largely what he likes.

Leah Tsemel argues strongly that the Palestinian Authority needs to develop a realistic strategy to counter the latest Israeli attempt at ethnic cleansing: the efforts to denude Jerusalem of its Palestinians. She is right, of course. But a realistic strategy is needed for the rest of Palestine too, and the Arab states also need to play a part, as does Europe. Otherwise, the next five years will be as bleak for the Palestinians as have been the last 50. At present, Israeli policy is to solidify its apartheid regime, under which the Palestinians will probably not even be allowed "bantustans" but will be confined to "Indian reservations". And subjection to apartheid may not be their worst fate. Until or unless there is a just peace, there will always be the possibility of a further expulsion, of further Israeli crimes and yet more lies. Curiously enough, Israel too needs a just peace. For, unless there is at least the semblance of one, apartheid, further expulsions and lies may well be successful at the time, but are unlikely to ensure its long-term survival. At present, though, such a peace is not in sight.

Ian Gilmour

Preface

In the 50-year long history of the conflict between Israel and the Palestinians, it is fair to say that no issue has been as important or as intractable as that of the refugees created by that conflict. The expulsion, either directly or by coercion, of three-quarters of a million Palestinians at the hands of Jewish and subsequently Israeli forces, starting in 1947, has left an indelible legacy of hostility and bitterness. This has been exacerbated by two factors: first, that the expulsions were repeated during the Arab–Israeli War of 1967 and again in the current "ethnic cleansing" of Jerusalem; and second, by the fact of Israel's persistent denial of responsibility for them. This denial is eloquently expressed in its refusal so far to pay compensation or make reparations to the dispossessed Palestinians.

The Palestinian sense of grievance at this behaviour was given a concrete basis from the start by the international community's support for their case. Throughout this book, the reader will find reiterations of the text of UN General Assembly Resolution 194, passed in December 1948, as well as repeated reference to the Fourth Geneva Convention and to the UN Declaration of Human Rights. All three, but especially the first, affirm the legal right of the displaced Palestinians to repatriation. The repetition of these references in the book is not due to a paucity of new ideas on the subject nor to any desire on the part of the authors to copy each other but rather to the fact that these remain the legal backbone of the Palestinian case, testimony to an international consensus on its rights and wrongs. Moreover, none of these resolutions and covenants has ceased to be operative; they remain as valid in international law today as they were in 1948. Although the most relevant of them, UN Resolution 194, which specifically rules on the right of Palestinians to return and to compensation, has never been implemented, it is still on the statute books. Indeed it can only be revoked by the body which created it, and this, despite Israeli and American efforts in that direction after the signing of the Oslo Accords in 1993, has not yet happened.

It is this basis in legality which gives the Palestinian case its strength. Despite repeated attempts at obfuscating the facts – by deliberate historical distortion (all ably dealt with in some of the essays which follow); by Israel's contended claims for the Jews who came from Arab countries (irrelevant to the Palestinian claims against Israel); or by recently trying to confine the issue within the limited bounds of the Oslo Accords – the basic, international, legal underpinning to the Palestinian right to return and to compensation remains unaltered. And indeed these rights cannot be superseded by a new Palestinian–Israeli agreement which does not take them into account. It is true, as several writers point out, that the Oslo agreement provided for a discussion of the refugee issue as part of the final status talks. But it is also clear that Israel has no intention of repatriating the refugees within its territory or of offering them compensation. Even if it contributed to an international compensation fund for the refugees, as has sometimes been mooted, this would be a minor contribution and would in no way be sufficient to make up for the tremendous human and material losses incurred by the dispossessed Palestinians and which Israel is morally bound to honour. Thus, any agreement stemming from the Oslo process which was predicated on these lines would inevitably ignore Palestinian rights as enshrined in UN resolutions.

And if an agreement which overrode international law in this way were drawn up and allowed to stand, then a dangerous precedent would have been created. It would seriously call into question the value and status of international agreements and undermine the standing of international law. If the latter means anything in the context of Iraqi violations of UN resolutions or of the agreements over Bosnia, both of which are current preoccupations on the international stage, then it must apply in equal measure to the case of Israel and the Palestinians. Otherwise, the UN has little credibility and international law would become a parody to be exploited and abused by whoever is the stronger party. For these reasons alone, and irrespective of the particular case which forms the subject of our book, this must not be allowed to happen.

As for the dispossessed Palestinians, the great danger they face today is that their leadership, negotiating from a position of weakness relative to Israel's strength and the Western support which underpins it, may be tempted to concur with agreements imposed on them and be favourable to Israel. There is evidence that other parties, external to the conflict, as some of the essays in this collection mention, have been persuaded to adopt the Israeli view that the return of the refugees to pre-1967 Israel is non-negotiable and they must be resettled forever elsewhere. It would be a great tragedy if this were allowed to happen. Not only would it be a gross betrayal of the norms of law and natural justice, but it would also leave an indelible legacy of hatred and resentment against Israelis and their descendants.

The final essay of this book seeks to avoid such an outcome. It proposes a solution which may seem utopian, but which is perhaps the only rational option that now remains. By reviving the concept of a single secular state which will be home to the two peoples, it underlines the fact, unpalatable to Israelis, that their brand of ethnic nationalism provides no basis for a permanent and equitable resolution of the crisis. Equally unpalatably, it demonstrates to Palestinians that the only path for the effective restitution of their outraged rights lies in a compromise which will deny them the opportunity to express their own separate nationalism.

Yet today, after 50 years of strife, there is no other way if political realities are to be accepted and historic wrongs are to be reversed.

Ghada Karmi

Acknowledgements

Our thanks are due to the International Campaign for Jerusalem (ICJ) and to the Centre of Islamic and Middle Eastern Law (CIMEL) at the School of Oriental and African Studies, University of London, for supporting the conference which was the basis for the present book. The ICJ was also responsible for generously funding the conference and the initial preparation for the book, for which we are most grateful.

We would also like to extend special thanks to Deborah Owen for her editorial assistance.

The Editors

Introduction

On 17 May 1997, the International Campaign for Jerusalem (ICJ) and the Centre of Islamic and Middle Eastern Law at the School of Oriental and African Studies (SOAS), University of London jointly convened a conference entitled "The Palestinians: A Continuing Exodus 1948–1997". This book consists of the papers presented at the conference, with two additional contributions from John Quigley (Chapter 6) and Rashid Khalidi (Chapter 9).

In Part I, the papers deal with the statistics, geography and history of the exodus from 1948 to 1997. Marie-Louise Weighill (Chapter 1) explores key aspects of the socio-economic, legal and political situation of the Palestinian refugees, the distribution of the refugees in the diaspora and especially in the neighbouring Arab countries and the problem of *tawteen* (adoption of new citizenship).

In Chapter 2, Ilan Pappe deals with the contemporary implications generated by the historiographical debate on the Palestinian refugee problem: in essence a confrontation between the Palestinian and the Zionist narratives. He says:

> The contradicting historical versions revealed not only a disagreement on facts. More than anything else they exposed the deep gap existing between the enormous importance the Palestinian national movement and its historians attributed to the solution of the problem against the almost total negligence shown by the State of Israel and its historians.

His paper tries to show that the recent stages of the historiographical debate, fed by the emergence of a revisionist, non-Zionist historiography in Israel, have helped to narrow this gap. This process has been strengthened by the Oslo Accords. Now probably dead to all intents and purposes, Oslo has nevertheless made the refugee problem a legitimate subject for future Israeli–Palestinian negotiations. This promise by itself, as we can see in the case of Jerusalem and the settlements, does not ensure an agreement or a solution. But it is clear that there is now an Israeli historical version, albeit not the official one but none the less a professional one, which is quite close to the version put forward for years by the Palestinian historiography.

Nur Masalha (Chapter 3) examines the causes of the 1967 exodus in the light of new historical evidence and more specifically against the background of actual evictions and "transfers" carried out by the Israeli army during and after the 1967 War and their overall impact on the exodus.

Leah Tsemel (Chapter 4) deals specifically with the ongoing expulsion of Palestinians from Jerusalem. She examines the legal status of Palestinian Jerusalemites since the Israeli annexation in 1967, the Palestinian "reality" in Jerusalem and preparing the ground for the final status negotiations. In her conclusion, she makes this plea:

> It is imperative to prevent Israel from completing its social, political and demographic transformation of Jerusalem. What is required is an immediate, concerted effort by local and international human rights organisations, political activists, the Palestinian Authority and Palestinian negotiators. They must jointly develop a realistic strategy to counter the new Israeli policy.

The second part of the book examines possible solutions to the refugee problem – from a political and legal viewpoint.

Anis Al-Qasem (Chapter 5) deals with the right of return in international law generally and specifically as it applies to Palestinians and the enforceability of that right through courts and UN organisations.

John Quigley (Chapter 6), while also dealing with the right of return, explores specifically the right of Palestinians to return to their home areas in Israel, despite the change of sovereignty and the changed character of the terrain. He examines also the right of return as an individual human right, the character of the right and resettlement as an alternative to repatriation.

Salman Abu-Sitta (Chapter 7) explodes the myth of the "imposs-ibility" of the return of the Palestinian refugees to their homes on the grounds that their homes and villages have been destroyed and new Jewish immigrants live there today. He demonstrates that the refugees can return without the dislocation of any Jews and the relocation of only 150,000 Jews.

In Chapter 8, Ghada Karmi discusses the question of compensation and reparations for the Palestinian refugees, by first considering the continuing international interest in the question of compensation of Jewish victims of Nazism for the seizure of their properties and possessions and the recent international row over the "Nazi gold" held in Swiss banks. She criticises the double standards shown by the international apathy for compensation to Palestinians and examines the Palestinian case for compensation, both moral and legal.

In his admirable finale (Chapter 9), Rashid Khalidi, in his search for truth, justice and reconciliation, outlines four elements for an essential solution to the Palestinian refugee problem: a formal recognition of Israel's primary responsibility for the creation of the Palestinian refugee problem; that Palestinian refugees and their descendants must have a right of return to their homes *in principle*; provision of compensation or reparations for all those who choose not to return or are not allowed to do so under a final negotiated settlement; a right to live in the newly independent Palestinian State and to become its citizens; and a special regime to be negotiated between a Palestinian State and Jordan and Lebanon for those refugees who are in Jordan and the Lebanon. To this fifth element I feel must be added all those who have become citizens of other states, whether Arab or non-Arab.

One of the principal criticisms of the Oslo peace process is that it did not attempt to resolve the two core problems of the refugees and Jerusalem, but left them for further negotiation. This is true. But at the very least, the Declaration of Principles[1] and subsequent Cairo Interim Agreement have placed the refugee problem on the agenda by the establishment of a "Continuing Committee" and by recognising that the 1948 refugees must at least be discussed in the final permanent status talks.[2] The Continuing Committee has been set up and has had several meetings, but has achieved nothing so far.[3] The final status talks have not even begun, due to the Netanyahu Government's failure to comply with the other important measures of the Interim Agreement, in particular withdrawal and redeployment, and this despite so-called "honest brokerage" by the US and the condemnation of Israel by the world community and UN General Assembly.[4]

The papers in this book do not attempt to provide a solution to the Palestinian refugee problem, whether at any future talks under the Oslo peace process or through any other machinery. But we hope that they are a useful beginning towards a deeper study of the problem – historical, geographical and legal – and perhaps a first step towards proposing elements of a just and lasting peace to the Palestinian/Israeli problem.

Eugene Cotran

NOTES

1 See Declaration of Principles, A 12 and Interim Report, A.
2 Declaration of Principles, A V.
3 It is reported that the Committee has not even reached agreement on who is a "displaced person".
4 See the US veto in the Security Council in the aftermath of the Jabal Abu Ghneim (Har Homa) proposed settlement in East Jerusalem and the two UN General Assembly Resolutions of April/May 1997, opposed only by Israel, the USA and Micronesia (A/Res/ES-10/2).

Part I

History of the Exodus 1948–1998

1

Palestinians in Exile:
Legal, Geographical and
Statistical Aspects

Marie-Louise Weighill

This paper will explore key aspects of the socio-economic, legal and political situation of Palestinian refugees and demonstrate how the problems currently faced by refugees are linked to their history since 1948. The Palestinian exile is the result of a single historical event – the loss of their country; yet a process has been at work since 1948 of a steady whittling away of the unity of the Palestinians as a group and their replacement with smaller groups of variable status.

Not only are the Palestinians scattered throughout their places of exile, their very status as a nation in exile is increasingly under attack. A hierarchy is being established within which the criteria by which an individual or community is judged to be Palestinian is dependent on how well they fit criteria established by others, outsiders over whom the Palestinians have no control. Since the loss of their country, Palestinians have been subjected to a grinding process of dispossession and fragmentation within an international community that is, as will be shown, too often a party to that process rather than a protector of Palestinians' legal rights to national self-determination.

Since the opening of the multilateral and bilateral peace negotiations which have for the first time envisaged negotiations on the "final status" of the Palestinian refugees, the process of fragmentation has reached its climax; Palestinians are viewed as factors in the politics of their internal host countries and as a set of different problems to be dealt with on a country-by-country basis. As will be shown, the ongoing peace process is intensifying the disaggregation of Palestinians into an inchoate set of groups with varying status and entitlement. The current impasse in the peace process, which seems increasingly to be a structural fault rather than a matter of stalled negotiations, raises the possibility that the Palestinians will face the next century as marginalised, unwanted and powerless minorities in exile.

The Problem: the Palestinians as Refugees

> It was then that we joined the world of the exile. The world of
> the occupied. The world of the refugee. The world of the ghetto.
> The world of the stateless.[1]

As has been comprehensively, and, one would hope, conclusively documented, the Palestinian refugees who arrived in the host countries in 1948 and 1949 had been forced to leave their homes either by direct action or intervention of the military forces or by a fear of such action that was nothing if not well-founded. In the context of this paper, the precise circumstances of the departure of the refugees is not of central importance save in the effect it had on the pattern of flight and the subsequent settlement of the refugees. More crucial to the process of Palestinian fragmentation and the nature of their existence in exile is why and how they were prevented from returning. The development of the barriers to repatriation and the institutionalisation of refugee status and assistance provision have contributed to the progressive atomisation of the Palestinians into separate and progressively less powerful communities.

After the fall of Haifa and Acre, the villagers of the Galilee were inexorably driven from village to village over the border into southern Lebanon and Syria. Refugees from the south of Palestine were driven out along with the Egyptian armies, while those from the central coastal plain took refuge in the east of the country (in the area that was to become known as the West Bank). The conditions faced by the refugees on their arrival were appalling; most had left their homes with only the barest minimum of supplies, others had spent weeks after fleeing their homes camping in villages and towns in which they sought safety from the Israeli Defence Forces' (IDF) advance. Those who had moveable or accessible resources travelled directly to cities such as Nablus, Beirut or Damascus; the rest were forced to seek shelter in the border areas.

Initially, the refugees were forced to rely on their own resources and the help organised by both individuals in the host countries and local or national charitable institutions. However, the help that could be provided was limited and the condition of the refugees soon reached acute levels.

> [They are in a] desolate situation. Early refugee groups had been accommodated in houses, but later groups congested and over-flowed all available forms of shelter and some 25 per cent were encamped under trees. Food and water supplies were inadequate, hygiene and the sanitary conditions were appalling. Hospital accommodation was completely insufficient to meet requirements of a refugee population consisting largely of vulnerable groups.[2]

In the years since the war of 1948, the Palestinians have become the most significant refugee population in existence. There are currently 3,308,133 registered refugees under the protection of the United Nations Relief and Works Agency for Palestine Refugees (UNRWA). Palestinians are also among the "oldest" refugee groups, having received sustained assistance and protection for 47 years. Since their status is inherited, the number of Palestinian refugees rises yearly. Fewer than 15 per cent of all those bearing the designation "Palestinian refugee" have any meaningful recollections of pre-1948 Palestine. Yet succeeding generations continue to be born as refugees, with all the political ramifications and social obstacles that designation brings.

The symbol of Palestinian refugee status is the existence of a United Nations Agency solely devoted to their assistance and support. UNRWA is, however, a somewhat ambiguous protector. Its most serious shortcoming in the current situation is the extent to which it offers assistance but not the security of an internationally recognised legal status. At the heart of UNRWA's relationship with Palestinian refugees is a fundamental clash between how the Agency defines its role and the expectations of the refugees – a clash which has existed since the establishment of UNRWA in 1950. From the start, refugees saw the UN's job as helping them to return to their homes. UNRWA's mandate, however, was essentially to keep them alive until a peace agreement could be reached.

In the case of UNRWA, this tension was exacerbated by its unique legal role which left it responsible for assistance to, but not protection of, the refugees. Palestinians explain their possession of a UN Agency solely responsible for them by pointing out that the United Nations is uniquely responsible for their situation. The point was forcefully articulated in 1950 by the Lebanese delegate to the United Nations.

> In all other [refugee] cases persons had become refugees as a result of action taken contrary to the principles of the United Nations, and the obligation of the Organisation towards them was a moral one only. The existence of the Palestine refugees, on the other hand, was the direct result of a decision taken by the United Nations itself with full knowledge of the consequences. The Palestine refugees were therefore a direct responsibility on the part of the United Nations and could not be placed in the general category of refugees without betrayal of that responsibility.[3]

The United Nations' responsibility for the Palestinian people derives from its role in 1947 in promoting the partition of Mandatory Palestine, preparing the way for the creation of the State of Israel and the ensuing dispossession of the Palestinians. The UN's failure to impose the implementation of UN Resolution 194 on the Israelis meant that the Palestinians were forced to remain in exile. UNRWA itself was born of the failure of the United Nations Palestine Conciliation Commission to – in the terms of its mandate – "facilitate the repatriation and rehabilitation of the refugees and the payment of compensation".

When UNRWA was established in December 1949, it was assumed that assistance "to prevent conditions of starvation and distress" would be temporary. Forty-seven years on, UNRWA continues to have its mandate regularly renewed and to operate as an assistance organisation to the third and fourth generations of Palestinian refugees born outside Palestine. The continued existence of UNRWA represents for Palestinians proof of the world's refusal to enforce their legal right to return to their homes.

UNRWA's own unique position as a UN agency responsible for a discrete set of specifically defined refugees has contributed to the tension between Palestinian perceptions of their rights and the UN's obligation on the one hand, and UNRWA's limited mandate and capacity for action on the other. Palestinians are famously excluded from the 1951 Geneva Convention on the status of refugees. Covering all other refugees in the world, the Convention states in Paragraph D of Article 1 that its provisions: . . . shall not apply to persons who are at present receiving from organs or agencies of the United Nations other than the United Nations High Commissioner for Refugees protection or assistance".

The implications of this for both the legal rights and the nature of assistance provided for refugees have been intently debated.[4] While the continuing existence of UNRWA represents for some an acceptance of international concern and responsibility for the Palestinians' rights, exclusion from the Convention definition has resulted in Palestinians being denied key civil and social rights in the country of asylum as refugees – rights which are accorded to other refugee groups who fall under the aegis of the UNHCR.

The 1951 Convention does, however, offer refugees significant economic and social rights protecting them against discrimination in the pursuit of gainful employment, in labour legislation and in social security,[5] rights which have often been withheld from Palestinians. Moreover, the specific regional remit of UNRWA has meant that UNRWA-registered refugees who leave its field of operation in the Middle East are not treated by the international community as "genuine refugees" and therefore cannot seek asylum outside the Middle East.[6]

Notably, the relevant paragraph in the Convention refers to the exclusion of groups receiving protection *or* assistance from other agencies. UNRWA was established by the General Assembly in December 1949 as a relief organisation "without prejudice to the rights of the refugees to repatriation or compensation" and not as an agency offering protection. As one analyst has noted, ". . . the fact that UNRWA was only intended to provide assistance and that, as a consequence of this provision, the Palestinians would lack international protection, was not considered."[7]

While the lack of protection for Palestinian refugees appears a remarkable, even sinister omission today, it should be remembered that the 1951 Convention was, at its inception at least, prompted by a specific historical situation which influenced its formulation, particularly its notion of protection. For the refugees and displacees in Europe at the end of the Second World War, the great fear and concern was that they might be forcibly returned (*refoulement*) to their states of origin, which in many cases were under Soviet control. Protection therefore was centred on enforcing the right of refugees to make new lives in the countries of asylum. For Palestinians, of course, the situation could hardly have been more different. The rights that they required protection for were security in the country of asylum and the right to return home. Yet in the context of a 50-year exile, exclusion from these rights has contributed to the diminution of Palestinian autonomy and self-reliance and their consequent marginalisation.

UNRWA's limited mandate and the uneasy connection between its own responsibilities and the wider responsibilities of the United Nations have led to misunderstandings and conflict between the Agency, other assistance agencies and the refugees themselves. For the refugees, it has resulted in the creation of an assistance agency focused on their own situation and yet one which is notable (in comparison with certain other assistance programmes administered by UNHCR, for example) for the lack of both participation in the design and implementation of assistance and the involvement of local and international NGOs in its assistance programmes.

The situations of other long-term refugee groups offer some striking contrasts. The South West Africa Peoples' Organisation (SWAPO), the Pan-Africanist Congress (PAC) and the African National Congress (ANC) have acted as the implementing partners of UNHCR in the provision of assistance within the refugee camps in Africa. Tibetan refugees have a government in exile which draws up development plans for its community, sets priorities for assistance and coordinates the assistance provided by the outside world. The Tibetan system has had remarkable success in securing the autonomy, integrity and prosperity of the refugee community. Palestinians, in contrast, have, save for the period 1969–82 in Lebanon, been largely excluded from the design and implementation of United Nations assistance which they regard as nothing more than interest on their losses. It is therefore hardly surprising that the interaction of Palestinians and "their assistance agency" has so often been fraught with misunderstanding. As late as the 1960s, UNRWA reports presented the Palestinian refugees as "unable to grasp their circumstances or comprehend concepts of relief", while for one Palestinian in Gaza, the purpose of assistance was to "stuff our mouths with bread so that we could not talk".

Insecurity of Status

Without the protection of an internationally agreed convention, Palestinian refugees' legal rights in exile have been at the mercy of political developments, both regional and domestic, over which they have no control. As will be shown below, Palestinian refugees have in the past five decades been subjected to a steady assault on their legal status which has left them in an increasingly marginal and vulnerable position.

The legal position of Palestinian refugees in the host countries (Jordan, Syria and Lebanon) has altered over time. The security of a refugee in the host countries is dependent on how valid his or her legal status is seen to be and residency can be changed, seemingly arbitrarily, by the host government. If a refugee community's right to remain in a particular country is uncertain, the host government is less likely to sanction any assistance programmes – such as improvement of living conditions or the provision of income-generating projects – which seem to establish that community more firmly in the country.

The initial response of host states to the Palestinian exodus was to offer them refuge and protection. This was based on the assumption that the refugees' stay would be temporary and that the Palestine Conciliation Commission (PCC) would find a solution. When this did not occur, it became necessary to define clearly the status of the refugees. Any such definition was, however, never intended to form the framework for the refugees' integration into the host community, but rather was intended to establish a viable means of identifying entitlement to assistance. Two central and intrinsically incompatible policies were adopted. First, Palestinians would be given full residency rights, and second, governments would oppose plans for the resettlement of the refugees.

The former principle was established in the Casablanca Protocol adopted by members of the League of Arab States in 1956, which referred in particular to the Palestinians' right to work, freedom of movement, and full residency status. Since then, successive collective and individual resolutions by Arab states have reiterated this position.

[13]

Simultaneously, however, the Arab governments refused to consider permanent settlement of the refugees and insisted on the implementation of the options contained in UN Resolution 194 (II), namely repatriation to Palestine or full compensation for losses incurred during the war of 1948. Reflecting the importance of the latter principle, Arab governments, with the exception of Jordan, have refused to give the refugees citizenship. Most Arab states (Egypt, Lebanon, Syria, Iraq and most recently Yemen) have instead issued Palestinians living within their borders with special refugee documentation (RD) or travel documents.

The definition of a refugee, fixed during the 1950s, has not been altered or extended to meet the developments of 40 years in exile. The legal image of a refugee remains one of an individual living in a camp entitled to work and protection but not to property or economic rights. The institutionalisation of a definition originally intended to address a fluid and temporary situation has resulted in major anomalies, notably the difficulty Palestinian refugees face in transferring their status from one country to another or in establishing themselves as independent economic actors. The commitment of the host states to allowing the Palestinian refugees full residency status and civil rights has weakened over time. After the Gulf War, Arab states officially revoked the 1965 Protocol, declaring it superseded by the internal law of each state. Various restrictions were imposed on Palestinians in the Arab states, especially RD holders. Since the signing of the Oslo Accords, refugees in the host countries, particularly Lebanon,[8] have seen even tighter restrictions on their status and freedoms. Disenfranchised by the stripping away of their rights in exile and deprived of support and representation by the Palestine Liberation Organisation (PLO) – which increasingly concentrates on the situation inside the West Bank and Gaza – Palestinian refugees in the host countries face an uncertain future.

Under Israeli occupation, Palestinian refugees in the West Bank and Gaza were subjected to extreme restrictions on their ability to improve their own lives and to function within the society. However, following the signing of the Declaration of Principles, the very status of refugees within the West Bank and Gaza has become dangerously marginalised. The accords between the PLO and Israel effectively deprive the Palestinians within the West Bank and Gaza of their rights as refugees, transforming them into "second-class citizens" of an as yet unformed state.

Diversity within the Palestinian Diaspora

While, as has been asserted above, the legal status of Palestinians is under attack from those who wish to fragment them into isolated communities, the living conditions faced by Palestinian refugees show considerable diversity, as is to be expected after 50 years in exile.

The image of Palestinians eking out a dependent existence in dusty, shack-filled refugee camps is very far from the truth. Refugees live in villas in Amman and slums in south Beirut; some refugee camps contain two-storey stone houses, while other refugees live in extreme poverty amongst the host community. Similarly, there are communities of Palestinians living in America, Australia, Canada and Europe, as well as all over the Arab world. However, over 80 per cent of the Palestinian refugees still live either within historical Palestine (Israel and the West Bank and Gaza) or within 100 miles of its borders.

FIGURE 1.1
Distribution of Palestinians

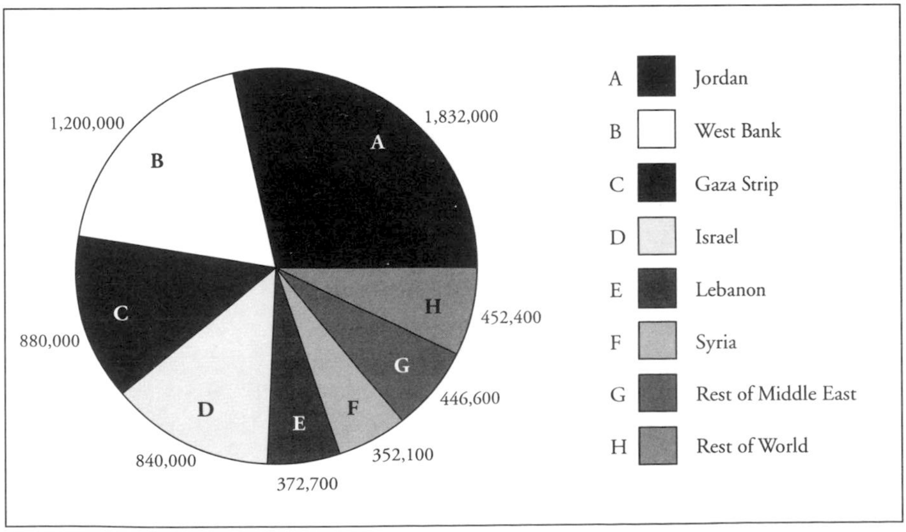

A	Jordan
B	West Bank
C	Gaza Strip
D	Israel
E	Lebanon
F	Syria
G	Rest of Middle East
H	Rest of World

A: 1,832,000
B: 1,200,000
C: 880,000
D: 840,000
E: 372,700
F: 352,100
G: 446,600
H: 452,400

Source: U.S. Bureau of Census and Population, 1996

[15]

In each country or area where Palestinians have been exiled, there are striking variations in refugee patterns of livelihood which can also exist inside a single country. Variables influencing the relative conditions of Palestinian refugees within a country include whether they are living in a rural or urban area, proximity to the capital or major city of the country, the economic situation of the areas in which they are living, the time at which they left the camp and the degree of security they enjoy in the host society.

Jordan

According to UNRWA estimates, Palestinian refugees constitute 28.2 per cent of Jordan's population. The major influxes of Palestinians to Jordan followed the 1948 and 1967 Wars, which brought an estimated 400,000 and 350,000 respectively to the kingdom. Others came from Lebanon in 1982 and from the West Bank since 1967. As a result of the Gulf War in 1991, an estimated 300,000 Palestinians returned from the Gulf to Jordan: around half are registered UNRWA refugees.

There are ten UNRWA camps in Jordan: four were established after 1948, and six after 1967. In addition to this, there are three government camps at Suknah, Henaikin and Madaba, housing around 24,500 people in total. All camps are formally administered by the Palestinian Affairs Department (PAD) and UNRWA facilities and services are available in all. In addition to the registered population, there are also low-income Jordanians, Egyptians, Sri Lankans and others living in the camps.

In Jordan there are two groups of Palestinian refugees whose position is radically different: the 1948 refugees who came to the East Bank (then Transjordan) after the creation of the State of Israel and the 1967 refugees who fled across the river as a result of the Six Day War. Among the latter group are people not considered by the government to be refugees, since they were living in Jordan up to 1967 and are currently "displaced persons" rather than refugees who have crossed an international frontier. The 1948 refugees were housed in large camps situated on the edge of major cities, while the 1967 refugees were placed in rural areas significantly called "emergency" rather than "refugee" camps. Their position is currently uncertain. Under the Quadripartite Agreement between Jordan and Israel, some should have the right to return to the West Bank.[9] The numbers of those entitled to

Distribution Map

TABLE 1.1
Jordan: UNRWA Camps and Registered Refugees

Area	Refugees in camps	Refugees outside camps	Total
North Amman	*92,217*	290,613	382,830
Jabal el-Hussein	28,754		
Beqaa	63,463		
South Amman	*40,901*	298,633	339,534
Amman New Camp (Wihdat)	39,861		
Talbieh	1,040		
Zarqa area	*45,605*	281,733	327,338
Zarqa	15,025		
Marka	30,580		
Irbid area	*59,465*	179,030	238,495
Irbid	19,762		
Husn (martyr Azmi al-Mufti)	16,039		
Jerash	11,471		
Souf	12,193		
TOTAL	**238,188**	**1,050,009**	**1,288,197**

Source: UNRWA, UNRWA's Area of Operations, June 1995.

do so is the subject of a sharp debate between the two parties. While the status of the "1967 displaced" is under discussion, they remain in limbo – excluded from the negotiations, they can only wait to see what the outcome will be. Meanwhile, their position within Jordan grows more precarious.

In an even more minimal position are the non-Jordanian registered refugees resident in Jordan – that is, refugees who were first registered in Gaza and hold Egyptian travel documents. Over 80,000 people in this position live in worse socio-economic conditions than other Jordanian/Palestinians. Many of the Gazans live in Jerash and Marka camps; others are among the numerous low-income Palestinians inhabiting squatter areas and similar poor districts of Amman and the larger towns. According to UNICEF, there may be 400,000 Palestinians living in such circumstances, of whom many but not all are registered with UNRWA. They represent "the most poorly housed, inadequately serviced and economically needy segment of the Palestinian refugee population, with the least access to public services and facilities . . . They are the hard core of Jordan's urban poor."[10]

These refugees are not considered Jordanian citizens and accordingly they do not have the same rights and duties as Jordanians. They travel on their Egyptian travel documents and must obtain a return visa before departing from Jordan if they wish to enter the country again. They are only allowed to work in the private sector, but the concession of work permits is in most cases subject to prior approval by the authorities concerned. The unemployment rate among this category may be as high as 40 to 50 per cent.

Lebanon

In Lebanon the refugees live in six distinct areas, excluding the Christian enclave of Dbayeh. (The Lebanese authorities classify them in four districts while UNWRA uses six for administrative purposes as can be seen in Table 1.2.) Each of these areas was effectively separated from the other during the latter stages of the civil war and each presents separate problems and challenges for the future provision of assistance. In South Lebanon the camps are clustered around the two major cities of Tyre and Sidon. These areas were the scene of serious internecine fighting between the Palestinian factions, the South Lebanese Army, the Druze Progressive Socialist Party and Amal. There

Distribution Map

TABLE 1.2
Lebanon: UNRWA Camps and Registered Refugees

Area	Refugees in camps	Refugees outside camps	Total
Beirut area	635	43,311	43,946
Mar Elias	635		
Mountain area	24,955	46,176	71,131
Burj al-Barajneh	13,820		
Dbayeh	3,949		
Shatila	7,186		
Saida area	42,446	40,551	82,997
Ein el-Hilweh	38,483		
Mieh Mieh	3,963		
Tyre area	46,991	40,697	87,688
El-Buss	8,135		
Rashidieh	22,524		
Burj el-Shemali	16,332		
Tripoli Area	38,432	8,160	46,592
Nahr el-Bared	25,000		
Beddawi	13,432		
Beqaa Area	7,105	13,810	20,915
Wavell	7,105		
TOTAL	175,747	170,417	353,269

Source: UNRWA, UNRWA's Area of Operations, June 1995.

remains considerable apprehension among the Palestinian community in South Lebanon that any future peace agreement between Syria, Lebanon and Israel will involve the clearing of all refugee camps south of Beirut and the relocation of the inhabitants of the camps to the Bekaa Valley.

The camps around Beirut suffered most from the 1982 invasion of Lebanon, the ensuing massacres and the destruction following the camp wars of 1985–7. Much of the camp infrastructure in Sabra and Shatila has been completely destroyed and there remain many homeless families scattered throughout south Beirut. The government has presented plans for the whole of south Beirut to be cleared and rebuilt; it has yet to offer specific guarantees that the refugees will be rehoused.

In the northern part of Lebanon the two camps around Tripoli suffered from the factional fighting among the Palestinian Resistance Movement during the early 1980s. Economic opportunities in the area are limited by the surrounding area's poverty. Finally, Wavell Camp, in the Bekaa Valley, is severely isolated and suffers from severe overcrowding and a consequent high incidence of acute and chronic respiratory problems. Almost the only available work is in the opium and hashish fields which surround the camp.

In Lebanon the Ministry of the Interior recently made the issuing of residency permits conditional on possession of an UNRWA ration card. This new measure will deprive up to 50,000 Palestinians, who for whatever reason do not hold an UNRWA ration card, of any residency rights and allow the authorities to deport them at any time.[11] Unknown numbers of Palestinians had their residency documents confiscated or stamped "not allowed to return" in the early 1980s. Other Palestinians were taken off the register of those Palestinians entitled to stay in Lebanon by the authorities if they had acquired residency or other citizenship abroad. According to the Directorate of Palestinian Refugee Affairs (DPRA), more than 7,000 Palestinians have been taken off the registry since 1980.

There is a clear correlation between insecurity of residence and economic vulnerability. Those Palestinians who are "downgraded" from full residency status tend to be the poorest and the least able to help themselves. Their uncertain position makes it difficult to obtain work permits or to gain access to government services, including secondary schools. This group also includes Palestinians who fled to

Lebanon as a result of the 1967 War and the events surrounding Black September in 1970. These people are not seen as "Lebanese" Palestinian refugees (i.e. those who came directly to Lebanon in 1948) and have correspondingly less security of residence.

Syria

Palestinian refugees account for an estimated 2.4 per cent of Syria's population. In addition to registered refugees, Syria has some 125,000 displaced persons from 1967. As Table 1.3 shows, only some 25 per cent of registered Palestinian refugees live in the ten official camps. In addition to these, there are three "unofficial camps", not recognised by UNRWA, but established by the government's General Administration for Palestine Arab Refugees (GAPAR). These are Yarmouk, in central Damascus, which contains over 70,000 registered refugees, and Latakia and Ein el-Tal, both in the north of the country, which together house around 7,550 persons. GAPAR also retains overall responsibility for the UNRWA-recognised camps.

Most refugees live in or near the major cities of Damascus, Hama and Homs. During the fieldwork it was observed that the socio-economic condition of the refugee camps and areas was intimately linked to the prevailing socio-economic situation of the surrounding area. The more isolated areas and camps were poorer than those close to cities. Palestinian refugees in Syria enjoy broadly the same rights in terms of residency, army service and association as Syrian citizens, the only difference being that Palestinians are not entitled to vote.

West Bank

The West Bank (including Arab Jerusalem) covers an area of approximately 5,500 square kilometres and is inhabited by an estimated 1.2 million Palestinians. In contrast to Gaza, the West Bank is still predominantly a rural society. Only 26 per cent of the refugees (10 per cent of the population) live in refugee camps. An estimated 60 per cent of the total population live in more than 400 villages (around 70 of which have a high concentration of refugees and receive UNRWA services), while 30 per cent live in the 24 cities and towns.

In the West Bank, refugees are dispersed in urban as well as rural areas. In the early years UNRWA worked with Jordan to avoid

TABLE 1.3
Syria: UNRWA Camps and Registered Refugees

Area	Refugees in camps	Refugees outside camps	Total
Damascus	*44,060*	217,559	261,619
Khan Eshieh	12,619		
Khan Danoun	6,014		
Sbeineh	7,303		
Qabr Essit	9,245		
Jaramana	8,879		
North	*14,378*	17,971	32,349
Neirab	14,378		
Homs/Hama	*17,251*	5,835	23,086
Homs	11,331		
Hama	5,920		
South	*7,622*	12,632	20,254
Deraa	4,177		
Deraa Emergency	3,445		
TOTAL	**83,311**	**253,997**	**337,308**

Source: UNRWA, UNRWA's Area of Operations, June 1995.

Distribution Map

TABLE 1.4
West Bank: UNRWA Camps and Registered Refugees

Distribution Map

Area	Refugees in camps	Refugees outside camps	Total
Nablus area	*68,600*	154,003	222,603
Askar	10,642		
Balata	16,405		
Fara	5,421		
Camp No. 1	5,089		
Tulkarm	6,483		
Nur Shams	13,113		
Jenin	11,447		
Jerusalem area	*30,233*	127,161	157,394
Shufat	7,682		
Amari	6,598		
Deir Ammar	1,696		
Jalazone	7,160		
Kalandia	7,097		
Hebron area	*25,422*	90,062	115,484
Dheisheh	8,694		
Aida	3,406		
Beit Jibrin	1,499		
Fawwar	5,048		
Arroub	6,775		
Jericho area	*5,011*	8,043	13,054
Aqabat Jabr	3,773		
Ein el-Sultan	1,238		
Nueima	*uninhabited*		
ex-Gaza	2,439	5,438	7,877
TOTAL	131,705	385,707	517,412

Source: UNRWA, UNRWA's Area of Operations, June 1995.

concentration of refugees on the border by establishing new smaller camps through the West Bank. Refugees along the "Green Line" were considered a security risk in case they attempted to recover their property from Israel, an endeavour which sometimes resulted in retaliatory raids by the Israeli army. Jordanian government policy during the 1950s supported the economic integration of refugees in order to benefit from international aid, refugee skills and to discourage Palestinian separatism and disaffection with the annexation of the West Bank.

The provision of camp sites in the West Bank is regulated by the 1951 Agreement in which UNRWA agrees to pay the Jordanian government the sum of 500 Jordanian dinars per month per head "towards all costs arising out of rents for land occupied by refugee camps and for charges of water consumed by refugees within the Hashemite Kingdom of Jordan", with the government taking all responsibility for renting the land and paying water charges in the first place. Since the early 1950s, therefore, the Jordanian government has been paying rent to the owners of the land on which the West Bank camps are built.

Refugees living in camps in rural areas of the West Bank often have little contact with local residents, growing up almost segregated from residents, using UNRWA schools and health services. When circumstances allow, most work in Israel and not locally; hence they remain in isolated communities, separated socially and economically from their neighbours. Urban refugee camps are mainly found around the towns which remained under Arab control after the 1948 War. They have become slum areas, containing some of the poorest elements of society. Demographic pressure and housing congestion have led to expansion, often making it difficult to perceive the boundary between camp and town. The refugees have daily contact with residents and compete with them for employment.

Gaza Strip

The Gaza Strip, a small piece of dusty land along the Mediterranean coast measuring 35 miles by eight, is unique for its population size, composition and social structure. It is the product of a war and the continuing aftershocks of that war which occurred long before the majority of its inhabitants can remember. The Strip has no internal logic or coherence as a geographical unit. It is part of the trauma of the

TABLE 1.5
Gaza: UNRWA Camps and Registered Refugees

Distribution Map

Area	Refugees in camps	Refugees outside camps	Total
Deir el-Balah area	31,446	27,091	58,537
Deir el-Balah	14,578		
Maghazi	16,868		
Khan Younis area	49,680	68,792	118,472
Khan Younis	49,680		
Nuseirat area	65,253	14,990	80,243
Nuseirat	41,323		
Bureij	23,930		
Rafah area	72,729	40,563	113,292
Rafah	72,729		
Rimal area	63,381	45,835	109,216
Beach	63,381		
Jabalia area	80,137	36,848	116,985
Jabalia	80,137		
Gaza town area		86,815	86,815
TOTAL	362,626	320,934	683,560

Source: UNRWA, UNRWA's Area of Operations, June 1995.

1948 catastrophe which exiled 85 per cent of the population of Palestine. The lives of and opportunities for every one of its inhabitants have been and continue to be shaped by the political process which first created it and has ensured its continued existence.

Before the Palestinian uprising, the *Intifada*, and the ensuing peace process, the Gaza Strip, if mentioned at all, was presented as a locus of neglect, impoverishment and hopelessness. The overcrowded cities and camps of the area were the subject of little research and minimal interest; most researchers contented themselves with a few days in Gaza to complement their time in the West Bank and transferred their insights from the larger area to the smaller, ignoring the profound differences in demography, economic opportunity and social structure. The most profound difference between the two areas was established in the years after 1948 and intensified thereafter by the operations of the assistance organisations and the ruling administrations, both Egyptian and Israeli. Gaza is fundamentally a large but confined refugee camp. Seventy per cent of the inhabitants are registered refugees, as will be explained in subsequent chapters; the remaining 30 per cent have a good claim to "refugeehood" or the status of displaced persons. Even after almost 50 years a substantial proportion of the registered refugee inhabitants live within the boundaries of the refugee camps established in 1948; the rest live in areas contiguous to them.

The Strip has shown, over the last 50 years, the essential characteristics of refugee camps – lack of personal and communal autonomy, limited decision-making capacity, social alienation, economic dependency and political impotence – multiplied exponentially by the size of the population and the seeming impossibility of a political solution. Gaza has been shaped by, indeed exists as, the outcome of the refugee influx of 1948 and the continued refusal of the international community since then to enforce their rights to return to their homes. To speak of the "liberation" of the Gaza Strip through the attainment of autonomy unaccompanied by an awareness of the fundamental instability and unsustainability of the area is to define the "liberation" of a prison camp as the removal of the guards to a reinforced and still impenetrable perimeter fence.

From the 1950s onwards, refugees in the Gaza Strip moved out of the camps, making use of economic gains from working with UNRWA or from business, to buy and build houses. Refugees have moved to wherever they could afford to purchase land, and have also built in areas such as the land to the west of Rafah without planning permission. In addition, around 12,000 refugee families have moved out of the camps into government housing projects since the 1970s, according to the Israeli government.

In the Gaza Strip, some refugees find casual day labour in agriculture, working for landowners for extremely low wages. Those who have been able to buy land outside the camps have made a profit from farming or raising animals. Rural camps, such as Faraa, may be situated in areas of high agricultural productivity – few of the refugees, however, are able to gain agricultural employment on the land because there is not enough work for the residents, and the owners tend to employ members of their extended family. Often there is little social or economic interaction between refugee camps and villages.

Within the West Bank and Gaza Strip, social integration between the refugees and residents remains limited. The two communities remain divided by the provision of assistance which is the exclusive preserve of one and closed to the other. Resident children cannot attend UNRWA primary schools and in the government secondary sector children from the two communities rarely interact. Economic links are confined to the purchase of some specialised items from the shops in big cities as each refugee camp has its own market where the necessities can be obtained. Opportunities for employment within camps, whether rural or urban, are very limited. The assistance provided by UNRWA continually produces generations of skilled and educated workers who leave the camps either to work in towns or Israel, or to seek employment abroad. However, despite their levels of education, FAFO, the Norwegian research institute, reports that UNRWA refugees "are heavily over-represented in the lowest wealth income category".[12]

Refugees and the Peace Process

Debate on the future of the Palestinian refugees has become sharper since the Oslo agreements. Within the multilateral process, debate on the nature of the final status of the 1948 refugees has been postponed until the rest of the negotiations have been completed. Progress on even minor points remains agonisingly slow and inconclusive. The Multilateral Working Group on Refugees is divided into seven themes, responsibility for which was assigned to various "shepherds".The seven themes are: Data Bases (overseen by Norway); Human Resources Development (USA); Vocational Training and Job Creation (USA); Family Reunification (France); Public Health (Italy); Child Welfare (Sweden); and finally Social and Economic Infrastructure (the European Union). Strikingly absent from this list are explicit categories for (a) repatriation and (b) protection. The focus of discussion up to the opening of negotiations on the "final status" of 1948 refugees has been the planning of assistance programmes to alleviate the living conditions of the refugees. As has been the case earlier in their history, the international community's focus has been on providing externally organised assistance to the Palestinian refugees rather than on ways to enforce their rights – rights for which the international community should be the guarantor.

While the Palestinian delegation to the multilateral process has continued to reiterate the importance of discussing assistance without "prejudice to the final status agreements on the political future of refugees", some Palestinian representatives have grown suspicious of the way in which negotiation has, in the words of Mohammed Hallaj, "centred on ways to assist the refugees rather than on confronting the issue of displacement and statelessness which makes the refugee question the volatile issue that it has been for more than 40 years". This has, continued Hallaj,

> corrupted the process by denying the moral and legal standards accepted by the international community for more than four decades. By shelving the United Nations resolutions, it put the future of Palestinian refugees at the mercy of the balance of power and confined refugee rights to what Israel is willing to concede.[13]

In his discussion of the place of assistance within the multilateral negotiations, Salim Tamari elucidates many of the arguments currently in play concerning the role of assistance to Palestinian refugees in the future. In his article he focuses on the "Bristol Report", a review of assistance in the West Bank, Gaza and the host countries written in 1994 under the auspices of the European Union within the "Social and Economic Infrastructure Development" theme.[14]

Tamari points out with reason that oft-reiterated claims that assistance will not and should not prejudice the final status negotiations are perhaps disingenuous, given the continual marginalisation of Resolution 194 during the multilateral negotiations and the propensity of the international community to ignore "facts created on the ground" long enough to allow themselves to claim that the changes, while contrary to international law, morality and even reason, are permanent and cannot be reversed.

Yet in his criticism of the external assistance planned for refugees, Tamari goes on to suggest that

> to claim that such aid shall not prejudice the future status of refugees (as is often stated in the multilateral negotiations) is not very accurate *since refugees with improved social and economic status are likely to move out of camps, to migrate to other countries, and in general to relegate their refugee condition to an abstract political commitment.* [Emphasis added.]

This suggestion goes beyond acknowledging the vital connection between the protection of rights and the provision of assistance. It proposes a causal connection between assistance that raises refugees' ability to improve their socio–economic position and the loss of desire or determination among refugees to return to their homes. This argument has been a common one beyond the Palestinian case, from host governments who fear the burden "integrated" refugees will place on their resources and from liberation movements or representatives of the refugees, who fear that refugees will "disappear into the woodwork" if they move beyond the camps.

The view that "urbanisation" means a conscious abrogation of rights has proved mistaken in several key instances. In the case of the Afghan refugees in Pakistan, it was refugees that were "self-settled" and had some independent means who were the first to return, since they had both the means to establish themselves in their own country and the security of being able to leave if the situation in their own country proved untenable. Similarly, the majority of those who repatriated to Mozambique were so–called "self-settled" refugees. The inhabitants of camps tend to be far less flexible; having been coerced into dependence on assistance, they have a great deal more to risk and therefore tend to resist repatriation unless it is organised on a huge scale. This is not to suggest that Palestinian camp refugees are less likely than other Palestinians to wish to return, but rather to question the assumption that the assistance that improves their physical security and well-being in the country of asylum will prevent them from returning.

Assistance and *Tawteen* – "If you build it, they will stay"

This assumption has its roots in the international communities' long-term policies towards the refugees. One of the most sensitive and enduring issues in the lexicon of Palestinian refugee assistance has always been that of *tawteen*, a term associated with the transfer of nationality or the adoption of new citizenship. The term is generally used in connection with the long-held suspicion among Palestinians and Arab governments that the international community intends to liquidate the "refugee problem" by incorporating the Palestinians within the host countries (Jordan, Syria and Lebanon) and the areas of Palestine in which they sought refuge (the West Bank and Gaza). This incorporation is taken to mean the cancellation of all rights or identity as refugees and their transformation into Syrians, Lebanese, and so on.

It is certainly true that within a few months of the war of 1948, there were attempts to promote the view that the Palestinians would be better off "blending" into the surrounding countries. As early as 1950 a Western delegate to the United Nations pronounced that it "would not be in the interest of the refugees to return" and the Israeli delegates worked hard to promote the view that since Israel was a fact, the other Arab countries would have to accommodate those refugees who had "streamed out". The Israeli representative insisted that "mass migrations have occurred in other situations in recent history and in no other case has the tide turned back to the *status quo ante*". Further, the Israelis sought to link prevailing ideologies of the "unmixing of peoples" and "a state for every nation" by turning the legal right to reside in the country of one's birth into a question of population balance and stability, arguing that the idea that "demographic homogeneity should be achieved in order to avoid a minority problem [was] a principle that should govern the process of repatriation".[15]

The Economic Survey Mission, appointed by the UN Conciliation Commission, was seen by the Arab host countries as aiming to resettle the majority of refugees outside Palestine and in doing so, to "end" the refugee problem by transforming the Palestinians into citizens of their host countries. The refugees themselves and the Arab government delegations who negotiated on their behalf at Lausanne thereafter succeeded in establishing the primacy of repatriation as a "fundamental and universal human right" and the primacy of Resolution 194 in discussions of the future of the Palestinians. Yet, as so often, the recognition of this right by the international community was not accompanied by any significant or effective measures to enforce it.

In the absence of a political settlement, the opposition to *tawteen* becomes a *sine qua non* of Palestinian political discourse. After the hardening of attitudes in the mid-1950s and the collapse of UNRWA's initial "works" schemes, a great deal of rhetoric was devoted to the protection of the refugees from resettlement and their defence against Western plots to incorporate them into the host societies. UNRWA's initial plan to have any refugees who were "assisted to become self supporting" removed from the refugee rolls, although quickly abandoned, contributed to this belief.

For the host governments also, the scale and form of refugee assistance was assessed and monitored for fear that new initiatives might lead to *tawteen*. In the aftermath of the peace agreements at Oslo and Washington, in which attention was focused on the situation of Palestinians inside the West Bank and Gaza, the Lebanese government in particular expressed concern that the refugees within Lebanon would be left for them to deal with. Recent discussion as to the liquidation of UNRWA and the "implementation of peace" in a new Middle East "without refugees"[16] has exacerbated these concerns.

The rejection of *tawteen*, however, has become associated with a broad range of approaches to the improvement of Palestinian refugees' conditions and living standards – approaches which were not connected with the abrogation of refugee status or the acquisition of a new citizenship. In particular, the concept of *tawteen* has been associated, if not confused, with that of integration. Integration, one of the broadest and most poorly defined concepts in refugee studies, has been interpreted in the Palestinian context as meaning the incorporation of the Palestinians into the host society in economic, social and legal terms. Yet integration in terms of linkages with the host society economy, social structure and physical space has, inevitably, resulted from almost 50 years of interaction. While the discourse of organised, externally funded assistance has not taken this interaction and de facto integration into account, it has been the unavoidable consequence of an assistance structure which relied on the refugees' ability to support themselves.

In turn, *tawteen* has been used by some Palestinians to cover assistance initiatives within the country of first asylum which do not involve the complete separation of refugees from their hosts. However, such separation was not an issue in most host countries where economic and social integration did take place between the Palestinians and their hosts in the years after 1948, for the simple reason that the internationally provided assistance was not sufficient for the Palestinians to live on. Palestinians worked within the host economies, albeit in a structurally vulnerable position; refugees lived outside the camps alongside hosts and shared some services, such as secondary education. All this took place with no diminution of Palestinian national awareness or conviction.

Yet, in the absence of political or legal protection of the Palestinian right to repatriate, any assistance initiative which might seem to promote "integration" has been criticised as a step towards *tawteen*. In the current uncertain climate, sensibilities regarding the provision of assistance to Palestinians in the host countries have become acute. Some have even proposed a so-called "moveable criterion" to judge the appropriateness of refugee assistance. If it is something that can be brought home when the refugees repatriate (such as literacy, education or training) then it is acceptable. Anything else is "resettlement by stealth".

Most particularly, the discourse concerning *tawteen* has focused on the infrastructure of refugee camps. The camps, regardless of the extent to which they have physically melded with the surrounding areas, act as powerful symbols of refugees' separate identity and destiny. Plans to link them with host community infrastructure are rejected as attempts to dissolve the status of refugees. Thus, even the linking of the sanitation systems of the camp and the city has been construed as *tawteen*. An oft-repeated, almost mythical example is the story of refugees cutting down trees planted by UNRWA in an attempt to either "brighten up" or make permanent the refugee camps. The refugees in this story uproot the trees in protest, a powerful symbol of their determination that the camps are to be nothing more than transit stops on a journey which, however long its duration, has only one possible destination. The resonance and appeal of this anecdote is undeniable; however, its meaning may be more complex than a first retelling would suggest. A visit to a refugee camp in Gaza revealed many refugees to have well-tended and much admired fully grown trees in their courtyards. No one suggested that these trees represented anything other than shade. Trees, then, are not the issue; the issue is who plants them, and where.

Efforts to uncouple the physical improvement of refugees' lives, particularly housing, from political considerations were not helped by Israeli policies in the Occupied Territories from the early 1970s onwards. With the construction of the government housing schemes such as Sheikh Radwan, in Gaza City, the Israelis hoped to "clear" the refugee camps and to neutralise the refugee problem. Initially at least, the schemes were in no way voluntary; the original inhabitants were those whose houses were demolished in the security clearances of the early 1970s and who were not permitted to rebuild their homes in the camps. Even those who voluntarily bought land in the settlements and built their own homes were forced to demolish their homes in the camps. This was certainly resettlement by force and both UNRWA and the PLO were vociferous in their opposition to it. Yet, if the purpose of the Israeli plan was to "pacify" the refugees by offering them material benefits in exchange for giving up their refugee identity, it was an unmitigated, if not spectacular, failure. After the start of the Palestinian uprising, Sheikh Radwan was one of the most consistently active areas in Gaza. A change of residence had done nothing to alter the refugees' sense of identity or entitlement.

As far as refugees in the host countries are concerned, links between refugee camps and towns and improvements made by refugees to their homes are used as a de facto argument by those who promote a "pragmatic" response to the Palestinian issue on the grounds that there is no refugee issue to solve, since the camps have elided with the local cities. This is the view propounded by Ginat.

> There is no doubt that the improvements made by the inhabitants in their homes in the refugee camps reflect their feelings. They regard themselves as permanent rather than temporary residents. The process of urbanization is a natural one when the inhabitants improve their well being. The variety of cultural elements in the

camps' population, that is, non–refugees who settled in the camps, and undoubtedly consider the camp their permanent home, also contributes to the urbanization process.[17]

For refugees, housing is housing. To argue, for example, that "refugees with improved social and economic status are more likely to move out of camps, to migrate to other countries, and in general to relegate their refugee condition to an abstract political commitment"[18] is to propose a causal connection between assistance that raises refugees' ability to improve their socio-economic position and the loss of desire or determination among those refugees to return to their homes.

Integration, although a notoriously vague and disputed concept, does not involve the dissolution of cultural identity, or the loss of rights. Indeed, security of rights is essential to integration, together with the ability of refugees to organise separately and to maintain their separate identity. Integration, then, means refugees "maintain their own identity, yet become part of the host society to the extent that host population and refugees can live together in an acceptable way".[19] At this stage of the peace process, in the absence of both a meaningful representative structure for the Palestinian refugees, whether in the host countries or the West Bank and Gaza, and a commitment on the part of the international community to enforce their rights, the future for Palestinian refugees appears to be a bleak choice between marginalisation and segregation.

NOTES

1 F. Turki, *The Disinherited* (New York: *Monthly Press*, 1972).
2 UN Document, St Aubin Report 1949, Introduction.
3 See Paul Weis (ed.), *Travaux Préparatoires of the Refugee Convention, 1951* (Cambridge: Grotius, 1995), p. 257.
4 See, for example, Khadija Elmadad, "Appropriate Solutions for the Palestinian Refugees", Paper presented to the IGCC Conference on "Promoting Regional Cooperation in the Middle East", Vouliagmeni (Greece), November 1994 (via IGCC). Internet on: gopher://gopher-igcc.ucsd.edu:70/OF-1%3A78291%3 AElmadad-Refugees.

5 I. C. Jackson, "The 1951 Convention Relating to the Status of Refugees", *International Journal of Refugee Law*, vol. 3, no. 3 (1991), p. 408.

6 J. Hathaway, *The Law of Refugee Status* (Toronto: Butterworth, 1991).

7 L. Takkenberg, "The Protection of Palestinian Refugees", *International Journal of Refugee Law*, vol. 3, no. 3 (1991), pp. 414–34.

8 S. Al-Natour, "The Legal Status of Palestinian Refugees", *Journal of Refugee Studies*, vol. 10, no. 3 (1997), pp. 360–78.

9 The Palestinian–Israeli Declaration of Principles (DOP) of September 1993 called for immediate negotiations between Israel, the Palestinians, Jordan and Egypt on the "modalities of admission of persons displaced from the West Bank and Gaza in 1967." Subsequently, a Continuing (or "Quadripartite") Committee was established to discuss these issues. The Committee first met in Amman in May 1995; subsequent meetings were held in Beersheba, Cairo, Gaza, Amman and Haifa. Work within the Committee was slow, with major differences over the definition of a "displaced person" and hence the number of potential returnees. By 1997, deterioration in the peace process saw work in the Committee grind to a virtual halt.

10 UNICEF, *Palestinians in Jordan and UNICEF: Summary Plan of Operations* (1992).

11 F. al-Khazen, "Permanent Settlement of the Palestinians in Lebanon: Recipe for Conflict", *Journal of Refugee Studies*, vol. 10, no. 3 (1997).

12 M. Heiberg and G. Ovenson, *Palestinian Society in Gaza, West Bank and Arab Jerusalem: A Study of Living Conditions* (Oslo: FAFO, 1993).

13 Mohammed Hallaj, quoted in Salim Tamari, *Return, Resettlement and Repatriation: The Future of Palestinian Refugees in the Peace Negotiations*, Final Status Strategic Studies (Berkeley, Calif.: Institute for Palestine Studies, 1996). Internet address: http://www.arts.mcgill.ca/MEPP/PRRN/papers/tamari2.html.

14 In discussing and to an extent critiquing his conclusions I must declare an interest in that I was responsible for writing the first draft of this report.

15 UNGAOR, 3rd Session, Part 1, 1st Committee, 201st Meeting (1948).

16 Marc Perron, "The Refugee Working Group, One Year Later", Notes for Remarks by Marc Perron, Assistant Deputy Minister (Africa and Middle East), Department of Foreign Affairs and International Trade to the Institute for Social and Economic Policy in the Middle East, John F. Kennedy School of Government, Harvard University, 24 February 1995. Internet address: http://www.arts.mcgill.ca/MEPP/PRRN/docs/peronharvard95.html.

17 J. Ginat, "A Proposal for a Permanent Settlement Plan for the Palestinian Refugees", Paper presented to the IGCC Conference on "Promoting Regional Cooperation in the Middle East", Vouliagmeni (Greece), November 1994 (via IGCC). Internet address: gopher://gopher-igcc.ucsd.edu:70/OF-1%3A78291%3AGinat-Refugees.

18 Tamari, *Return, Resettlement and Repatriation*.

19 T. Kuhlman, *Asylum or Aid? The Economic Integration of Ethiopian and Eritrean Refugees in the Sudan* (Leiden: African Studies Centre, 1994), p. 56.

2

Were They Expelled?:
The History, Historiography and
Relevance of the Palestinian
Refugee Problem

Ilan Pappe

This essay is concerned with contemporary implications generated
by the historiographical debate on the Palestinian refugee problem.
The debate, ever since it started in the 1960s, has been, in essence, a
confrontation between two narratives: the Palestinian one and the
Zionist one. Historians on both sides have been presenting documents
and facts, but have also adhered to their own political positions on
the subject. The contradictory historical versions reveal not only a
disagreement on facts, but more significantly a deep gap between
the enormous importance the Palestinian national movement and its
historians attribute to the solution of the problem and the almost total
lack of interest shown by the State of Israel and its historians. It will be
suggested here that the recent stages of the historiographical debate,
fed by the emergence of a revisionist non-Zionist historiography
in Israel, have helped to narrow this gap. This process has been
strengthened by the Oslo Accords. Although it is now probably dead
to all intents and purposes, Oslo has nevertheless made the refugee
problem a legitimate subject for future Israeli–Palestinian negotiations.
This promise by itself, as we can see in the case of Jerusalem and the
settlements, does not ensure an agreement or a solution. But should
the refugee question be brought to the negotiating table in the
future, there is now an Israeli historical version (albeit not the official
one), which is quite close to the version put forward for years by
Palestinian historiography. Historians on both sides would not, of
course, determine the outcome of the peace process, should it be
renewed, but they have an impact, as I have tried to show elsewhere.[1]

This article is therefore an historiographical, rather than an historical assessment of the making of the Palestinian refugee problem. It begins by considering the most recent historiographical contribution to the debate – which is the reaction of Zionist historians in Israel today to the tendency of Israeli revisionist historians to accept many of the claims made over the years by the Palestinian historiography on the subject. Although in this section the paper questions some of the assumptions made by mainstream Israeli historians today, it is mainly concerned with exploring the logic and ideology underlying this official hegemonic Israeli position on the subject – a logic still directing the present political system in Israel. It propounds an ideology accepted by the two main parties in the country, Labour and Likud, which is also deeply rooted in the perceptions of many members of the Israeli peace camp (centred around the "Peace Now" movement).

This sweeping loyalty to a position of denial in Israel is not just a case of court historians faithful to Zionist ideology. There is an overall tendency to deny that there ever was an expulsion – with many insisting that there was just a flight. This denial is driven by an apprehension, characteristic of many Israelis belonging to the Zionist left, from where most academicians still come, of facing the Palestinian demand for the "right of return" – a demand that after all had been supported by United Nations General Assembly Resolution 194 (11 December 1948) and at least since 1987, in the wake of the peace policy adopted by the PLO, seemed negotiable in the context of a successful peace process.[2]

The second part of this paper returns after ten years to revisit the historiographical picture on the question of expulsion as it was portrayed by the "new historians" in Israel.[3] The article surveys the Palestinian – mainly professional historians' – reaction to this picture, analyses the positions of both sides and puts forward a kind of "bridging" narrative of its own for what happened in 1948, based on a common ground found between these two points of view.

The final section deals with the wider implications of the historiographical debate, at all its stages. The debate has and will have an impact on the current Israeli and Palestinian positions towards the so-called Oslo "peace process". We are here mainly concerned with whether or not the Israelis can come to terms with the evil and negative role appropriated to them in the Palestinian historical narrative on the making of the refugee problem. The bottom line argument of this article is that the crisis of identity in Israel, as well as the chances of a genuine peace process, is closely connected to a courageous and sincere Israeli review of the Zionist role in the making of the refugee problem, and that such a review would considerably affect the nature of the solution for the Palestinian refugee problem.

The Current Official Israeli Line of Argument

The official Israeli version shuns any responsibility for the Palestinian refugee problem. According to this version, the refugees were not expelled, but fled before and during the 1948 War, encouraged by the local and external Arab leadership. It claimed that the Arab League had conveyed a message of self-confidence, assuring those who had left that they would return triumphantly once the dust of war had settled.

It was David Ben-Gurion who provided this version which, in its basic arguments, is still accepted today by many professional historians in Israel. On 11 October 1961 he declared in the Knesset:

> The Arabs' exit from Palestine . . . began immediately after the UN Resolution, from the areas earmarked for the Jewish state. And we have explicit documents testifying that they left Palestine following instructions by the Arab leaders, with the Mufti at their head, under the assumption that the invasion of the Arab armies at the expiration of the Mandate will destroy the Jewish state and push all the Jews into the sea, dead or alive.

Ben-Gurion added also the "domino effect" theory: once the first wave of refugees left – between October 1947 and March 1948 – others soon followed suit. The call from the Arab leaders on the one hand and the "domino effect" on the other appear in Ephraim Karsh's book, the most recent attempt to defend the Israeli official version of the war.[4]

Professional Israeli historians added logical and methodological reasoning to the Zionist narrative constructed so skilfully by David Ben-Gurion. The making of the refugee problem was inevitable, claims Netanel Lorch, the chief historian of the Israeli army. Despite his official position and his loyalty in his account to the Israeli of the 1948 War, even his interpretation was not "patriotic" enough for his masters. As a result, in 1959 he was forced to publish the account of the war he had prepared for the Israeli Defence Forces (IDF) as a private publication.[5] He ran into trouble, so to speak, as he challenged several "truisms" regarding the Israeli view on the military history of the war. However, when it came to an analysis of the refugee problem he abided faithfully by the official line. Thus, as we stated, he argues that the refugee problem was inevitable. This was due to the demographic mosaic prevailing in Mandatory Palestine. The refugees were the inescapable victims of a war fought against a very tense geographical proximity of Jewish settlements to Palestinian villages, as well as a strained co-existence in the mixed Arab-Jewish towns of Haifa, Jaffa, Tiberias and Safad. There were also Jewish refugees, Lorch reminded us, as a proof that it was demography, rather than ideology or policy, which made the problem.[6] An Israeli geographer, Arnon Golan, has made a similar claim quite recently in a doctoral thesis, where he equated, methodologically and thematically, the plight of the Jewish refugees with that of the Palestinians.[7] The Jewish refugees were the inhabitants of the Jewish Quarter in the Old City of Jerusalem, of isolated settlements such as Gush Etzion and Mishmar Ha-Yarden, as well as others in the Negev which were captured by the Egyptian army in the summer of 1948.

Let us examine these two arguments: the first about the inevitability of civilian casualties in any civil war, and the other, stemming from it, that there were therefore also Jewish refugees. Indeed, one could agree that any war fought in an inhabited area is bound to create a refugee problem. In some cases, the civilians who flee or leave their homes return once the fighting is over; in others they become refugees, uprooted from their country and waiting to be either repatriated or resettled elsewhere. However, the "inevitability argument" ignores the scope of the human tragedy. The 1948 War was not the Second World War, which inevitably created masses of refugees. Nor was it a war similar in its magnitude to the regional wars of the second half of the twentieth century. We are talking here of a limited civil war followed by scattered campaigns after 15 May 1948 between regular Arab armies and Jewish forces. This military activity on both sides cannot serve as a satisfactory explanation for the Palestinian mass exodus. After all, almost all the Palestinians (90 per cent) were uprooted from their original homes in the areas occupied by Jewish forces during the war. Moreover, the inevitability argument does not explain why the Palestinians could not return to their homes.

As for the equation of Jewish and Palestinian refugees, this seems to be an even more dubious line of reasoning. The Jewish refugees remained in Palestine and most of them were returned to their homes once they were repatriated as part of a prisoner-of-war exchange at the end of the fighting. They were prisoners of war, and were treated as such. Moreover, the disparity in numbers speaks for itself: 750,000 Palestinian refugees compared with 5,000 Jewish refugees.

Another argument which has been produced lately by Ephraim Karsh in his attack on the "new history" in Israel (i.e. the work of the revisionist Israeli historians who challenge the official Zionist narrative) is that there could not have been a Jewish policy of expulsion since the official policy of the Hagana (the main Jewish underground movement) was to encourage the Arab population to surrender. This line of argument is based on a simplistic reading of Plan D. We shall deal more deeply with this plan in the second part of this article which will reassess the findings of the "new historians" and the Palestinian reactions to them. Here it will suffice to explain that Plan D was prepared by the Hagana in March 1948 as a general guideline for the Jewish forces in anticipation of a war both against the Palestinian community and the Arab armies.[8]

Our readers may contemplate the following instructions in Plan D and think whether this could be understood as a plan sensitive to the fate of civilians in the 1948 War.

> Operations against enemy population centres located inside or near our defensive system will be taken [that was an area within the designated Arab state according to the UN partition plan and which was adjacent to the Jewish state; it was seen by the Jewish Agency as a buffer zone] and will be carried out in order to prevent them from being used as bases by an active armed force. These operations can be carried out in the following manner: either by destroying villages (by setting fire to them, by blowing them up, and by planting mines in the debris) or, in the case especially of those population centres which are difficult to control, operations should be carried out according to the following guidelines: siege of the villages, conducting a search inside. In case of resistance, the armed force must be wiped out and the population expelled outside the borders of the state.[9]

Almost all the Arab villages were regarded as military targets and the mixed towns fell within the areas regarded as crucial for military purposes. Only total surrender ensured survival for these villages, but even that was not always granted.[10] Thus Itzhak Rabin ordered the evacuation and destruction of the villages of Abu Gosh, the most pro-Zionist village in Palestine (only a very intensive effort by Jewish intelligence officers close to the *mukhtar* averted the deed). Other less cooperative villages, within areas regarded as of crucial strategic importance, were doomed to be destroyed and evacuated regardless of the willingness of some to surrender. Many other Palestinian villages and neighbourhoods faced the fate awaiting them in Plan D, some because they resisted, others because they simply did not display a willingness to surrender openly (by waving a white flag).[11]

None the less, Israeli historians attach great importance to the fact that the Jewish military command differentiated between "friendly" and "hostile" villages as a proof of the sensitivity and morality of Zionist conduct. The differentiation between friendly and hostile villages was committed to paper but seems to have been totally ignored by the energetic officials working in the Jewish Agency's Land Department. It was in particular the Head of the Department, Yossef Weitz, who tried to evict as many Arabs as possible regardless of their "friendliness" or "hostility". Weitz was very active in searching for fertile land, in encouraging local commanders to evacuate Arabs and generally in exploiting the state of anarchy for the acquisition of more and more land. The Jewish policy of reprisals provided the best opportunity for such activity. Thus, in places where the reprisals had already resulted in a large number of ruined and empty villages, as in Yadjur and Balad al-Shyakh, near Haifa, all that remained to be done was to take over the land of the villages. It seems that if Weitz had had his way, even more evictions would have taken place but there was not a plan as ambitious as that on the Jewish side.[12]

When a group of revisionist historians in Israel challenged many of these official Israeli arguments, a more elaborate and sophisticated version of denial was presented by mainstream academicians. It was Shabtai Teveth who took the lead in counter-arguing, according to the official version. In an article published in *Middle Eastern Studies*, he provided a list of causes which led to the exodus. The bottom line of his argument is that only the Palestinians and the Arab governments were to blame for what happened in 1948.[13]

The principal factor was the flight of the urban upper class, who had already begun leaving in September 1947. This was a voluntary exodus of about 70,000 Palestinians, mainly from the mixed towns of Palestine. For Teveth, the departure of this group is crucial to understanding what happened next. He has no doubt, as he states clearly in the article, that had the elite stayed, the picture would have been different. But how different? Teveth sees the elite's behaviour as setting a code of conduct for the rest of the population. Here Teveth reproduces the "domino effect" put forward by Ben-Gurion in 1961 and mentioned above. It started a series of flights, as he calls it. The elite's departure undermined the moral and economic foundations of the society as a whole. The elite evacuated vital civil service positions in the economic infrastructure of the towns. The collapse occurred around March and April 1948, and it was the fall of Haifa (on 21 April 1948) which played a particularly important role in accelerating the process.

This line of argument accounts for the flight of a tenth of the whole refugee population. It plays with "what if?" history – had the elite stayed, things would have been different – never an easy causal connection to make. Nor is the "voluntary" exodus argument so convincing. Some of the 70,000 left when the fighting had already begun. One cannot argue with the accusation that the elite did not show enough resilience or commitment to the cause. Thus, Teveth presents us with a harsh verdict on the Palestinian elite's behaviour. He may or may not have a point, but what has this to do with the question of whether or not the Israelis were responsible for the exodus? Does it mean that with such an elite, the rest of the Palestinians deserved expulsion? Or does it mean that had they stayed – as 'Abd al-Qadir al-Husayni did, for instance – and fought, they could have changed the balance of power or foiled Zionist intentions? Elites leave their communities on the eve of disasters and can be condemned for that, but the important point here is who brought the calamity upon the community in the first place.

Teveth goes on to explain that without the elite, the rest of the community fled. But they did not flee, they were partly put on trucks, partly frightened by shows of force (such as large explosions nearby), and partly they ran away from the fate which befell the people of Deir Yassin.[14] Could a more solid leadership have prevented a massacre, had it stayed behind, or would it have been massacred together with the rest?

Teveth is Ben-Gurion's biographer, so it is no wonder that he also reproduces Ben-Gurion's argument about the Arab leaders' encouragement to the Palestinians to leave.[15] He provides one piece of evidence: a call by the Mufti to women, children and old men to stay out of areas of danger – hardly a call for a mass exodus of villages and city neighbourhoods. Teveth argues that the Mufti saw the whole of Palestine as an area of danger and hence this was a call for a general evacuation. He also explains that the Mufti hoped that a mass exodus of women and children would embarrass the Jews in the face of world public opinion and would give the pretext for an Arab "invasion" of Palestine. Teveth further asserts that the Arab generals wanted such an evacuation, so that their armies would have a smooth ride into Palestine.

Erskine Childers has already proved to us that there was no call beyond the one mentioned by Teveth.[16] Moreover, this particular, limited order, like so many orders of the Mufti, was not implemented. Before women and children could be evacuated, they were expelled with the men from their homes.

It is also quite difficult to find evidence or logic in the presentation of tactical calculations accompanying the eviction plan: either embarrassing the Jews in the eyes of the world or providing a pretext for invasion. Already in October 1947, the Arab leaders, including the Secretary-General of the Arab League, Azzam Pasha, had informed the UN that partitioning Palestine was a *casus belli* as far as they were concerned. They refrained from any action, hoping that the UN would recognise the impracticability of partition in the face of the developing civil war in Palestine. Nor were they willing to risk a direct confrontation with the British forces still left behind in Palestine. As for public opinion in general, unlike the Zionist leaders and unfortunately for the Palestinians themselves, Arab and Palestinian leaders showed very little interest in world diplomacy. They failed to send a diplomat to the most crucial of the UN discussions on Palestine's fate, when they had a clear indication that the USA might change its pro-partition policy.[17] The diplomatic arena was dominated by the Jewish Agency skilfully exploiting the effect of the Jewish Holocaust on world public opinion.

As for the argument that the Arab military establishment demanded evacuation in order to aid an uninterrupted implementation of the invasion plan, there seems to be a slight problem. There was no "invasion plan" of any kind, nor was there any serious strategic thinking on the part of any of the Arab military high command. Only on 30 April 1948 was a plan devised.[18] This argument therefore does not hold water, nor do most of these arguments, as has been shown by the work of the "new historians" in Israel, particularly by Benny Morris's *The Birth of the Palestinian Refugee Problem*.[19]

Revisiting the "New History" and its Palestinian Critiques

The declassification of military documents in the Israeli archives relating to the 1948 War has shed new light on Israeli refugee policy. These documents were systematically mined by Benny Morris in his book which refutes many of the official Israeli explanations given until then for the making of the refugee problem. When the book appeared several years later in Hebrew, it was the first time ever that the Israeli public had been exposed to a counter-narrative of the Israeli role in the making of the problem – and it was not a sympathetic one.

Like the Irish journalist, Erskine Childers, before him, Morris found no evidence of instructions or directions by the Arab Higher Committee, or any Arab government for that matter, to the local population of Palestine to leave the country. All he could trace were instructions by the Arab Higher Committee to local commanders to secure the evacuation of women, children and old men from areas of danger. His book is a diligent and comprehensive analysis of Israeli actions in almost every Palestinian village and neighbourhood. The work lists a long number of cases where Palestinian civilians had been forcefully driven out of their homes and expelled outside Palestine.

Morris's book contains three elements: a discussion of the causes of the exodus; revelations of Israeli atrocities during the fighting; and a charge sheet blaming the Israelis for their anti-repatriation policy. It is difficult to find a clear-cut answer in his book to the question of cause. Morris writes about the prominent role in compulsory transfer played in Zionist policy, particularly since the 1930s, but in his conclusions he gives the impression that the exodus was a mixture of flight and expulsion. The presence of the concept of "transfer" as an option in Zionist strategic thinking created an expulsionary mood, so to speak, but was not translated into a plan. There was no master plan, concludes Morris. The expulsions were the inevitable result of the war – they were local initiatives which won retrospective affirmation and understanding from the superior concerned.

Morris's position differs in its conclusions from the main claims made by Palestinian historians, some of whose work, for example that of Nur Masalha, was based on similar documentation.[20] Masalha's argument is quite straightforward. Ever since its very beginning, the Zionist movement had considered the compulsory transfer of the local population as the only possible way of settling the conflict in Palestine. It became an integral part of the Zionist strategy of survival and hence the uprooting of the local population was *conditio sine qua non* for the success of the Zionist project. The hope was that a voluntary transfer would be agreed upon, but towards the end of the Mandate it was recognised that only a compulsory one could work.

Masalha sees the transfer idea as a Zionist simplification, or reduction, of the "Arab problem", an attempt by Zionist leaders to sell to their community, and to world public opinion at large, a schematic, clear-cut solution to the conflict. The conflict was thus presented as a "zero sum game". The schematic solution was born after a more complicated, mainly Marxist, analysis of the conflict, based on the hope of creating affinity with the Arab working class, failed to attract Jews and Arabs alike. While Morris limits the category of expulsion to direct expulsion, Masalha widens the scope and includes in it psychological warfare, massacres and the cutting of water and food supplies, as well as the undermining of the economic infrastructure.[21] Using such categories, many more Palestinians can be seen to be victims of direct expulsionary Zionist policy. In fact, apart from the 70,000 who left in the first wave, it includes everyone else.

The end result of the war led historians who had written before the declassification of the new material to assume that only a transferist Zionist policy could have caused such a mass exodus. After the declassification, those who criticised Benny Morris, such as Norman Finkelstein, claimed that the documents Morris himself had unearthed indicated how systematic was the Israeli policy of expulsion.[22]

But the main counter-argument to Morris's version did not use new documentation. It was the one put forward by Walid Khalidi (which, like other Palestinian critiques of Morris, at times does not take into account how far Morris went as an Israeli historian). In my book, *The Making of the Arab–Israeli Conflict, 1947–1951*, I have devoted several pages to the Morris–Khalidi debate.[23] Let me here just capture the main points, now that almost ten years have passed since that debate started.

Walid Khalidi did not alter his main argument, made in the 1960s, about the existence of a Zionist master plan for the expulsion of the refugees. The declassification of new material and the appearance of Morris's work did not change his position either. The reason is that he always based his conclusions on the published document of Plan D. Plan D was accessible in Hebrew and Khalidi translated it into English in the 1960s. As we showed above, this is a straightforward document providing a series of military methods by which Jewish forces can deal with the local population. Morris writes, however, that the plan was a military programme,

> not a political blueprint for the expulsion of Palestine's Arabs: it was governed by military considerations and was geared to achieving military ends. But given the nature of the war and admixture of the two populations, securing the interior of the Jewish state for the impending battle along its borders in practice meant the depopulation and destruction of the villages that hosted local militia and irregular forces.[24]

Eventually, and this is the main point made by Morris, Plan D was not implemented at all. He describes a Jewish leadership confused under conditions of war and thus failing to give direct instructions on anything. Therefore he attributes most of the expulsion decisions to local commanders who were probably not aware of Plan D. As I have written in my book, I found this argument hardly convincing and I would like to put the counter-argument again: "If I plan to throw someone out of his flat, the fact that he left before I had a chance to expel him in no way alters the fact of my intention."[25]

Walid Khalidi also rejects Morris's point of view. Like Nur Masalha after him, he puts the plan in a wider historical perspective and writes:

> Plan D . . . was the name given by the Zionist High Command to the general plan for military operations within the framework of which the Zionists launched successive offensives in April and May 1948 in various parts of Palestine. These offensives, which entailed the destruction of the bulk of the Palestine Arabs, were calculated to achieve the military *fait accompli* upon which the state of Israel was to be based.[26]

Khalidi and Morris agree that there was a mass expulsion later on in June 1948 and until April 1949. But Khalidi is more interested in what happened in April and May, and not later on. The reason is that Morris and Khalidi agree that 70,000 refugees fled in the first wave, and that about 250,000 were expelled in the final stages of the war – but this accounts for only half of the refugee population. The argument is about the 350,000 or so who left Palestine between March and June 1948. While Morris thinks this half left of its own accord, Khalidi argues that it was expelled as well (a particularly heated argument has been going on about the refugees of Haifa, around 65,000 in number). Zionist historiography cited Haifa as an example of a Jewish effort to persuade Arabs to stay – Morris, in this case, accepts the official version. Khalidi does not – he describes, as does Nur Masalha more elaborately, the means by which the Haifa population was driven out. Haifa was evacuated in the wake of Plan D, as was the Palestinian population of the mixed towns of Jaffa, Safad and Tiberias.[27]

Plan D refers specifically to the fate of the mixed towns and views them against a certain political background which developed in March 1948, when the plan was composed. In that month, the diplomatic fortunes of Zionism were dwindling. After the impressive success at the end of 1947, when the Jewish Agency recruited both the USA and the USSR to support the partition plan, in March 1948 the American President, Harry Truman, had second thoughts on the subject. He was willing to keep to recommendations made by the State Department to replace partition with an international trusteeship over Palestine. Plan D was based on the assumption that military operations had to be swift and decisive before a possible change in American policy could freeze the military situation on the ground.

So, Plan D was in many ways what Khalidi claims it was – a master plan for the expulsion of as many Palestinians as possible. Moreover, the plan legitimised, *a priori*, some of the more horrible atrocities committed by Jewish soldiery. It called explicitly for the expulsion of the Palestinians from the mixed towns and from locations deemed strategic by the military command. It was implemented – either by commanders who did so because they knew of the plan, or by those who were not aware of it. They all implemented a policy of destruction and expulsion recommended by the Jewish Agency, as is clearly manifested in Plan D. Was this the policy for the war itself – that is, for the period stretching from May 1948 to March 1949? Given the conduct of the Israeli army and its systematic expulsions, so pedantically described in Morris's book, one can at least say it had a significant bearing on the IDF's policy.

But Khalidi and Masalha raise another important issue. They see Plan D as epitomising Zionist ideology. Masalha, as mentioned in a counter-argument to that of Morris, presented Plan D as an ultimate expulsion scheme relating to all the previous Zionist transfer programmes. A plan materialised once the power to implement it was there. The impotence of the Arab world, the pro-Zionist world public opinion in the wake of the Holocaust, and the impressive build up of a state infrastructure on the Jewish side created the ideal conditions for its implementation. Khalidi shares this view, and the *Palestine Encyclopedia* goes even further and relates the original transfer plans to Herzl.[28] Was Plan D born out of Zionist ideology, as claimed by Khalidi, as well? Or was it an ordinary military plan, as argued by Morris?

Masalha and Khalidi, it seems, may have a somewhat reductionist view of Zionism. Zionist ideology did not centre only around the idea of transfer. Throughout the Mandatory period, Zionist leaders offered other solutions as well, not all of them directly associated with transfer. Moreover, the leaders displayed ambiguity more than anything else. Thus, Moshe Sharett moved from the extreme of a considerable compromise to the other extreme of transfer throughout his career as Head of the Political Department of the Jewish Agency.[29] But Masalha is right in claiming that expulsion was seen as a legitimate means, with no moral scruples. Transfer was conceived of as one of the more feasible solutions. I think he has clearly established a connection in his book between the expulsion of 1948 and the popularity of transfer in Zionist thought. Plan D was written in anticipation of the final confrontation between Zionists and Palestinians as to who was going to rule Palestine. In view of such an all-out confrontation, any means seemed legitimate and useful. Unlike more peaceful times in the Mandatory period, on the eve of the 1948 War, expulsion became the most favoured solution in the eyes of the military commanders and probably of David Ben-Gurion. On the other hand, his second-in-command, Moshe Sharett, still preferred a negotiated agreement on the partitioning of Palestine to transfer.

Plan D offered Zionist survival at all costs, but for some prominent members in the movement, survival could be achieved also by reaching an agreement with the other side. These leaders even predicted that there was a good chance that a local consensus would be elicited. It would be given in recognition of the modernising role Zionism played in Palestine and would be held by what the Zionists called "moderate" Arabs, a moderation generously financed by the Jewish Agency when necessary. It was, in a way, a typical colonialist "divide and rule" policy based on modernising perceptions of reality. However, should there be resistance (or, in Zionist discourse, should the extremist have the upper hand) the Zionist settlers were prepared to expel the local population from the very beginning.

Thus, to sum up this section, we may say that expulsion was an inevitable result of the Zionist presence, although it was not the principal aim of the Zionist movement. The distinction bears relevance to the third part of this article: do we seek a solution to the unjust presence of the Zionists in Palestine, or do we seek a solution for the refugees? But before approaching this last part, I would like to present a bridging narrative which is based on the common assumptions and claims of the "new historians" and the Palestinian historians.

The common version agrees that the Palestinian exodus began with what can be called a voluntary flight of large segments of the elite (probably about 70,000 altogether who left the country by January 1948). The exodus of the elite undermined the steadfastness of the population, although it is very doubtful that they had the power to face the Jewish takeover of the country had they stayed behind. Being a voluntary departure, it cannot be directly related to Jewish policies, nor is there any documentation that expulsion was discussed among Zionist leaders immediately after the partition plan was accepted by the UN in November 1947. The elite left in the hope of returning – they left without their possessions, and did not sell their property. They were never allowed to return.

The unanticipated departure so early on in the war by tens of thousands of Palestinians does not exclude the possibility that the leaders of the Jewish community, sitting on their war plans in March 1948, were not contemplating the depopulation of Palestine. Their discussions reveal the dissatisfaction of the Jewish Agency with the state allocated to the Zionist movement by the UN partition plan: the designated state envisaged the citizenship of almost an equal number of Palestinians and Jews. This is why, despite the first wave of voluntary refugees, the Jewish authorities soon after that prepared an expulsion plan. The Palestinians had to be expelled, they could not be persuaded to leave. Most of them were villagers strongly attached to their land and homes and not easily intimidated by acts of war; nor did they have the means to travel.

It is easier to find common ground in the historical narrative about what happened after 15 May 1948. From that moment, "new historians" in Israel and Palestinian historians share a clear notion of "what happened". It seems that a coherent Israeli policy developed through May 1948, beginning with the appointment of Yossef Weitz to head "transfer committees". Where expulsion failed, transfer was encouraged by every possible means (even by setting fire to the fields of Palestinian villages which were considered prosperous, or by cutting the water supply to city neighbourhoods). In May 1948 Weitz convinced the Israeli government that it should confiscate any looted Arab harvest for the needs of the newly born state.[30] This policy of burning or confiscating fields continued throughout the summer. Between April and the end of May, 300,000 more Palestinians became refugees. All were expelled – if we accept that fleeing one's house because the house of one's neighbour was ransacked is expulsion. Towards the end of the war, with mass operations by Israel in the north and south of Palestine, several massacres were committed, adding an incentive to the flight of the population. In 'Ilabun, Sa'sa'a,

Dawamiyya, Safsaf and Zurief, Palestinians were massacred.[31] The atrocities (at least on that we may all agree) were not part of a master plan. In their case we can apply Morris's explanation for most of the expulsions – "*A la guerre comme à la guerre*".

In the last stages, expulsion was even more systematic and the war ended with 750,000 Palestinians (half of the Arab population of Mandatory Palestine) becoming refugees. This figure is a conservative estimate provided by the UN which is challenged by Palestinian demographers, who tend to speak of one million.[32] It began with the expulsion of 150,000 in the operations of October and November 1948 and ended with scattered transfer operations which continued as late as the mid-1950s, long after the fighting had subsided.

This was part of the anti-repatriation policy of the Israeli government in the face of the international effort to settle the conflict in Palestine. Whoever was involved in this peace process, be it the UN or the US and Europe, they all agreed that unconditional repatriation of the Palestinian refugees would be an integral part of any solution. From June 1948, Israel was engaged in a policy aiming at creating a *fait accompli* that would render repatriation impossible. In that month, Yossef Weitz wrote in a memorandum that there was a consensus among those responsible for the "Arab problem" that the best way to deal with abandoned Arab villages was by "destruction, renovation and settlement by Jews".[33] In August, the Israeli government decided to implement Weitz's ideas to the letter.

The prime objective was to demolish what was left of the abandoned Palestinian villages, almost 350 in all, so that the term repatriation itself would become meaningless. Moreover, Israel's policy-makers required the land and the property for the absorption of the waves of new Jewish immigrants from Europe and from the Arab countries.[34]

Whether this was an old Zionist dream come true, as claimed by the PLO Charter, Masalha and Khalidi, or whether it is, as I see it, a specific plan designed for the 1948 War, the important point is the growing consensus among Israeli and Palestinian historians about the Israeli expulsion of the Palestinians in 1948 and the destruction of villages and towns. The desire to expel them before and during the war seems to be quite evident: expulsion followed by an anti-repatriation policy and a refusal to enter into meaningful peace negotiations after the war. If indeed this was the ideological bent of the Zionists, it means that even if the Palestinians had accepted partition they would have been expelled. But here we enter the dangerous zone of alternative history, not always a useful field of research. We can only repeat that the Jewish state was designated to be a bi-national state (with the Arabs constituting 45 per cent of its population), a scenario which would have defeated the Zionist dream of creating a Jewish nation state. Nor did the Israeli army distinguish, as we have shown, between those who were and those who were not involved in actual fighting in its expulsion policy.

The common ground is a consensus between the "new historians" in Israel and many Palestinian historians that Israel bore the main responsibility for the making of the problem. If Plan D is not seen as a master plan for expulsion (even Benny Morris agrees that it was not born out of the blue), at least expulsion was considered as one of the principal means of building a Jewish homeland in Palestine. The plan reflected the mood of the Jewish soldiers before and after the war, a mood which is echoed concisely in Ezra Danin's words to Ben-Gurion, "the Arabs of the Land of Israel, they have but one task left – to run away".[35]

The British and the Palestinian leadership share the responsibility – the British for the period which lasted until 15 May, at least, when they were responsible for law and order. Expelling people meant that they were not fulfilling these functions. In fact, British policy-makers were concerned only with the safety of their withdrawing troops and clerks, and nothing more. As in India, chaos, anarchy and bloodshed were left behind with little thought in Whitehall for Britain's negative legacy.

The Palestinian leadership played a negative and important role in the dynamics of the exodus. Not only did the political elite forsake its constituency in its most crucial hour, it also failed to give coherent guidance from its exile to the besieged communities in Palestine. The escape of those who were able to flee in relative security – the professional and business classes from the major cities – augmented the terror and confusion.

An Israeli recognition of the central role the refugees play in the national ethos and memory of the Palestinians could be one of the many fruits of the historiographical debate on the question of

[53]

causality and responsibility. Another would be a recognition of Israeli guilt. A third would be a revision of the PLO's demand for a transfer of the Jews out of Palestine as the only rectification of past evils. I would like to conclude this essay with some reflections on the contemporary implications of this debate.

Coming to Terms with the "Original Sin"

There is no need to "de-Zionise" Israel in order to get Israelis to accept the bridging narrative above as a feasible version of past events – including the allocation of responsibility for what happened in 1948 to Israel. But recognition of that responsibility can undoubtedly contribute to a process of de-Zionisation: a contemporary wish to dissociate oneself from an unpleasant past in an attempt to build a more just future. As I argued above, Zionism was concerned with more than just the expulsion of Palestinians. Many Zionists genuinely believed, like all colonialists, that they were modernising Palestine and the Palestinians. I would therefore separate the discussion on the 1948 exodus from a debate on the nature of Zionism. The colonialist perspective of Zionism and its inherent contradiction between a desire to be a democratic state and at the same time a Jewish nation state are a better means for exploring the moral validity of Zionism as a past ideology or a present institutionalised interpretation of reality. Israelis, like the "new historians", can come closer to the Palestinian version of what happened in 1948 without necessarily sharing the Palestinian perspective on Zionism as a whole. This new Israeli perception may increase the chances of Israelis accepting, at least in principle, the right of return for the refugees of 1948.

Moving from historiography to politics, we would say that the political implication of the consensus described above is an Israeli recognition of the Palestinian historical interpretation of the 1948 War as *al-Nakba*, the catastrophe. It also implies acknowledging that the main component of this catastrophe is the making of the refugee problem – a problem which is at the root of the Arab–Israeli conflict. For many Israelis, particularly the young generation, this is not an easy concession. For them, even if they see themselves as belonging to the peace camp, the formative year of the conflict, what it is all about is the occupation of the West Bank and the Gaza Strip in the 1967 War.

One can, however, make a connection between these two dates – 1948 and 1967 – for they have much in common. On both occasions, each of the two sides felt that the other had aimed at its annihilation. At both junctures, the Israelis came out with the upper hand surviving the battle and retaliating by a mass uprooting of the local population. For the Palestinians, both the 1948 and the 1967 Wars ended with the making of a huge refugee problem. The refugee reality was the fertile ground on which the Palestinian national movement was re-born, as it was the background against which it was easy to recruit the masses to the relentless struggle against the State of Israel.

Israel became a *fait accompli* in 1948 at the expense of 750,000 Palestinian refugees. Israel ended the 1967 War victoriously and the price was an additional 400,000 refugees. On each occasion, the population was intentionally expelled and systematically uprooted. Two million Palestinians, at a very conservative estimate which includes natural demographic growth, are the living victims of the two wars. Some of them are the victims of their leaders' stupidity; most of them are the victims of their foes' callousness.

Fatah, founded in 1959 and overtaking the PLO in 1968, was the principal institutional manifestation of the Palestinian longing for revenge and the return of the lost time of pre-1948 Palestine. The PLO's Charter spoke of an armed struggle for the sake of the return of the refugees to their homes and of the elimination of the "Zionist entity" which was founded by "nazi and fascist means".[36] The Charter predicted the establishment of a secular, democratic Arab state instead of Israel. The Charter was taught in the refugee camps' schools, and its precepts fed the imagination of playwrights, novelists and poets in their efforts to express the living spirit of Palestinian nationalism.

The Palestinian armed struggle had many sources of inspiration. One of them was the psycho-historical explanation of Franz Fanon and others like him of the purifying and homogenising effect national armed struggle can have in the crystallisation of a new identity for deprived anti-colonialist peoples. It seems that the leaders of the Palestinian armed struggle were also influenced by liberation struggles all over the Third World; the charismatic dogma of Mao Tze-tung, for example. Mao's "peasant revolt" was emulated by Arafat in 1967, in the wake of the Israeli occupation, with little success.

The failure of the Maoist approach brought Palestinians ever closer to the Algerian model of guerrilla warfare. A daily struggle against the Israeli army but also terrorist acts against the civil population (including the hijacking of aeroplanes) was the mixture used between 1968 and 1978 by the PLO in an attempt to change the reality in post-Mandatory Palestine. But it was to no avail. The guerrilla and terror campaigns were not supported by world public opinion, nor did they help to bring a solution to the refugee problem. The UN, from the very moment the 1948 War ended, endorsed the right of all Palestinian refugees to return to their previous homes. But what really counted were the positions of the two superpowers. Both supported the idea of partitioning Palestine and neither related to the fate of the refugees. The biggest success of the PLO has been in convincing at least the European Union, although a very marginal player in the politics of the conflict, to add the right of return to the outlines of a future settlement. But, in general, world public opinion after 1967, very much to Israel's convenience, dealt with the conflict as a process beginning in 1967 and not before. An Israeli withdrawal from those territories occupied in 1967 in return for peace was the formula. A large number of Israelis, enough to bring a Labour government to power in 1992, believed that this was what the conflict was about, and this was the only way to solve it.

The focus on the fate of the occupied territories relegated the refugee problem to the margins of regional and international diplomacy. Palestinians had a share in this process, too, because there was a clash between conflicting Palestinian interests. Those under the harsh Israeli occupation of the West Bank and the Gaza Strip were interested in its termination more than anything else, and found the PLO in Beirut, and later in Tunis, incapable of helping. They preferred direct confrontation as well as direct negotiations with the Israelis. They were more successful than the PLO in bringing the Israelis and the Americans to the negotiating table, exactly because it was convenient for the Israelis to deal with the post-1967 reality, as well as to put aside and perhaps to forget the Palestinian victims of 1948. Nonetheless, the leadership of the occupied territories, once institutionalised in the form of *Lajnat al-Tawjih*,[37] sought a way of coordinating its policy with the PLO. The level of coordination reached its peak in the Madrid peace process, but had already come to the fore in the 18th Palestine

National Council (PNC), which recognised the principle of partition on the basis of the exchange of land for peace, and accepted the creation of two states in post–Mandatory Palestine. The leadership inside and outside Palestine had a common strategy for a while which marginalised the right of return.

The Oslo Accords have so far had catastrophic effects on that common strategy. It has shown the "insiders" and "outsiders" that their expectations have diverged after more than 25 years of different existence as national communities. Each has been affected by the reality of being "inside" and "outside", each developing its own set of expectations from the peace reality unfolding but by now disappearing before their very eyes. Those "inside" longed for the end of occupation and the creation of the state; those "outside", still responsible for the fate of all the Palestinians, wished for a peace reality which would enable the return of the refugees to their homes.

Until Oslo, the PLO was committed to the return of the refugees, not only in word, but also in deed. The armed struggle from Amman, Beirut and Tunis was for their sake and in their name. More than 40,000 young Palestinians died in this struggle. All this time, the refugee camps delivered a message of impermanence: huts built from temporary materials and an educational system conveying the message that there is no normal and real existence without return. Even though the huts are now made of brick, they are still not made of stone, and even when the camps become integral neighbourhoods of Amman, Beirut and Damascus, they still carried in their names and socio-geographical structure the Palestine of the past and of the future. What may seem to the outside observer to be a fictional construction of reality is in essence the only solid basis on which life can be sustained in the poor Palestinian refugee camps inside and outside Palestine.

This is not the place to explain why the Oslo agreement came about. Suffice it to mention that at first a coordination between the PLO leadership in Tunis and the Unified National Command, the body leading the *Intifada*, produced a series of steps, beginning with the Declaration of Independence of 1988, continuing with the first ever open US–PLO dialogue, and culminating in the Madrid Conference. The Israeli elections of 1992, the impotence of American pressure on Israel, the disintegration of the USSR and the mis-policy of Arafat in the Gulf Crisis all brought the PLO closer to direct negotiations with Israel. Clause 5, sub-clause 3 of the Declaration of Principles signed by the PLO and Israel on 13 September 1993 in Washington mentioned for the first time Israel's recognition of the right of the Palestinians to bring the future of the refugees to the negotiating table. No more and no less.

Until now, Israel (both Labour and Likud) has not been ready even to deal with less contentious subjects, such as settlements. Hence it is probably very far from willing to tackle the issue of refugees. The weakness of the Palestinian Authority *vis-à-vis* Israel and its total reliance on it ensure that this clause will not be dealt with in the near future. But the issue has now been highlighted and it can continue to be promoted by two groups: the "new historians" and their work, as already mentioned; and the Israeli Palestinians who have rediscovered their Palestinian nationality and are now playing a more confident role in Israeli politics. The issue will stay in the forefront also because of growing Palestinian dissatisfaction with the Oslo Accords and the futility of the present peace process. The solution of the refugee problem will remain the prime condition for the successful pursuit of a genuine and comprehensive peace.

Israelis – leaders and people alike – have a genuine psychological problem when faced with the refugee issue. This is indeed for them the "original sin". It puts a huge question mark over the Israeli self-image of moral superiority and human sensitivity. It ridicules Israel's oxymorons, such as the "purity of arms" or misnomers, such as the "Israeli Defence Forces", and raises doubts over the religious notion of the "chosen people" and the political pretension of being the only democracy in the Middle East which should be wholeheartedly supported by the West. In the past, it has produced a series of repressions and self denials as well as the promotion of unrealistic political solutions, the most prominent of which was the alliance with the Hashemites in Jordan at the expense of the Palestinians. It was accompanied by an intellectual struggle against the Palestinians, epitomised by the official Israeli fabrication of the history of the land and the conflict. It culminated in 1982 with Ariel Sharon's war of annihilation aiming at a physical destruction of both the PLO and the refugee land of Lebanon.

Palestinian guerrilla warfare and terrorism has helped the Israelis evade the issue. Palestinian peacemaking also helps the Israelis to evade the issue as long as the peace sponsors accept the Israeli formula that only the results of the 1967 War are negotiable. But regardless of Zionist repression and PLO misconduct, both sides will have to solve the problem. Even the President of the very limited and crippled Palestinian Authority knows he cannot sustain a reasonable amount of credibility and legitimacy if he openly or implicitly forgets the refugees. Israel will not help him. Israelis will find it difficult to relate to a tragedy or to an historical narrative in which they play an evil role. At some point, both sides will have to face the issue, and even with the American desire that everything should be dealt with in a business-like manner, without emotion or sentiment, it will be a highly charged subject to deal with because it is a moral one.

Martin Buber was aware of the need for Israel to relate not only to the problem itself in a material and political manner, but also to the moral aspects of it. He wrote to David Ben-Gurion in 1958 that peace was not just a matter of compromise (partition or reparations), but also of reconciliation. He did not go far in this approach, but it was a start. In recognition of Israel's responsibility, he suggested two courses of action: firstly, that Israel would ask the UN to begin a peace process centred on a solution to the refugee problem. This was in 1958, when the problem had been totally forgotten by the world, and when David Ben-Gurion was only too happy to let the world forget about it. An Israeli initiative, Buber claimed, would indicate a willingness to bear responsibility. Secondly, he said that Israel should allow a symbolic repatriation of refugees to its own territory as a principal recognition of the right of return, while demanding the resettlement of the others in Arab states and the repatriation of the rest to the (then) Jordanian West Bank and Egyptian Gaza Strip.

In a way, historiographical revisionism in Israel manifests a symbolic recognition of Israel's responsibility. How it can be translated into a concrete peace settlement, whether one according to Buber's suggestions or those of others, is beyond the terms of this article. An Israeli recognition of the centrality of the refugee problem in the Palestinian historical narrative, collective memory and national ethos is the first step. A revision of the Israeli historical narrative is the second. These two steps have been taken by some, but not enough, Israelis. The rest would follow, given a continued Palestinian willingness for reconciliation and a strong will for peace on both sides.

NOTES

1 See Ilan Pappe, "Post-Zionist Critique on Israel and the Palestinians, Part 1: The Academic Debate", *Journal of Palestine Studies*, vol. XXVI/2, no. 102 (Winter 1997), pp. 29–41.

2 I refer here to the 18th and 19th PNC resolutions on peace with Israel.

3 On the "new historians", see Pappe, "Post-Zionist Critique". The first Palestinian critique on this version was presented in a special issue of the *Journal of Palestine Studies* commemorating 40 years of *al-Nakba*, vol. 18, no. 1 (Autumn 1988). The most important input there was by Walid Khalidi, "Plan Dalet: Master Plan for the Conquest of Palestine", *Journal of Palestine Studies*, vol. 18, no. 1, Autumn 1988, pp. 4–20. Then came Nur Masalha's "Debate on the 1948 Exodus", *The Journal of Palestine Studies*, vol. 21, no. 1 (Autumn 1991), pp. 90–7.

4 Efraim Karsh, *Fabricating Israeli History* (London: Frank Cass, 1997).

5 This book by N. Lorch appeared in English as *The Edge of the Sword* (Tel Aviv, 1968).

6 Lorch, *Edge of the Sword*, pp. 300–30.

7 Arnon Golan, *The New Settlement Map of the Area Abandoned by Arab Population within the Territory of the State of Israel During Israel's War of Independence and After (1948–1950)* (Ph.D., Hebrew University, Jerusalem, 1993) (in Hebrew), pp. 95–114.

8 Plan Dalet was translated into English by Walid Khalidi and appears in the special issue of the *Journal of Palestine Studies*, vol. 18, no. 1, pp. 4–20.

9 Y. Slutzky, *The Book of the Hagana* (Tel Aviv, 1972) (in Hebrew), vol. 3, pp. 1955–9.

10 The story of four such villages appears in Benny Morris, *1948 and After: Israel and the Palestinians*, (Oxford: Clarendon Press, 1990), pp. 191–222.

11 A detailed description of the fate of each Palestinian village in 1948 can be found in Walid Khalidi, *All that Remains: The Palestinian Village Occupied and Depopulated by Israel in 1948* (Washington: Institute of Palestine Studies, 1992).

12 Benny Morris, "Yossef Weitz and the Transfer Committee, 1948–1949", *Middle Eastern Studies*, 22,4 (October 1986), pp. 522–61.

13 Shabtai Teveth, "The Palestinian Arab Refugee Problem and its Origins", *Middle Eastern Studies*, 26,2 (April 1990), pp. 220–6.

14 On 9 April 1948, over 200 men, women and children were massacred by the Irgun with the knowledge of the leadership as part of the bid to take over the area overlooking the road between Tel Aviv and Jerusalem. See Ilan Pappe, *The Making of the Arab–Israeli Conflict, 1947–1951* (London and New York: I. B. Tauris), pp. 85–6.

15 Teveth, "The Palestinian Arab Refugee Problem", pp. 227–9.

16 His original contribution is reproduced in the special issue of the *Journal of Palestine Studies* devoted to 1948: vol. 18, no. 1.

17 Pappe, *The Making of the Arab–Israeli Conflict*, p. 43.

18 Ibid., pp. 102–34.

19 Benny Morris, *The Birth of the Palestinian Refugee Problem* (Cambridge University Press, 1988).

20 Nur Masalha, *Expulsion of the Palestinians* (Washington: Institute of Palestine Studies, 1992), pp. 175–90.
21 Masalha, "Debate on the 1948 Exodus".
22 Norman G. Finkelstein, *Image and Reality in the Israeli–Palestine Conflict* (New York: Verso, 1995), pp. 51–87.
23 Pappe, *The Making of the Arab–Israeli Conflict*, pp. 87–101.
24 Morris, *The Birth of the Palestinian Refugee Problem*, pp. 62–3.
25 Pappe, *The Making of the Arab–Israeli Conflict*, p. 94.
26 Khalidi, "Plan Dalet", p. 8.
27 Pappe, *The Making of the Arab–Israeli Conflict*, p. 94.
28 See the entry for Zionism in *Al-Mawsu'at al-Filastiniyya* (Damascus: The PLO Publications, 1982).
29 On Sharett, see Ilan Pappe, "Moshe Sharett, David Ben-Gurion and the 'Palestinian Option', 1948–1956", *Studies in Zionism*, 7,1 (1986), pp. 77–97.
30 Morris, *1948 and After*, pp. 173–90.
31 Morris, *The Birth of the Palestinian Refugee Problem*, pp. 233–9.
32 On the question of figures, see Pappe, *The Making of the Arab–Israeli Conflict*, pp. 244–51.
33 Morris, "Weitz and the Transfer Committee", p. 539.
34 On the anti-repatriation policy adopted by Israel in August 1948, see Israel State Archive, File 2444/19, Meeting at the Prime Minister's Office.
35 Quoted in Morris, *The Birth of the Palestinian Refugee Problem*, p. 522.
36 PLO Charter, 1968, Clause 22.
37 See Emil F. Sahliyeh, *The PLO after the Lebanon War* (Boulder, Colo.: Westview Press, 1986), pp. 115–38.

3

The 1967 Palestinian
Exodus

*Nur Masalha**

In his study of the 1967 exodus, William Harris found that the exodus from the West Bank involved up to 250,000 people and was by far the largest out-movement of Palestinians caused by the 1967 hostilities. Harris also estimated the population loss of the Gaza Strip between June and December 1967 at 70,000.[1] In total, some 320,000 Palestinians fled or were expelled from the West Bank and Gaza in the course of the hostilities or shortly after.[2] In contrast to the large number of books written on the Palestinian refugee exodus of 1948, only meagre historical research has been carried out on the 1967 exodus. In fact Peter Dodd and Halim Barakat's *River Without Bridges* (1969)[3] and William Harris's *Taking Root: Israeli Settlement in the West Bank, the Golan and Gaza–Sinai, 1967–1980* (1980) are the only serious scholarly investigations of the 1967 exodus. No comparative work on the two phenomena has ever been attempted. The paucity of published works on the 1967 exodus may be explained by the following: the 1967 exodus was much smaller than the 1948 one, with manifestly different demographic and political consequences for Palestinian society in the West Bank and Gaza Strip; the relevant Israeli state archival sources are still classified; the 1967 exodus is perceived by Israelis and Palestinians alike to be somewhat less controversial than the 1948 one; and the widespread (mis)perception that the 1967 exodus was largely "voluntary", as opposed to the "forcible" nature of the 1948 exodus.

An important body of new evidence has been unearthed in recent years, much of it appearing in the form of investigative articles in the Hebrew press, which sheds new light on the events surrounding

* The support of the Palestine Studies Trust, UK, and the Institute for Palestine Studies, Washington DC, is gratefully acknowledged by the author.

the 1967 exodus. This chapter is an attempt to examine the causes of the 1967 exodus in the light of this new historical evidence and, more specifically, against the background of actual evictions and "transfer" operations carried out by the Israeli army during and after the 1967 War and their overall impact on the exodus.

The Hebrew press has been an important source for the events of 1967. This was supplemented by secondary sources in Hebrew, Arabic and English. However, any definitive conclusions on the 1967 exodus will have to wait until Palestinians produce some good oral history on the events of 1967 and until Israel declassifies its relevant official documents.

The Ideological Context: The Revival of the "Transfer" Concept

"Jerusalem of Gold"

The June War of 1967 marks a decisive turn in the history of Zionism, the Israeli State and the Palestinians, particularly those living in the occupied West Bank and Gaza Strip. Zionism had at last achieved its aim of controlling the whole of Palestine. Moreover, the overwhelming Israeli victory in the war, the seizure of the remainder of Palestine with its sizeable Arab population, the resultant outburst, and later upsurge, of messianic Zionism and the growing Israeli confidence all contributed to the prompt and inevitable revival of the "transfer" concept. In the wake of the 1967 conquests, the perception of Eretz Yisrael (the Land of Israel) as a whole was found not only in the maximalist Revisionist camp of Herut (later Likud), but increasingly gained ground in all mainstream Zionist parties, particularly the traditionally pragmatic ruling Labour Party. Given the fact that ideological/historical and security claims to the occupied areas were to be put forward, action had to be taken to "redeem the land" – through Jewish settlement without which the "redemption" process was impossible. At the same time, official and public concern at being faced with what is called "the demographic problem" – that is, the problem of absorbing too many non-Jews within the Jewish state – became manifestly stronger.

Although some 320,000 Palestinians fled or were expelled in the course of hostilities or shortly after, the Palestinian inhabitants of the territories – contrary to the 1948 exodus – remained *in situ*. The number of Palestinians living within the new cease-fire lines (including those citizens of Israel) was 1.3 million in 1967,[4] and given the high Arab birth rate, the prospect of the Palestinians becoming at least 50 per cent of the population – a Zionist/Israeli nightmare – was perceived as a feasible reality. The "conquest of the land" (*Kibbush Haadamah*) had always been Zionism's central task. The Zionists needed, as in 1948, to hold the land they had conquered, to people it with Jews and "develop" it, and to "transfer", or otherwise suppress, the native population who might oppose them. Indeed, for the Israeli leaders one of the key questions from June 1967 onwards was not whether Israel should maintain a presence in the newly acquired territories, but how it could be maintained without adding over one million Palestinians to the Arab minority of Israel. The old Zionist dilemma of non-Jews in a Jewish state had to be resolved. Against this background of Zionist expansionism, transfer ideas were revived in public debates, in popular songs, in articles in the Hebrew press and, most importantly, in cabinet discussions and government schemes.

For the settler who is coming to "redeem the land", the native inhabitants earmarked for dispossession are usually invisible. Marked for uprooting and dislocation, they are simultaneously divested of their human and national reality and classed as a marginal nonentity. Indeed, Zionist historiography provides ample evidence suggesting that from the very beginning of the Zionist *Yishuv* (settlement) in Palestine, the attitude of the majority of the Zionist groups towards the native Arab population ranged from a mixture of indifference and patronising superiority, to outright denial of their national rights, to uprooting and transferring them to neighbouring countries. Leading figures, such as Israel Zangwill, a prominent Anglo-Jewish writer – a close lieutenant of Theodor Herzl (the founder of political Zionism) and propagator of the transfer solution – worked relentlessly to propagandise the slogan that Palestine was "a land without a people for a people without a land". A reference to the same notion of an "empty country" was made in 1914 by Chaim Weizmann, later President of the World Zionist Congress and the first President of the State of Israel.

> In its initial stage, Zionism was conceived by its pioneers as a movement wholly depending on mechanical factors: there is a

country which happens to be called Palestine, a country without a people, and on the other hand there exists the Jewish people, and it has no country. What else is necessary, then, than to fit the gem into the ring, to unite this people with this country?"[5]

More revealing, however, is the anecdote Weizmann once told to Arthur Ruppin, the head of the Colonisation Department of the Jewish Agency, about how he (Weizmann) obtained the Balfour Declaration in 1917. When Ruppin asked what he thought about the indigenous Palestinians, Weizmann said: "The British told us that there are some hundred thousand negroes [*kushim*] and for those there is no value."[6] A few years after the Zionist movement obtained the Balfour Declaration, Zangwill wrote: "If Lord Shaftesbury was literally inexact in describing Palestine as a country without a people, he was essentially correct, for there is no Arab people living in intimate fusion with the country, utilising its resources and stamping it with a characteristic impress; there is at best an Arab encampment."[7] This and other pronouncements by Weizmann and other leading Zionists embodying European supremacy planted in the Zionist mind the racist notion of an empty territory – empty not necessarily in the actual absence of its inhabitants, but rather in a kind of civilisational barrenness – justifying Zionist colonisation and obliviousness to the fate of the native population and their eventual removal.

The same axiom of "empty territory" ("a land without a people for a people without a land") runs through Zionist state education in Israel and finds strong expression in children's literature. One such work for children contains the following excerpt:

Joseph and some of his men thus crossed the land [Palestine] on foot, until they reached Galilee. They climbed mountains, beautiful but empty mountains, where nobody lived . . . Joseph said: "We want to establish this Kibbutz and conquer this emptiness. We shall call this place Tel Hai [Living Hill] . . . The land is empty; its children have deserted it [the reference is, of course, to Jews]. They are dispersed and no longer tend it. No one protects or tends the land now."[8]

In similar vein, Israel's leading satirist, Dan Ben-Amotz, observed in 1982 that "the Arabs do not exist in our text books [for children].

This is apparently in accordance with the Jewish-Zionist-socialist principles we have received. 'A people without a land returns to a land without people.'"[9]

In October 1991, Prime Minister Yitzhak Shamir, in his address to the Madrid Peace Conference, resorted to quoting from *Innocents Abroad* by Mark Twain. (Twain visited Palestine in 1867 and his description of its natives was either marked by invective or was humorously pejorative.) Shamir's aim was to prove that Palestine was an empty territory, a kind of civilisational barrenness that (in Shamir's words) "no one wanted"; "A desolate country which sits in sackcloth and ashes – a silent, mournful expanse which not even imagination can grace with the pomp of life".[10] The same axiom of "ruined"/ "desolate"/"empty" country was used by both Shamir and the current Israeli Prime Minister, Binyamin Netanyahu, to justify Zionist colonisation of Palestine and the obliviousness to the fate of its native inhabitants.[11]

These images and formulas of empty and untended land gave those who propounded them a simple and self-explanatory Zionism. These contentions not only justified Zionist settlement but also helped to suppress conscience-pricking among Israeli Jews for the dispossession of the Palestinians before, during and after 1948 and since 1967: if the land had been empty, then no Zionist wrongdoing had taken place.

A few weeks after the June 1967 War, Israel's leading novelist, Amos Oz, wrote an article in the Hebrew daily *Davar* in which he drew attention to the revival of transfer thoughts in Israel: "one often hears talk about pushing the Palestinian masses back to rich Kuwait or fertile Iraq".[12] Oz tried to explain this "talk" about transfer against the background of the deep-seated inclination among Israeli Jews to see Palestine as a country without its indigenous inhabitants.

> When I was a child, some of my teachers taught me that after our Temple was destroyed and we were banished from our country, strangers came into what was our heritage and defiled it. The desert-born Arabs laid the land waste and let the terraces on the hillsides go to ruin. Their flocks destroyed the beautiful forests. When our first pioneers came to the land to rebuild it and to redeem it from desolation, they found an abandoned wasteland. True, a few backward, uncouth nomads wandered in it.

Some of our first arrivals thought that, by right, the Arabs should return to the desert and give the land back to its owners, and, if not, that they (the Zionists) should "arise and inherit", like those who conquered Canaan in storm: "A melody of blood and fire . . . climb the mountain, crush the plain. All you see – inherit . . . and conquer the land by the strength of your arm . . ." (Tchernichovsky, "I Have a Tune").[13]

Oz also drew attention to Na'omi Shemer's song "Jerusalem of Gold", which encapsulated this deep-seated inclination among Israeli Jews to see Palestine as a country without its Arab inhabitants. The song, "Jerusalem of Gold", which came to be defined as a kind of "national anthem of the Six Day War",[14] was commissioned by the municipality of Jewish Jerusalem, written for a music festival held on the eve of the war,[15] and became a national hit after the Israeli seizure of Arab East Jerusalem, the West Bank and Gaza Strip. It is the most popular song ever produced in Israel and in 1967 it swept the country like lightning, genuinely expressing Israeli national aspirations following the new conquests. Na'omi Shemer herself received the Israel Prize for her unique contribution to an Israeli song which carries these passages:

Jerusalem of Gold . . .
How did the water cisterns dry out, the market-place is empty,
And no-one visits the Holy Mount [al-Haram al-Sharif] in the
    Old City.
And through the cave within the rock winds are whining,
And no-one goes down to the Dead Sea by way of Jericho.

. . .

Jerusalem of Gold . . .
We have returned to the water cisterns, to the market-place and
    the square.
A shofar[16] sounds on the Holy Mount in the Old City.
And in the caves within the rock a thousands suns do glow,
We shall again descend to the Dead Sea en route for Jericho.[17]

In his *Davar* article, Oz offers a liberal Zionist explanation of the connection between the "land without a people" formula, the popularity of Shemer's song "Jerusalem of Gold", and the emergence of the transfer "talk" after the war:

It seems that the enchantment of "renewing the days of old" is what gave Zionism its deep-seated inclination to see a country without inhabitants before it . . . How fitting would it have been for the Return to Zion to have taken the land from the Roman legions or the nations of Canaan and Philistia. And to come to a completely empty country would have been even better. From there, it is only a short step to the kind of self-induced blindness that consists in disregarding the existence of the country's Arab population, or in discounting it and its importance on the dubious grounds that it "has created no valuable cultural assets here," as if that would permit us to take no notice of its very existence. In time, Na'omi Shemer would express this state of mind in her song, "Jerusalem of Gold . . . the market-place is empty/And no-one goes down to the Dead Sea by way of Jericho." Meaning, of course, that the market-place is empty of Jews and that no Jew goes down to the Dead Sea by way of Jericho. A remarkable revelation of a remarkably characteristic way of thinking.[18]

This "characteristic way of thinking" echoes strongly the deep-seated formula of "a land without a people" and naturally leads to the revival of the transfer concept, a fact illustrated by the attitude of Na'omi Shemer, the poet laureate of Greater Israel's supporters, towards the indigenous inhabitants of Palestine. In January 1979, one of the famous heroes of the Israeli army, Meir Har-Tzion,[19] who owns a large cattle ranch situated on the lands of the destroyed Arab village of Kawkab al-Hawa in the Beisan Valley (the inhabitants of which were driven out in 1948) stated: "I do not say that we should put them [the Arabs] on trucks and kill them . . . We must create a situation for them in which it would not be worth living here, but [to leave] to Jordan or Saudi Arabia or any other Arab state."[20] Har-Tzion was promptly applauded by Shemer in an article in the Histadrut (Labour-controlled) daily, Davar.

Arab emigration from Israel, if it is done with mutual respect and positive will . . . is likely to be the right solution . . . It is possible that it will be recognised as a most humane possibility after much suffering and only after hard and bitter civil war – but talking about it is permitted and must be done now . . . Why is the exodus of one million French from Algeria a progressive and humane solution and the exodus of one million Arabs from Israel not?[21]

Shemer and Har-Tzion are not marginal figures in Israel. Shemer is Israel's most famous and popular songwriter and Har-Tzion, who was brought up and educated in Kibbutz Ein Harod and fought in the Ariel Sharon-commanded Unit 101, set up by the army in the 1950s to carry out "retaliatory" attacks against Arab targets, was described by the late Moshe Dayan as "the brightest soldier in Jewish history since Bar-Kohkva".[22]

The argument that the support for the "transfer" concept does not come only from a fringe group is also illustrated by the fact that the other veterans of Unit 101 and the Paratroops Corps, the elite force of the Israeli army which carried out most of the "retaliatory" operations against Arab targets in the 1950s and 1960s, have emerged in the 1970s and 1980s as among the most persistent public exponents of Arab "transfer". The most important veteran commanders of the paratroopers were: Ariel Sharon, Defence Minister in 1981–2; Raphael Eitan, Chief of Staff in 1978–83; and Colonel Aharon Davidi, a former head of the Paratroops Corps, who became a senior lecturer in geography at Tel Aviv University. In an interview in the mass-circulation daily *Maariv*, Davidi said how he would solve the Palestinian problem: "In the simplest and most humane manner: the transfer of all the Palestinians from their present locations to the Arab countries." When interviewer Dov Goldstein remarked that the Arabs would not accept such a solution, Davidi responded:

> They will. The transfer is very important for both the Jews and the Arabs. They will accept it if they have no choice. The Arab states are spread out over a territory of more than 10 million square kilometres. The density of the Arabs is the lowest in the world. Would it be a problem to absorb one million there, and to arrange housing and employment for them, with the help of great wealth?[23]

Davidi's assertions echo classical mainstream Zionist argumentation in justification of Arab removal. Such support for the "transfer" concept does not come only from a fringe group; some of the nation's leading authors, novelists and poets, such as Natan Alterman, Haim Hazaz, Yigal Mossenson and Moshe Shamir (all of whom supported Israel's retention of all the territories seized in 1967), publicly endorsed the idea of transfer in the post-1967 era.[24] These leading literary figures were also closely associated with mainstream Labour or left-wing Zionism in the pre-1948 period and the first two decades of the State of Israel.

Natan Alterman (1910–70), whose poetry had a powerful impact on Jewish society during the *Yishuv* period and the first three decades of the State of Israel, wrote in an article in *Maariv* shortly after the 1967 War: "The transfer solution is only possible in an ideal peace situation between us and the Arab states which will agree to cooperate with us in a great project of population transfer". Alterman had served on the editorial board of the liberal daily *Haaretz* from 1934 to 1943, when he joined the Histadrut daily *Davar* (virtually the mouthpiece of the ruling Mapai Party), and had been closely associated with the two most important leaders of Mapai, David Ben-Gurion and Berl Katznelson, the founder of *Davar* and hero of labour Zionism in the Mandatory period.

In justification of his views of the morality of Arab removal in the post-1967 period, Alterman cited statements made by Berl Katznelson in 1943 (the year Alterman joined *Davar*):

> Our contemporary history has known a number of transfers . . . [for instance] the USSR arranged the transfer of one million Germans living in the Volga region and transferred them to very distant places . . . One could assume that this transfer was done against the will of the transferees . . . There could be possible situations that would make [Arab] population transfer desirable for both sides . . . Who is the socialist who is interested in rejecting the very idea beforehand and stigmatising it as something unfair? Has Merhavyah not been built on transfer? Were it not for these many transfers, Hashomer Hatza'ir [a Zionist group which founded the Mapai Party in 1948] would not be residing today in Merhavyah, or Mishmar Ha'emek or other places . . . and if what has been done for a settlement of Hashomer Hatza'ir is a fair deed, why would it not be fair when it is done on a much larger and greater scale, not just of Hashomer Hatza'ir but for the whole of Israel?[25]

Haim Hazaz (1898–1973) was another leading author who supported the "transfer" concept in the post-1967 era. A prolific Hebrew novelist, his works won him numerous awards, including the Bialik Prize and the Israel Prize, the top prize awarded by the State of Israel. Hazaz, in an article published in *Davar* on 10 November 1967, echoed the Labour Zionist apologia of the pre-1948 period:

> There is the question of Judea and Ephraim [the West Bank], with a large Arab population which must be evacuated to neighbouring Arab states. This is not an exile like the exile of the Jews among the Gentiles . . . They will be coming to their brothers, to large and wide and little-populated countries. One culture, one language and religion. This is "transfer" such as that which took place between Turkey and Greece, between India and Pakistan . . . putting the world aright in one place through exchanging [the Arab population] to its designated place. We will assume responsibility for this task and assist in its planning, organising and financing.[26]

Hazaz repeated his transfer proposal in a simplistic way in an interview in 1968: "The [1967] war cost us 3 billion [Israeli] pounds – let's take three billion more pounds and give them to the Arabs and tell them to get out."[27] Hazaz was willing to allow a small Arab minority to remain in Israel provided it "would not disrupt or change the Jewish character of the Land of Israel".[28]

Another strand of support for the "transfer" idea comes from some of the ideologists, public figures and old-timers of the ruling Mapai Party, like Eli'ezer Livneh, Haim Yahil and Tzvi Shiloah, who publicly endorsed the transfer concept in the immediate post-1967 period.[29]

Eli'ezer Livneh (1902–75), who headed the political and educational department of the Hagana in the Mandatory period, was a Mapai Knesset member of the first and second Knessets (1949–55).[30] He served on the influential Foreign Affairs and Defence Committee between 1951 and 1955 (during which period he was closely associated with Ben-Gurion) and put forward in the summer of 1967 a plan for the transfer of 600,000 Palestinian refugees from the West Bank and Gaza Strip. In an article in the mass-circulation daily *Maariv* of 22 June 1967 (less than two weeks after the June War conquests), Livneh wrote: "They [the refugees] will choose, willingly, resettlement in whatever Arab country, or emigration to countries overseas. The Prime Minister of Australia has already suggested cooperation." A few weeks later, Livneh reiterated the proposal:

The refugees are now within our boundaries. We could rehabilitate some of them in our country [in Sinai, Egypt], and transfer others for productive life overseas or resettle them in neighbouring countries with which we will come to an arrangement . . . Jordan . . . is likely to be the chief beneficiary [as it would be able] to populate its wide territories.[31]

Livneh developed his proposal further into a fully-fledged plan in an article in the liberal daily *Haaretz* on 28 August 1967 (p. 2). He writes that in the last 19 years

tens of thousands of refugees have crossed . . . to Saudi Arabia, Kuwait, Bahrain, Qatar, Abu Dhabi, Dubai and the [other] oil principalities. Tens of thousands of their families, who remained in the camps [in the West Bank and Gaza] have lived off money remitted by their distant relatives . . . Just as half a million Jews immigrated to the Land of Israel from Arab countries . . . hundreds of thousands of "Palestinian" Arabs were crossing to Arab countries. The parallel is amazing . . . What is happening in the refugee camps in a sporadic and limited way without the support of a governmental body [in Arab states] should be widened and developed by us as regards dimensions and means. This means: (a) constructive emigration should be directed to all the countries in need of a workforce including the United States, Canada, Australia and Latin America; (b) the emigrants should be entitled to financial support from Israel . . . (c) the implementation must be planned over a long time, let us say 18 years; (d) the number of countries designated for migration and resettlement should be as large as possible.

Livneh continued: "If these Arabs [would-be transferees] want to maintain their Arabness in the United States, Canada, Brazil and Australia, it is up to them." Elsewhere, he made another small "concession":

To the extent that there might be a number of refugees who want, in spite of everything, to link agricultural roots in a landscape close to their spirit and tradition, it is worth offering them settlement in north Sinai . . . In the opinion of cautious experts there is water, land and other conditions there for the settlement of tens of thousands (approximately 60,000 persons).

Livneh argued that the "carrying out of the [transfer] task" depended mainly on Israel and on the conditions it could create.

(a) The allocation of large sums and (b) patience. If we spend 5,000 dollars on the emigration of a family of 6–7 persons on average (1,500 dollars on the journey and the rest for the exclusive use of the emigrating family) we would be able to finance every year the emigration of tens of thousands of families, or 60–70,000 persons by 50 million dollars (or 150 million Israeli Lira, three per cent of our state budget). There would be no lack of candidates and they would increase when encouraging information from abroad on the settlement of the first ones arrived . . . If we placed such encouraging sums . . . within 8–9 years about 600,000 persons would be likely to emigrate at this rate, meaning all the refugees from the [Gaza] Strip, the Hebron mountain, the mountains of Ephraim [in the West Bank] and the Jordan Valley.

Although in his earlier proposal Livneh had suggested that the world powers should finance the transfer and resettlement, in the August 1967 plan he proposed that Israel and world Jewry should shoulder "financing the project":

There is no need to explain its importance from the national, security and propaganda point of view. It should be placed at the top of our national priorities. In so far as we need [financial] means for it greater than the estimate given here, we are entitled to appeal to world Jewry. This is more justified and blessed than the use of fundraising to raise the standard of living [of Israelis] . . . The Jews of the diaspora will respond to this with understanding, and even with enthusiasm.

For Livneh, the success of the "project" would depend on its

planning with a long breath. In the beginning there will certainly be various difficulties in running it . . . Our reckoning should not be for one month or one season. We will develop the project as our responsibility, without making it conditional on the participation of other elements. To the extent that we carry it out, we will gain the cooperation of others. The United Nations' action in the refugee camps (UNRWA) would then assume constructive and purposeful meaning . . . The training in the schools of UNRWA would be adjusted to the needs of emigration and resettlement.

From other references it is obvious that Livneh was not content with the removal of 600,000 Palestinian refugees from the West Bank and Gaza, as he proposed in his euphemistically termed "emigration project", but sought to transform the demographic and political reality of the occupied territories by clearing out other residents as well.[32] What is also noticeable is the absence of any discussion in his plan of the resistance the Palestinians would be likely to put up against such a mass removal. Such a deliberate attempt to ignore Palestinian resistance to transfer is – as will be seen again – common to other transfer proposals put forward publicly in the euphoric period following the spectacular conquests of the 1967 War.

Mainstream Zionism rejected the views of the liberal minority – to which Amos Oz belongs – which argued that Palestine is also the homeland of the Palestinian people. Therefore one needs to go beyond Oz's explanation to understand the background against which "transfer" thoughts and debates promptly resurfaced after 1967. This background consists of the standard mainstream Zionist "solution for the Palestinian problem", which was predicated on the claim for monopolised Zionist/Jewish ownership and Israeli/Jewish domination of Eretz Yisrael/Palestine. This being the case, Zionism was bound to base its conception of Jerusalem on a non-existent entity, "Jerusalem of Gold", and to involve abstract historical and ideological rights in the newly acquired territories, as well as resting its claim on territorial expansion and domination and the actual "redemption of land" through settlement. One implication of the claim for monopolised ownership of a country shared by another people is the "transfer" solution. Against this background, transfer proposals and plans were inevitably put forward by mainstream Labour Party leaders – including ministers – immediately after the 1967 victory.

The Israeli Cabinet Meetings of 15–19 June 1967 and Moshe Dayan's Activities

General Moshe Dayan was appointed Defence Minister on the eve of the 1967 War and retained this powerful post until 1974. He was the archetypal exponent of Israeli post-1967 expansionism and the de facto integration of the occupied territories into Israel. Dayan instituted a policy of "creeping annexation", a process by which Israeli administration, jurisdiction and law gradually, incrementally and in a draconian fashion were imposed on the West Bank and the Gaza Strip in ever-expanding areas, yet without a comprehensive act of legal annexation. This process, also described as a de facto annexation, is generally seen in the actual transformation of the demographic and physical realities of these areas.

The Israeli government, the Dayan-headed Defence Ministry and Mossad (the Israeli external secret service) resorted, by and large, to discreet "transfer" activities in the aftermath of the June War. This method of secret transfer activities, as well as transfer discussions at cabinet level, has gradually been revealed by Israeli journalists and researchers as well as politicians. Examples of these revelations are the researches of Meir Avidan, published in *Davar* on 2, 5 and 19 June 1987, and the articles published by two Israeli journalists, Yossi Melman and Dan Raviv, who published an article in the *Washington Post* on 7 February 1988 entitled "Expelling Palestinians". The same article appeared in the *Guardian Weekly* (London) two weeks later under the title "A final solution of the Palestinian Problem?" and was similar to an article in the Hebrew daily *Davar* by the authors, which appeared around the same time and was entitled "This is the history of transfer".[33]

Avidan, Melman and Raviv reveal that less than two weeks after the Israeli victory in the war of June 1967, the Eshkol cabinet convened for a number of secret meetings, held between 15 and 19 June, to discuss a major issue: what to do about the "demographic problem" – the fact that the bulk of the Arab population of the territories, contrary to 1948, remained *in situ*. The official transcript of the meeting remains secret. However, according to private diaries kept and notes taken by Yaacov Hertzog, brother of Haim Hertzog, President of Israel from 1983 to 1993, who was at the time Director-General of the Prime Minister's office, both the Finance Minister, Pinhas Sapir, and the Foreign Minister, Abba Eban, called for the settlement of the Palestinian refugees in neighbouring countries.[34] Relying on Avidan's research, Melman and Raviv point out that at these meetings, "sentiment seemed to favour Deputy Prime Minister Yigal Allon's proposal that Palestinian refugees be transported to the Sinai Desert and that Palestinians should be persuaded to move abroad".[35] According to Hertzog's notes, Allon complained at the meeting of 15 June: "We do not do enough among the Arabs to encourage emigration".[36] At the same meeting, Menahem Begin, then Minister Without Portfolio, recommended the demolition of the refugee camps and the transfer of their residents to El Arish, in Sinai, which had been captured from Egypt.[37] Begin's proposal was also supported by the Labour leader and Minister of Transport, Moshe Carmel, at these discussions.[38]

Avidan also reveals that the Ministerial Committee for Defence decided on 15 June 1967 that: "Israel will demand that the Arab countries and the superpowers start preparing an elementary plan to solve the refugee problem, which would include the settlement of refugees in Iraq, Syria, (Egypt?), Algeria, Morocco, Jordan and other countries. In the presentation of this demand emphasis will be made on the fact of population exchange" (that is, that the settlement of the refugees will come in the place of the Jews who left Arab countries).[39] Apparently, a ministerial committee was set up to look into ways of "solving the refugee problem".[40] A few weeks after the June discussions, Dayan went even further, publicly declaring that the resettlement of the refugees must be carried out in the Jordanian kingdom across the river.[41]

The product of the June discussions was not a total relocation of the refugee camps' residents to the Sinai Desert but rather a "voluntary" transfer plan, designed to "thin out" the population of the Old City of Jerusalem, the West Bank and Gaza, which later became known as the Moshe Dayan plan. Immediately after the June 1967 War, Dayan consolidated a plan for encouraging Arab emigration from the occupied territories to South America.[42] The scheme began with the formation of a secret unit charged with "encouraging" the departure of the Palestinians for foreign shores. The secret unit was composed of representatives of the Prime Minister's office, the Defence Ministry and the Israel Defence Forces. Some patchy revelations about the same secret scheme were also made by General Uzi Narkiss, Commanding General of the Central Command until 1968 (with responsibility for the West Bank), who told an interviewer in October 1988 that after the June 1967 War,

> some of the Mossad men came to me . . . and then they offered some [Arab] individuals sums [of money] in exchange for them leaving their property [in the Old City of Jerusalem and the West Bank] . . . These sums were part of the government allocation for

this matter. Some agreed but the experiment failed; it succeeded only with several scores of people, until one of our daughters was killed in revenge in our embassy in Paraguay. Then the operation was stopped.[43]

According to reports in the Israeli press, a total of about one thousand Palestinians were "transferred" to South America during the three years of the plan.[44]

Yossef Weitz's Proposal, September 1967

Yossef Weitz (1889–1972), former head of the Jewish National Fund's Land Department and a leading Zionist proponent of transfer, with experience in dealing with the "Arab problem" spanning four decades, realised immediately after the war that the "Arab problem" had acquired a new quality. On 29 September 1967 he published an article in *Davar* in which he reiterated his 1940 proposal to transfer all the Palestinians and urged the public to consider the idea in the wake of the new conquests. The article was based on a six-page memorandum written by Weitz 12 days earlier,[45] and possibly submitted to the Israeli government for consideration.

> Amongst ourselves it must be clear that there is no room for both peoples in this country . . . With the Arabs transferring, the country will be wide open for us. With the Arabs staying, the country will be narrow and restricted . . . The only solution is the Land of Israel, or at least the Western Land of Israel [that is, the whole of Palestine], without Arabs. The Zionist work . . . must come simultaneously in the manner of redemption (here is the meaning of the messianic idea); the only way is to transfer the Arabs from here to neighbouring countries, all of them, except perhaps Bethlehem, Nazareth and old Jerusalem. Not a single village or a single tribe must be left. And the transfer must be done through their absorption in Iraq and Syria and even in Transjordan. For that goal, money will be found and even a lot of money. And only then will the country be able to absorb millions of Jews . . . There is no other solution.[46]

From this perspective, Weitz explained in his *Davar* article, a solution of "transfer" was advocated in the early 1940s and was supported by Berl Katznelson,[47] Yitzhak Volcani[48] and Menahem Ussishkin,[49] and "investigations were undertaken to put this concept into effect".[50] Weitz argued that

> any suggestion for the settlement of the liberated territories (the West Bank and Gaza Strip) must be subjected necessarily to a definite policy which addresses and solves three fundamental problems rendered more acute by the June War: regional security, the demographic problem and the "resettlement of the refugees" . . . [As to] the demographic problem, there are some who assume that the non-Jewish population, even in large percentage, can be more effectively under our surveillance if it is within our boundaries, and there are some who assume the contrary . . . The author of this article tends to support the second assumption and has an additional argument to support his position: the need to sustain the character of the state, which will henceforth and obviously in the near future be Jewish, by the majority of its inhabitants, with a non-Jewish minority limited to 15 per cent.[51]

Early on, Israeli leaders realised that the refugee communities in the West Bank and Gaza[52] presented the most serious problem for Israel in more than one way. The refugee camps were – and still are – the most overcrowded parts of the territories, and are therefore the most difficult to control. In addition, because the refugees did not accept their sojourn in the territories as an indefinite one, Israeli leaders saw a greater long-term challenge from the refugees than from the indigenous population. In his *Davar* article, Weitz referred to a memorandum drawn up by Ezra Danin, Zalman Lifschitz and himself – all members of the Israeli government Transfer Committee of 1948 – called "Memorandum of Settlement of the Arab Refugees", dated October 1948, the composition of which was preceded by investigations, surveys and research based on data considered reliable at the time.[53] In 1967, Weitz believed that

> the logical and possible way of rehabilitating the refugees in the Arab countries is blocked by their rulers, and will be blocked for a long time to come. With no alternative, the way leads at least initially to the West Bank side of the Jordan Valley. In this region, the arable lands could be increased by means of desalination and some of the refugees could be settled there.

[79]

However, for Weitz, the solution for most residents in the territories' refugee camps remained transfer. Although willing to cede some of the heavily populated regions of the territories to Jordan, Weitz argued that in order to forestall the Arab demographic problem

> we should consider as an essential action towards the solution of the refugee problem making financial assistance available to families who are prepared to emigrate to countries outside the Arab world. Every financial investment in these [transfer] activities will be of great blessing to our state today and in the future.[54]

It should be pointed out that not everyone in Israel was satisfied merely with financial incentives and encouragement of the kind proposed by Weitz. An opinion poll carried out three weeks after the 1967 victory showed 28 per cent of the Israeli Jewish electorate in favour of expelling the Palestinian citizens of Israel, and 22 per cent favouring expulsion of Palestinians from the occupied territories.[55] In a way, Weitz's practical and usually discreet approach to Arab transfer activities characterised the pragmatism of Labour Zionism and its handling of this very prickly and explosive issue. Although in 1940 he had advocated "total" Arab removal from the whole of Palestine, in 1967 he opted for "partial" transfer. It is likely that decades of immersion in the attempts to implement secret plans of Arab transfer taught Weitz to take pragmatic constraints into consideration – including opposition among the Palestinians themselves and rejection from Arab states, as well as the sensitivity of Western public opinion. All these factors rendered the transfer task exceedingly difficult.

The Israeli Army's Schemes and Operations, June–September 1967

The Destruction of the Ancient al-Magharbeh Quarter
The June 1967 War began suddenly and ended quickly. In his recent book, *Intimate Enemies* (1995), Meron Benvenisti, former Deputy Mayor of Jerusalem, writes:

> At the end of the 1967 War there were attempts to implement a forced population transfer. Residents of cities and villages in areas

near the cease-fire line were expelled from their homes and their communities destroyed; the Israeli authorities offered financial "incentives" and free transportation to Palestinians willing to leave.[56]

In fact, in the course of hostilities and in the immediate aftermath of the June 1967 War, with its rapidly changing circumstances and particularly given the fact that most Western governments applauded the overwhelming Israeli victory, Defence Minister Dayan and other army generals (including Uzi Narkiss, Haim Hertzog and Shlomo Lahat) found an ideal opportunity to drive out tens of thousands of Arabs from their villages, towns and refugee camps in the West Bank and Gaza Strip. In their article "This is the History of Transfer" (*Davar*, 19 February 1988) the Israeli journalists Yossi Melman and Dan Raviv pointed out that the Israeli conception of

> exploiting opportunities to transfer Arab populations, which was first employed in 1948, resurfaced shortly after the 1967 War: commanders in various ranks of the army believed that the wind blowing from the political echelons was calling for the exploitation of the opportunity to thin out the Palestinian population.

Among the first people evicted were the residents of the ancient al-Magharbeh Quarter in the Old City of Jerusalem. They were turned out of their homes on 11 June, two days after the capture of East Jerusalem by the Israeli military, with three hours' notice.[57] Apparently, the quarter was completely demolished because it was located immediately adjacent to the southern part of the Wailing Wall, the Western Wall of al-Haram al-Sharif (the Noble Sanctuary). Its inhabitants, about 135 families (or some 650 to 1,000 persons), were the beneficiaries of an ancient and important Islamic Waqf foundation originally established in 1193 by al-Malik al-Afdal, the son of Salah al-Din. Its obliteration in June 1967 resulted also in the destruction of several historic religious sites (including two mosques, two *zawiyas* and a great number of endowed buildings) which the Quarter contained.[58]

The Old City of Jerusalem was captured by the Israeli army on 7 June 1967. In his book, *Jerusalem: A City Without a Wall*, Uzi Benziman, a prominent journalist on the daily *Haaretz*, described in detail the circumstances surrounding the destruction of this Muslim quarter.[59] The story began on 7 June while Israeli paratroopers were advancing through the alleys of the Old City of Jerusalem. An engineering corps officer in the Central Command, Eytan Ben-Moshe, approached Shlomo Lahat, a senior military officer in the Central Command and the designated Military Governor of Jerusalem (subsequently Mayor of Tel Aviv) and proposed the demolition of a building used as a "public toilet", which was part of the al-Magharbeh Quarter and was adjacent to the Wailing Wall. In fact, even before Lahat had arrived in Jerusalem, Defence Minister Dayan had asked him to "clear pathways" to the Wailing Wall so that 200,000 Jews would be able to visit the Wall during the forthcoming feast of Shavuoth (Pentecost).[60] This seemed to suggest that the original idea to level at least part of the quarter came from Dayan. Furthermore, according to Benziman's account, several senior Israeli commanders in the Jerusalem district (including Uzi Narkiss, the Commanding General of the Central Command, Shlomo Lahat and Haim Hertzog), as well as Dayan, the Mayor of West Jerusalem Teddy Kollek and former Prime Minister David Ben-Gurion were all involved, either in the initial decision or in the actual implementation of the systematic operation to destroy the Arab quarter.

To begin with, Lahat approved Ben-Moshe's idea and sent the demolition plan to Uzi Narkiss (who also gave the orders to bulldoze the three Arab villages of Bayt Nuba, Imwas and Yalu, below). Moreover, on 8 June, former Premier Ben-Gurion, accompanied by Teddy Kollek and Reserve Colonel Yaacov Yannai, Director of the National Parks Authority,[61] visited the Wailing Wall. Both Ben-Gurion and Kollek were strongly in favour of the removal of Arab buildings adjacent to the Wailing Wall.[62] Kollek, who had long been closely associated with Ben-Gurion and who had been elected Mayor of West Jerusalem in 1965, appeared to have played a central role in the formulation and implementation of the decision to demolish the al-Magharbeh Quarter in June 1967. Apparently, he also informed the then Minister of Justice, Yaacov Shimshon Shapira, who replied: "I am not certain of the legal position, but do what should be done quickly, and let the God of Israel be with you."[63] In addition to Defence Minister Dayan, who represented the civil authority as well as approving and controlling the conduct of the field commanders, and, as we shall see, oversaw the progress of the demolition, Shapira's answer suggests at least some indirect and tacit ministerial approval of the action.

However, the actual order to capture the quarter and destroy its houses was given by Shlomo Lahat, the then Commander of Jerusalem, with the express approval of Uzi Narkiss, whose approval was given at a meeting with Lahat on 9 June.[64] On the following day, Saturday 10 June, Mayor Kollek assembled a group of "experts" at his apartment to discuss basic information about the Wailing Wall and the al-Magharbeh Quarter. The group included Dan "Max" Tanai, the engineer of the National Parks Authority; the historian and archaeologist Professor Michael Avi-Yonah; Yaacov Yannai; Aryeh Sharon, Chairman of the National Parks Authority; and Yaacov Salman, Deputy Military Governor of East Jerusalem and Lahat's assistant. Kollek explained to the participants the reasons for this urgent meeting.

> The al-Magharbeh Quarter adjacent to the Wailing Wall must be demolished. The responsibility for executing the plan will be in the hands of the National Parks Authority in order to give the matter as far as possible an unofficial character. The Department of Antiquities in the Ministry of Education and the Israeli Defence Force are not interested in involvement, publicly, in the execution of the plan, although they both bless it and will accord it practical assistance.[65]

Kollek put Tanai in charge of executing the operation, possibly seeking to bestow upon it a civilian legitimacy. Central to the planning and mode of procedure by Kollek and his technical "experts" was the need to act speedily in order to stave off internal criticism and potential obstruction and avoid attracting too much attention by the foreign media. At noon on 10 June, Kollek and his colleagues proceeded to the area of the Wailing Wall and decided on the spot to bulldoze the entire Arab quarter with the aim of creating a vast plaza for the Wailing Wall.[66] Kollek also got in touch with several Jerusalem construction companies, asking them to make earth-moving equipment available and to undertake the demolition task as "a donation to the city".[67]

While the actual demolition job was partly assigned to a civilian body called the Guild of Builders and Contractors, the Israeli army, particularly its Central Command's engineering corps, rendered the necessary assistance. Some time during the afternoon or the evening of the same day, an army officer went from one house to another, ordering the residents of the quarter to move out. When many families refused to leave their homes, an army unit moved in and evicted the bulk of the inhabitants by force. Meanwhile, two bulldozers and other heavy tools were assembled by the engineering corps and those in charge of the operation sought to complete the whole work on the night of 10 June. Commenting on this urgency of action by those responsible for the deed, Benziman explained:

> Those who presided over the destruction of the [Arab] neighbourhood assumed that their action was motivated neither by security [considerations] nor by mere town planning. They were driven that night [10–11 June] by an almost mystical feeling; that, in their eyes, they were the representatives of the Jewish people, who came to assert [Jewish] sovereignty over its most sacred site . . . The fate of 135 Arab families, who were the victims of these desires, was of no concern to them.[68]

The speed with which the Israeli authorities sought to carry out the levelling of the Arab residential houses was also evident in the fact that in the same evening one demolished wall of a house revealed an unconscious, badly injured, middle-aged Arab woman. By midnight, she was dead.

General Uzi Narkiss, came to the site in the early morning of Sunday 11 June and ordered that the levelling be completed speedily. More men and heavy tools were brought in. On the afternoon of the same day, Defence Minister Dayan appeared at the site. He also ordered Lahat to complete the levelling of the quarter with all speed,[69] possibly so that foreign journalists would not see the remains of the destroyed Arab quarter. In fact, only muted internal questioning of the levelling of the quarter was made by the Minister of Religious Affairs, as well as the Prime Minister, Levi Eshkol himself, who asked Uzi Narkiss on the telephone: "Why are residential houses being demolished?" The Ministry of Religious Affairs in particular appeared to be concerned that the action could tarnish Israel's image abroad.[70] However, backed by the powerful Defence Minister Dayan – who conducted the June 1967 War with great independence – Narkiss and Lahat easily managed to ignore the criticism and pursue the policy of levelling and forcible evacuation with and without the approval of the civilian authorities. (In the case of the al-Magharbeh Quarter there was active cooperation with Kollek and other civil authorities.) Benziman believed that

> the policy of evacuation and demolition continued for several days after the [Israeli army] entrance into the city within the walls. It was executed at the initiative of middle military echelons and with the tacit approval of senior level command. There was a lack of communication between the civil authorities and the military government; in practice, the latter exercised civilian functions. The military authorities, on their own responsibility, encouraged the Arab residents to get out of Jerusalem and other cities in the West Bank and to go to the East Bank [of Jordan].[71]

The evicted residents of the al-Magharbeh Quarter were dispersed in West Bank villages close to Jerusalem such as Shu'fat, Bayt Hanina and Silwan, as well as in the Muslim Quarter of the Old City of Jerusalem. None of the Israeli government ministries was prepared to accept responsibility for the demolition of the quarter, and no attempt was made to offer the evicted residents alternative accommodation.[72] Like the eviction of the three large villages in the Latrun area (see below), this removal should be treated as an internal expulsion rather than transfer out of the occupied territories. However, it is extremely important to remember that these cases of internal expulsion had a psychological effect on the 1967 exodus from the West Bank to Jordan – helping, almost certainly, to precipitate and encourage further exodus out of the country, especially in the first few weeks following the war.

The eviction and levelling of the al-Magharbeh Quarter were only the beginning of the sweeping changes carried out by the Israeli authorities in the Old City of Jerusalem. On 17 June 1967 at 4 a.m., the Israeli army ordered the inhabitants of the former Jewish Quarter and the surrounding houses to leave the premises within 24 hours. Apparently this measure affected several hundred Palestinian families who, according to the 1967 "Jerusalem Diary" of Sister Marie-Thérèse, could be observed all day carrying their belongings through the alleys of Jerusalem. Some of them were able to find refuge with relatives and friends. But the majority had to leave the town.[73] In the Old City's

Jewish Quarter and its surrounding districts, some 4,000 Palestinians were evicted to enable the reconstruction of a vastly enlarged and purely "Jewish" quarter, excluding its former Arab residents.[74]

The destruction of the al-Magharbeh Quarter should be seen as part of a wider internal debate that took place during and after the 1967 War about the future of the Muslim shrines in the Old City of Jerusalem, particularly the al-Aqsa Mosque and the Dome of the Rock, the third holiest Islamic site. In this connection, a recent article in the Hebrew daily *Haaretz* (31 December 1997) revealed the details of an extraordinary conversation that took place between General Narkiss and the Israeli army's Chief Rabbi, Shlomo Goren (later to become Ashkenazi Chief Rabbi of Israel from 1973 to 1983). In an interview given to *Haaretz* shortly before his death in late 1997, Narkiss recalled that only a few hours after the Old City was captured by the Israeli army in June 1967, he was urged by Rabbi Goren to blow up the Dome of the Rock. Narkiss had this to say:

> The paratroopers wandered around the plaza (on the Temple Mount) as if in a dream . . . Rabbi Shlomo Goren was among them. I was alone for a moment, lost in thought, when Rabbi Goren approached me. "Uzi," Rabbi Goren said, "now is the time to put 100kg of explosives into the Mosque of Omar (the Dome of the Rock) so we may rid ourselves of it once and for all." I said to him, "Rabbi, enough." He said, "Uzi, you will go down in history if you do this . . . This is an opportunity that can be taken advantage of now, at this moment. Tomorrow it will be too late." . . . I said, "Rabbi, if you don't stop, I'll take you to jail" . . . He simply walked away silently. He was completely serious.[75]

Also on 31 December 1967, Israel's army radio played a recording of a speech Rabbi Goren made in 1967 to a military convention in which the army's Chief Rabbi referred to the Dome of the Rock and the al-Aqsa Mosque, saying: "Certainly we should have blown it up. It is a tragedy that we did not do so."[76] Whether or not Islam's third holiest shrine came close to being blown up by Israeli paratroopers immediately after the shrines were captured in June 1967 remains an open question. However, in the 1980s, members of a militant Jewish group (Hamahteret Hayehudit) were arrested and put on trial for plotting to blow them up. Clearly the destruction of these Muslim holy places remains a most vivid fear for Palestinians and Muslims and an ambition for most extremist Jewish fundamentalists in Israel.

Bayt Nuba, Imwas, Yalu, Habla, Jiftlik, Bayt Marsam, Bayt Awa and al-Burj

Among the first to go were the inhabitants of the three ancient villages of Imwas (Emmaus of the New Testament), Yalu and Bayt Nuba, situated near the Green Line in the Latrun area north-west of Jerusalem. In 1987, these evicted villagers and their descendants numbered about 11,000 and were living in Amman, Jordan, with 2,000 living on the West Bank, near Ramallah.[77] Latrun was on a West Bank salient, 20 miles from Tel Aviv and some 15 miles from West Jerusalem. In 1948 it had been the gateway to Jerusalem which the Israelis failed repeatedly to capture; so they had to realign the roadway to bypass Latrun. For many years before 1967, the Israeli army had plans for taking over the Latrun enclave and straightening the border. According to military historian Meir Pa'il, there had been a "minimum plan" which included occupation of the Latrun enclave and the destruction of its Arab villages without moving on beyond the enclave.[78] June 1967 created the opportunity to realise these plans. The Latrun salient was captured by the Israeli army on the morning of 6 June 1967. On orders (not in writing, of course) from the Commanding General of the Central Command, Uzi Narkiss, the army bulldozers moved in and wiped out the three large villages on the grounds that their location was of "strategic" significance and that there was need to "straighten the [Green Line] border", according to the Israeli officer in charge of the operation.[79] Narkiss, a Labour Party man who later became Director-General of the Jewish Agency's (JA) Department of Immigration and Absorption, and in 1995 Chairman of the JA's Department of Information, also commanded the troops who captured Jerusalem and clearly approved of the order to evacuate the al-Magharbeh Quarter.[80]

The demolition of the Latrun villages was carried out by an engineering unit using explosives and bulldozers, and this involved the destruction of 539 houses in Yalu, 375 in Imwas and 550 in Bayt Nuba.[81] On 6 June some 2,000 families (over 6,000 persons) from the three villages found themselves on the road to Ramallah.[82] Those who could, rushed to the East Bank. The rest wandered from village to village in the Ramallah area. Amos Kenan, a well-known Israeli journalist who, as a reservist soldier, took part in the fighting in the Latrun area, revealed in graphic detail the story of Bayt Nuba.

> We were ordered to block the entrances of the villages and prevent inhabitants returning to the village from their hideouts after they had heard Israeli broadcasts urging them to go back to their homes. The order was to shoot over their heads and tell them not to enter the village. Beit Nuba [sic] is built of fine quarry stones; some of the houses are magnificent. Every house is surrounded by an orchard, olive trees, apricots, vines and cypresses. They are well-kept. Among the trees there are carefully tended vegetable beds . . . At noon the first bulldozer arrived and pulled down the first house on the edge of the village. Within ten minutes the house was turned into rubble, including its entire contents; the olive trees, cypresses were all uprooted . . . After the destruction of three houses, the first column arrived from the direction of Ramallah . . . Some Arabic-speaking soldiers went over to notify them of the warning. There were old people who could hardly walk, murmuring old women, mothers carrying babies, small children. The children wept and asked for water. They all carried white flags.
>
> We told them to go to Beit Sura. They told us that they were driven out everywhere, forbidden to enter any village, that they were wandering around like this for four days, without food, without water, some dying on the road. They asked to return to the village and said we had better kill them . . . We did not allow them to enter the village and take anything . . . More and more columns of refugees arrived, until there were hundreds of them . . . The platoon commander decided to go to headquarters and find out if there were any orders about what to do with them, where to send them, and whether it was possible to arrange transport for the women and food for the children. He returned saying that there were no orders in writing, simply that they were to be driven out.
>
> We drove them out. They went on wandering in the south like lost cattle. The weak died. In the evening we found that they had not been allowed into Beit Sura, for there too, bulldozers had begun to destroy the place. We found out that not only in our sector was the border [the Green Line] straightened out for security reasons but in all other sectors too.[83]

In her 1967 "Jerusalem Diary", Sister Marie-Thérèse wrote:

And now we see what the Israelis do not want to see: three villages [Imwas, Yalu and Bayt Nuba] systematically destroyed by dynamite and bulldozers. Alone, in dead silence, donkeys wander among the ruins. Here and there, smashed furniture, a torn cushion protrude from the rubble of stones and cement. A kitchen pot and a blanket abandoned in the middle of the road. They had no time to carry anything away.[84]

According to General Narkiss, the evicted inhabitants of the "four [sic] villages of the Latrun area" were evacuated to Ramallah and some of them crossed the river to Jordan.[85] In his book, *The Liberation of Jerusalem*, Narkiss wrote: "I was determined that the Latrun enclave, that years-old thorn in our flesh, would never be returned [to Arab sovereignty]."[86]

Canada Park was created with the help of the Canadian Jewish National Fund on the site of the three bulldozed villages and their 20,000 *dunums* of agricultural lands (four *dunums* equal one acre).[87] Professor Benjamin Beit-Hallahmi of Haifa University commented:

During most Saturdays every year, hundreds of Israeli families enjoy picnics in the beautiful Canada Park, midway between Tel Aviv and Jerusalem. The park is a popular place even during the week, and offers visitors olive trees, water springs, Roman antiquities, Byzantine churches and sports facilities . . . Canada Park . . . has been developed on the site where three Palestinian villages – Bet Nuba, Yalu and Emmaus [sic] stood before June 1967. Immediately after the June War, these villages were bulldozed and their 5,000 inhabitants turned into refugees. The Jewish National Fund got to work; millions were spent turning the land into a huge park, erasing every trace of the villages but lovingly preserving the antiquities.[88]

More recently, plans were announced to plant another section of the same site with trees and name it "Scharansky Hope Forest" (after Nathan Scharansky, the well-known Zionist activist and former Soviet prisoner[89] who is Minister of Trade and Industry in the current Likud cabinet of Binyamin Netanyahu).

Also in 1967, several other West Bank villages – Bayt Marsam, Bayt Awa, Jiftlik and al-Burj – were cleared and razed to the ground,[90] and only the intervention of a group of liberal Jewish intellectuals and academics saved the West Bank town of Qalqilyah from a similar fate when an order by the army Central Command to expel the inhabitants and the total destruction of the whole town was cancelled by Dayan.[91] Apparently, Zeev Shaham, commander of a force that operated in the area of Qalqilyah-Jenin, had received an order to destroy Qalqilyah from Uzi Narkiss, head of the Central Command.[92] Indeed, between 9 June and 18 July 1967 (before the cancellation of the order by Dayan), at least 850 out of 2,000 dwellings in Qalqilyah had been blown up by the Israeli army[93] and dozens of residents were forcibly transported from the town to the Jordan River.[94] At one point, Dayan gave the order not to destroy Qalqilyah because the whole operation had become widely known and public pressure had been mounting.[95] Sister Marie-Thérèse records:

> At Nablus we saw hundreds of families under olive trees; they slept in the open. They told us they were from Qalkilya [sic] and were not allowed to go back. We went to Qalkilya to see what was happening; we received a sinister impression. The city was being blown up by dynamite.[96]

Moreover, on 16 June the Israeli military totally destroyed the two villages of Bayt Awa (in the Hebron district) and Bayt Marsam; most of Habla met a similar fate on 22 June 1967; al-Burj was destroyed on 28 June 1967; and Jiftlik on 26 November 1967 and the following days.[97] Reporting simultaneously in the *New York Times* and *L'Orient* on 3 December 1967, Terence Smith wrote:

> The village of Jiftlik on the Occupied West Bank of Jordan, with about 6,000 refugee inhabitants, has been completely destroyed by the Israeli army. During the last two weeks, army bulldozers have razed about 800 buildings there . . . According to certain information, the Israeli army have also destroyed other villages near Latroun [sic] and Hebron. Since these villages had already been severely damaged during the war, some Israelis are saying that it might have been more sensible to have left half-destroyed the standing houses.

In mid-July 1967, John Reddaway, Deputy Commissioner General of UNRWA, estimated that some 16,000 persons had been left homeless after the Israeli army demolished buildings in West Bank villages.[98]

Attempts to "thin out" the teeming population of Gaza were also made in the summer of 1967, as a resident of the Strip, Abu Hassan, recalls:

> A few weeks after the Strip had been occupied, the Israelis embarked on a programme of forced deportation. On one occasion, the Israeli army rounded up all the men from my quarter and herded us into Jaffa School. The Israelis had two local *mukhtars* with them who told the officer in charge each man's profession – "he's a labourer, that one's a teacher" and so on. The Israelis picked out the ones they wanted, put them on trucks and sent them to Jordan. I remember another time the army arrived on trucks early in the morning and grabbed all the young men they could find. Those of us who were around began protesting, but the Israelis told us not to worry because they were only taking the youths for a few hours to help in the disposal of those killed in the Sinai during the war. We never saw those young men again. As soon as the work had been done, their identity papers were confiscated and they were forced to cross the canal into Egypt.[99]

"Transfer of 100,000 Without Anybody Saying a Single Word": The Operation of Haim Hertzog, Shlomo Lahat and Uzi Narkiss, June 1967

Haim Hertzog was the army's first Military Governor of the West Bank after the June 1967 War. Hertzog had been a political and military broadcaster during the war and published a record of the war, *Israel's Finest Hour* (1967). He was also a regular radio and television commentator in Israel and abroad and managed to amass honorary doctorates from several universities in Israel and other countries.[100] At a public debate on the Palestinian issue held in Jerusalem on 3 April 1970, this first Military Governor of the West Bank and influential figure of the Labour establishment did not refrain from revealing openly his heart's wishes: "If we had the possibility of taking one million Arabs [from the territories] and clearing them out, this would be the best."[101] However, it was only 21 years later, in early November 1991, a few days after the Madrid Peace Conference, that President Hertzog revealed publicly and proudly one of Israel's little-known secrets: that he, as Military Governor of the West Bank, efficiently organised and carried out, in cooperation with Shlomo Lahat, the Commander of Jerusalem, the operation of transferring 200,000 Palestinians from the West Bank in the immediate aftermath of the War. According to a statement confirming that this operation was indeed carried out, the President's office said:

> His [Hertzog's] considerations were that in the departing wave, many of the PLO men would leave and this would make it easier for the military administration. For days and weeks, lines of buses ran from the Damascus Gate [in East Jerusalem] to the Allenby Bridge [on the River Jordan]. Altogether during this period, 200,000 Palestinians left Judea and Samaria voluntarily, including 100,000 refugees whose camps were in the Jericho Valley.[102]

Hertzog claims that he had been prompted to organise this operation during a meeting with Anwar al-Khatib, the former Arab Governor of the Jerusalem district, at the Ambassador Hotel in Jerusalem on Friday 9 June 1967. According to Hertzog, al-Khatib raised at this meeting, *inter alia*, the problem of the families of Arab consuls stranded in Jerusalem and the problem of the families of the Jordanian officers, who fled and left their dependants behind, and asked the Israeli Military Governor to allow these families to leave Jerusalem for Jordan via the Allenby Bridge. Hertzog agreed and told al-Khatib that from the morning of Sunday 11 June, buses would be waiting near the Damascus Gate to transport any Arab wishing to depart to Jordan, on condition that each departing Arab signed a statement to the effect that he was leaving voluntarily. Hertzog also revealed that Shlomo Lahat, then the Commander of Jerusalem and Mayor of Tel Aviv from 1974 until 1993, was put in charge of implementing the operation and that "no contrary order was given by [Defence Minister] Moshe Dayan at any stage [to halt the operation]".[103]

Moreover, the superior Commanding General of Hertzog and Lahat, the aforementioned Commanding General of the Central Command, Uzi Narkiss, told an interviewer in October 1988 that he himself had supervised the implementation of the transfer operation in 1967, which, according to the interviewer, had resulted in the total "transfer of 100,000 [Palestinians to Jordan] without anybody saying a single word". Narkiss told the same interviewer in October 1988:

I placed several buses in Jerusalem and in other cities [of the West Bank] with "To Amman – Free of Charge" written on them. The bus used to carry them to the [partly] destroyed Allenby Bridge and then they would cross it [to Jordan]. I spread the news about these buses through individuals with wide contacts with the inhabitants, such as members of trade unions and chambers of commerce ... In this [bus] operation between 20,000 and 25,000 people got out.[104]

Calling again on the testimony of Sister Marie-Thérèse, it is reported that on Sunday 18 June 1967, Israeli soldiers circulated in East Jerusalem firing shots, while loudspeakers broadcast the following: "It is forbidden to go out during the curfew which will last all day tomorrow. Those who wish to go to Amman may do so. Buses are available for them."[105] One of the extraordinary revelations made by Narkiss in connection with his transfer operation was the daily telephone calls he used to receive after the war from the dovish Finance Minister, Pinhas Sapir, whose concerns were primarily the so-called "demographic problem" and the question of the maintenance of the Zionist-Jewish character of the Israeli state.[106]

Pinhas Sapir used to phone me twice a day to ask: how many [Arabs] got out today? Is the number of the inhabitants of the West Bank diminishing? The number [of those being transported by the buses?] began with 600 and 700 persons a day, and it began to decline until it reached a few score, and after two or three months the [bus?] operation stopped.[107]

The statement of the President's office elicited wide publicity in Israel in November 1991 and surprised Israeli historians. Hertzog's claim that Anwar al-Khatib was a partner in such an organised operation of mass transfer was denied by the latter. He promptly convened a press conference at which he said that he had only asked Hertzog at their Ambassador Hotel meeting for the release of the consuls of Egypt, Syria, Lebanon, Iraq and Saudi Arabia, all of whom had been detained by the Israeli army, and had asked Hertzog to permit 15 Jordanian officials, who had worked in Jerusalem, to reunite with their families living in Jordan. Al-Khatib added that he had been surprised, a few days after his meeting with Hertzog, to find out that the military administration had organised buses and trucks for mass transportation of Arabs to the Allenby Bridge.[108]

A former Israeli soldier described the "voluntary" and "humane" aspects of this operation in a November 1991 interview with *Kol Ha'ir*:

> My job was to take their [each Palestinian's] thumb and immerse its edge in ink and fingerprint it on the departure statement . . . Every day tens of buses arrived. There were days on which it seemed to me that thousands were departing . . . There were those departees who were leaving voluntarily, but there were also not a few people who were simply expelled . . . We forced them to sign. I will tell you how exactly this was conducted: [for instance] a bus [carrying men] would arrive and only men would get off. I emphasise, only men, aged 20 to 70, accompanied by border guard soldiers. We were told that these were saboteurs, fedayeen, and it would be better for them to be outside the state. They [the Arab men] did not want to leave, and were dragged from the buses while being kicked and hit by revolver butts. By the time they arrived at my [signing] stall, they were usually already completely confused [as a result of beatings] at this stage and did not care much about the signing. It seemed to them part of the process. In many cases the violence used against them produced desirable results from our point of view. The distance between the border point and the [Allenby] Bridge was about 100 metres and they crossed to the other side, running out of fear; the border guardsmen and the paratroopers were all the time in the vicinity. When someone refused to give me his hand [for fingerprinting] they came and beat him up badly. Then I took his thumb forcibly, immersing it in ink and fingerprinting him. This way the refuseniks were removed . . . I have no doubt that tens of thousands of men were removed against their will.[109]

The Three Large Refugee Camps near Jericho: 'Ayn Sultan, Nu'aymah and 'Aqbat Jabir

Between 1949 and 1967, the Palestinian population in the West Jordan Valley was dominated by three huge refugee camps surrounding the town of Jericho: 'Ayn Sultan, Nu'aymah and 'Aqbat Jabir. The residents of these camps had been driven out from present-day Israel in 1948–9. During the 1967 hostilities or shortly after, virtually all residents of these camps, approximately 50,000 people, fled or were expelled to the East Bank, along with more than 50 per cent of the native rural population of the Jordan Valley, reducing the region's total population by 88 per cent to 10,778.[110] In this context it is worth noting the reactions of two Israeli historians to the 1991 revelations surrounding the "transfer" operation of Hertzog, Lahat and Narkiss, and to the relevance of this operation to the almost total depopulation of the three refugee camps near Jericho. Uri Milstein had this to say:

> I remember that five days after the Six Day War I was in Jericho. It was empty there and we were told that the refugee residents of 'Ayn Sultan, Nu'aymah and 'Aqbat Jabir had fled. It is more likely that they [the Israeli army] drove them away. In the War of Independence [the 1948 War] there was no organised transfer, people [Israeli commanders] volunteered to carry it out on their own initiative. In the Six Day War there were similar situations. Many thought that we had not completed the job in the War of Independence. It is known that there was a plan to conquer Qalqilyah [town] and destroy it. There was also a plan to carry out transfer in Hebron in revenge for the massacre [of Jews] in [19]29. I have not read about the evacuation of 200,000 refugees in buses and I am not aware that this has been published anywhere.

Meir Pa'il stated:

> This story is new to me, but that does not mean that it is incorrect, particularly in the light of the facts that the refugee camps in Jericho ['Ayn Sultan, Nu'aymah and 'Aqbat Jabir] were emptied of their residents in one to two weeks after the Six Day War. The travel route of the buses which operated as described here from the Damascus Gate to the Allenby Bridge, had to pass via the Jericho Valley and the large refugee camps that were there and this is another confirmation of the story. If one of the four men, President Hertzog, Shlomo Lahat, his deputy Shmuel Albak, or Uzi Narkiss, confirms this thing, then this story is true and genuine.[111]

The strafing and firing on refugee columns were in fact reported in the foreign press. According to *The Guardian* (14 June 1967), "Israeli aircraft frequently strafed the refugees on the road from Jerusalem to Jericho, destroying and burning." The London *Times* (22 June, 1967) carried this report:

Israeli troops supervising the crossing [of the Jordan River] introduced a dangerous new element today [21 June] by firing their sub-machine guns over the heads of the straggling line of refugees . . . The disturbing feature is that there was no obvious point to this display of strength. The refugees were already bewildered enough and to risk causing a panic among already frightened people borders on military lunacy.

Hundreds of thousands of Palestinians fled or were expelled from the occupied territories during and after the June 1967 War. In their book, *River Without Bridges*, Peter Dodd and Halim Barakat study the 1967 exodus of the Palestinian refugees and attempt to answer the question: why did this exodus take place? The answer, according to them, is as follows:

The exodus was a response to the severe situational pressures existing at the time. The situational pressures were generated by the aerial attacks upon a defenceless country, including the extensive use of napalm, the occupation of the West Bank villages by the Israeli army, and the actions of the occupying forces. Certainly the most drastic of these actions was the eviction of civilians and the deliberate destruction of a number of villages [Imwas, Yalu, Bayt Nuba, Bayt Marsam, Bayt Awa, Habla, al-Burj and Jiftlik]. Other actions, such as threats and the mass detention of male civilians, also created situational pressures.[112]

Dodd and Barakat (who were not aware of the "transfer" operation of Hertzog, Lahat and Narkiss) added that there were other indirect reasons. The Palestinian villagers were not equipped and were ill-prepared to resist and cope with these situational pressures; they were ill-informed and unfamiliar with the terrifying nature of the aerial attacks. To this should be added the social structure of Arab society: the family-centred social structure diminished attachment to community and nation, and some Palestinians left to protect their family, particularly the honour of their womenfolk.

In his investigation of the 1967 exodus, William Wilson Harris (who also made no mention of the "transfer" activities of Hertzog, Lahat and Narkiss), estimated that of a pre-war population of approximately 1.4 million, about 430,000 left the territories occupied in the War (including the Golan Heights and Sinai) between June and December

1967. Most of these refugees left in June 1967. He pointed out that the 1967 refugee exodus varied from one region to another: for example, over 90,000 people (almost 90 per cent of the population) fled the Golan Heights, while the Gaza Strip lost less than 20 per cent of its 400,000 residents. Harris also noted local variations in the West Bank, attributable to a number of factors. The high population losses in some regions were the result of a "psychological legacy of pre-war events, a legacy of assorted fears". For instance, in the Hebron district and in the region surrounding the village of Qibya (situated about midway between the Latrun salient and Qalqilyah) in the West Bank, the Israeli army had carried out a large and infamous massacre in October 1953 in which 65 villagers, mostly women and children, were killed.[113] Another example was in the Latrun salient, where the residents of Yalu, Imwas and Bayt Nuba were ordered to leave their villages by the Israeli army and where the knock-on effect of their movement across the West Bank can still be traced in the higher losses from other villages on the Latrun–Ramallah–Jerusalem highway.[114]

The destruction of the Latrun villages and the al-Magharbeh Quarter and the encouragement of Arab departure by the Israeli army were raised in a Knesset debate on 21 June 1967 by two Jewish Communist Knesset members, Shmuel Mikunis and Meir Vilner, both protesting strongly against Israeli treatment of civilians in the newly occupied territories. Vilner stated:

> As regards the Arab inhabitants of the occupied Arab territories, especially on the West Bank of the River Jordan, it has been broadcast over the radio and published in the press that the Military Governor has frequently announced that anyone wishing to cross the river would be welcome to do so; there is no need to comply with any complicated procedure. What does it mean when, in a time of military occupation, we give the inhabitants the choice of leaving their homes? It means that pressure is being exerted on the inhabitants. It is, perhaps, no accident that the other [Arab] side should call on the inhabitants not to leave the places where they live. According to reports in the [Israeli] press, 100,000 people have crossed or been forced to cross the frontier and this number is increasing . . . There have been reports of the blowing up of villages in the Latrun area, for example, for "strategic, tactical and security reasons" . . . Villages were destroyed not only in the Latrun area after the military operations had

ended . . . Old and young, men, women and children, the sick and feeble were moved out of the former Jewish Quarter in the Old City in a horrifying way . . . Houses have been destroyed in the area around the Western Wall [the al-Magharbeh Quarter] and there seems to be a general confusion and disorganisation.[115]

However, both Vilner's proposal to debate the subject in the Knesset plenum and Mikunis's proposal to transfer the subject to a parliamentary committee were defeated by a parliamentary majority.[116] In a subsequent parliamentary question, another Communist member of the Knesset, Tawfiq Tubi, requested that the inhabitants of Yalu, Imwas and Bayt Nuba be allowed by Defence Minister Dayan to return to their villages. Once again, Dayan rejected this proposal.[117] Since 1967, the evicted inhabitants of Imwas, Yalu and Bayt Nuba have been campaigning for the return to, and the reconstruction of, their villages,[118] but none of the Israeli ministries has been prepared to take any responsibility for the destruction of these villages. The Israeli government and those army commanders who had the verbal order to destroy the Latrun villages must have thought that it was possible to rearrange both history and geography; that if they cart away the rubble and rake over the ground and plant seedlings where the homes of thousands of Palestinians had been, they would be able to get away with it.[119]

Encouragement of Arab departure by the Israeli authorities was also reported in the Hebrew and foreign press. According to *Davar* (13 June 1967), many of those who had left the West Bank claimed that the Israeli authorities were forcing residents of Jenin, Qalqilyah and Tulkarm (the so-called three towns of "strategic importance") to leave their homes. *Haaretz* (20 June 1967) reported that those who had left their homes on the West Bank had not been allowed to return. *The New York Times* of 26 August 1967 reported that each day for the previous two weeks some 500 residents had left the Gaza Strip, adding that "any reduction in Gaza area's population is a benefit to everyone in Israel's view". Several months later, the London *Observer* (17 December 1967) reported:

The opportunity of reprisals on security grounds has been taken to hasten the departure of more people from the West Bank and the Gaza Strip and to prevent the return of those who had fled. The

Israeli authorities believe that whatever the eventual political status of the Gaza Strip, the refugees there should be moved elsewhere.

One month later (28 January 1968) the same paper reported: "It is estimated that between 30,000 and 35,000 people have left the [Gaza] Strip as a result of the measures taken by the Israeli authorities." *The Guardian's* Middle East correspondent Michael Adams wrote:

> No Israeli, when he deals frankly with you (and many do) will deny that he would prefer to accept "the dowry without the bride", meaning that, from Israel's point of view, the ideal solution to the problem of the occupied territories would be their absorption by Israel but without their Arab population.[120]

In addition to the active encouragement of Arab departure, the Israeli army took tough measures to prevent the return of those who had fled during the war or shortly after. After the war, Israeli troops on the Jordan River apparently routinely shot civilians trying to slip back home on the West Bank.[121] A statement made by an anonymous soldier who had served in the 5th Reserve Division on the Jordan River, issued from the Tel Aviv office of the Hebrew magazine *Ha'olam Hazeh* on 10 September 1967, read:

> We fired such shots every night on men, women and children. Even during moonlit nights when we could identify the people, that is, distinguish between men, women and children. In the mornings we searched the area and, by explicit order from the officer on the spot, shot the living, including those who hid or were wounded, again including the women and children.[122]

General Uzi Narkiss also told an interviewer in October 1988 that after the 1967 War, Israeli troops on the Jordan River had killed civilians trying to slip back to the West Bank.[123]

Conclusion

All Palestinian areas occupied by Israel in June 1967 experienced immediate and substantial out-movements of Arab inhabitants, both the native population and those Palestinian refugees who had been driven out from Israel in 1948–9. Yet the most distinguishing feature of the 1967 exodus was its selective geographical character, with geographical variations in losses of native and refugee populations,[124] as opposed to the wholesale nature of the 1948 exodus.[125] For instance, the Gaza Strip and the West Bank highlands, where most population centres were distant from the 1967 war zone, experienced a comparatively moderate exodus. The Gaza Strip also showed the smallest population reduction, partly because the area – in contrast to the West Bank – is furthest from any potential sanctuary.[126] In contrast to the highlands of the West Bank, where population loss was between 20 and 25 per cent, 88 per cent of the Palestinian population in the west Jordan Valley was driven out from a region "highly attractive to Israel owing to its strategic attributes".[127] Both the Hebron district and the Deir Qaddis administrative divisions, on the western border with Israel, also ranked among the highest loss areas.[128]

There is no evidence to suggest that there were wholesale or blanket expulsion orders adopted or carried out by the Israeli army in June 1967, although the policy of selective eviction, demolition and encouragement of "transfer" continued for several weeks after the Israeli army occupied the West Bank and Gaza. In fact, some leading Israeli politicians, who were thrilled by the spectacular military victory, were clearly disappointed with the demographic outcome of the war. Indeed, Dayan himself was criticised by Deputy Prime Minister Yigal Allon for not driving out all the Palestinian inhabitants of East Jerusalem and Hebron.

During the 1948 War, Allon had commanded the operation that conquered the twin towns of Lydda and Ramle. According to Israeli historian Benny Morris, on 12 and 13 July 1948, shortly after the two towns were captured, Israeli troops "carried out their orders, expelling the 50,000 or 60,000 remaining inhabitants of and refugees camped in and around the two towns".[129] Allon's disappointment at the demographic outcome of the 1967 War, which, unlike the 1948 War, did not bring about the evacuation of most of the Palestinian inhabitants of the newly acquired territories, was expressed at a meeting with a delegation of the Whole Land of Israel movement, apparently in November 1967: "Is this the way to occupy Hebron? A couple of artillery bombardments on Hebron and not a single 'Hebronite' would have remained there. Is this the way to occupy [East] Jerusalem [without driving most of the Arabs out?]."[130]

In 1967, evictions and demolitions were evident in numerous geographical locations in the West Bank – the Latrun villages, the al-Magharbeh Quarter and the former Jewish Quarter in the Old City of Jerusalem, the border towns of Qalqilyah and Tulkarm, the west Jordan Valley and the refugee camps near Jericho and the Hebron district. Young men from several cities and refugee camps were also targeted for deportation.[131] The Palestinian population was still in shock and disarray in the face of Israeli military force, reeling from the military occupation and in no position to resist it.

Evacuations and demolitions were executed at the level of middle and senior military officers with the tacit approval of top-level command and Defence Minister Dayan, who conducted the 1967 War with great confidence and controlled the field commanders during and after the war, managing to shape its immediate consequences. Throughout this process of evacuation and demolition, there was some lack of communication between the civil authorities, particularly the Israeli cabinet, and the military commanders;[132] in practice the military exercised civilian functions. The military echelons, backed by Dayan, encouraged Arabs to get out of East Jerusalem and other cities of the West Bank as well as the refugee camps near Jericho, and to go to Jordan.

The forcible eviction of the inhabitants of the Latrun villages, the destruction of the al-Magharbeh Quarter and the initial destruction of most of the town of Qalqilyah represented one example of the ideology of force, which reached its apogee between the 1967 War and the October War of 1973. Dayan, who virtually dominated the Labour government's policies in the occupied territories until 1974, represented in his own style that ideology of force inherited from Ben-Gurion, which was based on the conviction that the defence of Israel depended exclusively on its own strength. The same ideology of force, which helped to reawaken thoughts of transfer during and after 1967, is rooted in the pre-state *Yishuv* and the events that led to the establishment of the State of Israel and the consequent Palestinian exodus of 1948. This ideology of force is predicated on a number of premises: (1) that Palestinians of the occupied territories would resign themselves to their fate, either being kept down or transferred if they dared to oppose Israel; (2) that Arabs only understand the language of force; (3) that the Arab world is very divided and Israel can create a *fait accompli*; and (4) that it does not matter what the Gentiles say, but what the Jews do, a well-known saying of Ben-Gurion.[133]

In 1969, two years after the destruction of the Latrun villages, Dayan felt it was necessary to remind his compatriots, including those who were opposed to Jewish settlements in the West Bank and the Rafah area in north Sinai, of what the younger generation never knew. Dayan had this to say in a 1969 speech at the Technion in Haifa:

> We came here to this country, which was settled by Arabs, and we are building a Jewish State . . . Jewish villages arose in the place of Arab villages. You do not even know the names [of these villages], and I do not blame you, because those geography books no longer exist. Not only do the books not exist, the Arab villages are not there either. Nahal [Dayan's own settlement] arose in the place of Mahlul, Gvat [a kibbutz] in the place of Jibta, Sarid [another kibbutz] in the place of Haneifis and Kfar-Yehoshu'a in the place of Tal-Shaman. There is not one single place built in this country that did not have a former Arab population.[134]

Given this unflinching perception of the uprooting and dispossession of Palestinian communities in the pre-state period, combined with the fact that Zionist objectives had always proceeded against the wishes of the local population; and given the emergence of the ideology of force and its occupation of the centre ground in Israeli policies toward the Palestinians, from there to the massive settlement and Judaisation of Arab Jerusalem and Israel's continuing eviction schemes was only a short step.

NOTES

1   W. W. Harris, *Taking Root: Israeli Settlement in the West Bank, the Golan and Gaza-Sinai 1967–1980* (Chichester: Research Studies Press, 1980), pp. 7 and 16–17.
2   Israeli estimates range from 173,000 to 200,000 while Jordanian and Palestinian estimates range from 250,000 to 408,000 (from June 1967 until the end of 1968); cited in Walid Salim, "The [Palestinians] Displaced in 1967: The Problem of Definition and Figures" in *The Palestinians Displaced* [in 1967] *and the Peace Negotiations* (Ramallah, West Bank: Palestinian and Diaspora Refugee Centre, 1996), p. 21. The real figure is probably somewhere around 320,000 people.

3   P. Dodd and H. Barakat, *River Without Bridges* (Beirut: Institute for Palestine Studies, 1968).

4   The Palestinian citizens of Israel numbered just below 400,000 in 1967. According to W. W. Harris, the Arab population of the West Bank immediately prior to the 1967 War was approximately 840,000. The 1967 refugee exodus reduced this population by between 200,000 and 250,000. However, by 1977, through a very high natural increase, the number of the West Bankers had recovered to over 820,000. See Harris, *Taking Root*, p. 7. The Gaza Strip inhabitants were about 400,000 in 1967.

5   A speech delivered at a meeting of the French Zionist Federation, Paris, 28 March 1914 in B. Litvinoff (ed.), *The Letters and Papers of Chaim Weizmann*, Series B, vol. 1 (Jerusalem: Israel University Press, 1983), Paper 24, pp. 115–16.

6   See protocol of Ruppin's statement at the Jewish Agency Executive's meeting, 20 May 1936 in Y. Heller, *Bamavak Lemedinah: Hamediniyut Hatziyonit 1936–48* [*The Struggle for the State: The Zionist Policy 1936–48*] (Jerusalem: Zalman Shazar Centre, 1984), p. 140.

7   I. Zangwill, *The Voice of Jerusalem* (London: William Heinemann, 1920), p. 104.

8   Y. Gurvitz and S. Nevon (eds.), *What Story Will I Tell My Children?* (Tel Aviv: Amihah, 1953), pp. 128, 132, 134, cited in Fouzi El-Asmar, "The Portrayal of Arabs in Hebrew Children's Literature", *Journal of Palestine Studies*, 16, no. 1 (Autumn 1986), p. 83.

9   D. Ben-Amotz, *Seporei Abu-Nimr* [*The Stories of Abu Nimr*] (Tel Aviv: Zmora-Bitan, 1982), p. 155.

10 For excerpts of Shamir's address, see *Journal of Palestine Studies*, 21, no. 2 (Winter 1992), pp. 128–31.

11 Ibid.; B. Netanyahu, *A Place Among the Nations* (London: Bantam Press, 1993), pp. 39–40.

12 A. Oz, "The Meaning of Homeland", *New Outlook*, vol. 31, no. 1 (January 1988), p. 22. Oz's article was originally published in *Davar* in 1967.

13 Ibid., p. 21.

14 Cited from the back cover of "Jerusalem of Gold", Fontana Records, SRF 67572, MGF 27572.

15 See *Maariv*, 11 June 1967.

16 The *shofar* is a horn used in Jewish high holidays to commemorate events of major significance.

17 Translated from Hebrew, Fontana Records in U. Davis and N. Mezvinsky (eds.), *Documents from Israel 1967–1973* (London: Ithaca Press, 1975), p. 220.

18 Oz, "The Meaning of Homeland".

19 Har-Tzion became a national hero after serving in "Unit 101" which, under the command of Ariel Sharon, carried out "retaliatory" operations against Arab targets in the 1950s. The unit was responsible for the attack on the Arab village of Qibya, to the south west of Hebron, in 1953, in which 63 villagers were slaughtered, and also carried out the expulsion of the al-'Azazmeh tribe from the Negev to Sinai.

20 *Maariv*, supplement, 22 January 1979, p. 6; cited also in M. Kahane, *Lesikim Be'enekhem* [*They Shall be Strings in Your Eyes*] (Jerusalem: Hamakhon Lara'ayon Hayehudi, 1980/81), p. 230.

21 *Davar*, 9 February 1979, p. 17.

22 Quoted in Z. Schiff and E. Haber (eds.), *Leksikon Levitahon Yisrael* [added title: Israel, Army and Defence: A Dictionary] (Tel Aviv: Zmora, Bitan, Modan, 1976), p. 178. In his book, *Heroes of Israel*, Haim Hertzog (President of Israel from 1983 to 1993) quotes Ariel Sharon's description of Har-Tzion as "The fighting symbol not only of the paratroopers, but of the entire Israel Defence Forces." See H. Hertzog, *Heroes of Israel: Profiles of Jewish Courage* (London: Weidenfeld and Nicolson, 1989), p. 271. See also M. Dayan, *Living with the Bible* (London: Weidenfeld and Nicolson, 1978), pp. 96–101. In March 1955 Har-Tzion and his colleagues were involved in a little-known massacre of Bedouin in the Negev (see Hanokh Bartov in *Maariv*, 26 January 1979, p. 14). In the wake of these atrocities the then Prime Minister, Moshe Sharett, entered in his personal diary: "I am dumbfounded about the essence and fate of these people, which is capable of having a noble soul . . . but in addition produces from the ranks of its best youth young men who are capable of murdering human beings in clear mind and cold-bloodedness by thrusting knives in the bodies of defenceless young Bedouins." (M. Sharett, *Yoman Ishi* [*Personal Diary*], vol. 3, entry for 8 March 1955 (Tel Aviv: Sifriyat Maariv, 1978), p. 823.

23 See *Maariv*, 6 December 1974; cited in Y. Kotler, *Heil Kahane* (New York: Adama Books, 1986), pp. 89–90.

24 See M. Nisan, *Hamedinah Hayehudit Vehabe'ayah Ha'arvit* [*The Jewish State and the Arab Problem*] (Tel Aviv: Hadar, 1986), pp. 119, 200; Shiloah, *Ashmat Yerushalayim*, p. 8; Moshe Shamir, *Hamakom Hayarok* [*The Green Place*] (Tel Aviv: Dvir Publishing House, 1991), pp. 95–9.

25 Quoted in T. Shiloah, *Ashmat Yerushalayim* [*The Guilt of Jerusalem*] (Tel Aviv: Karni Press, 1989), p. 45.

26 Quoted in A. Ben-'Ami (ed.), *Sefer Eretz-Yisrael Hashlemah* [*The Book of the Whole Land of Israel*] (Tel Aviv: Friedman Press, 1977), pp. 20–1.

27 Cited by Ephraim Urbach (a professor of Talmud and Midrash at the Hebrew University of Jerusalem) in *Midstream* (a monthly Jewish review), April 1968, p. 15. Urbach thought that "this sort of thing is very harmful and not at all edifying".

28 Cited in Ben-'Ami, *Sefer Eretz-Yisrael Hashlemah*, pp. 20–1.

29 For further discussion of the transfer proposals put forward by Yahil and Shiloah, see Haim Yahil, "Demography and Israel's Uniqueness" in Ben-'Ami, *Sefer Eretz-Yisrael Hashlemah*, pp. 312–13; and H. Yahil, *Hazon Umaavak: Mivhar Ketavim* [*Vision and Struggle: Selected Writings, 1965–74*] (Tel Aviv: Karni Press, 1977), p. 105; Shiloah, *Ashmat Yerushalayim*, p. 24; id., *Eretz Gdolah Le'am Gadol* [*A Great Land for a Great People*] (Tel Aviv: Otpaz, 1970), pp. 107–8; id. in *Moledet*, no. 12 (October 1989), p. 11.

30 See Ehud Sprinzak, *The Ascendance of Israel's Radical Right* (New York and Oxford: Oxford University Press, 1991), p. 57.

31 See Eli'ezer Livneh in *Moznayim* (literary monthly published by the Hebrew Writers' Association in Israel) (July 1967), p. 104.

32 See, for instance, Shim'on Ballas in *Haumah*, no. 2 (November 1967), p. 217.

33 Yossi Melman and Dan Raviv, "Expelling Palestinians", *Guardian Weekly* (London), 21 February 1988; *Davar*, 19 February 1988, pp. 10–11.

34 Melman and Raviv, "Expelling Palestinians", *Davar*, 19 February 1988.

35 Ibid.
36 Ibid.; Avidan, *Davar*, 2 June 1987.
37 Avidan, *Davar*, 2 June 1987.
38 Ibid.
39 Ibid.
40 See Shim'on Ballas in *Haumah*, no. 2, November 1967, p. 216.
41 Ibid.
42 *Maariv*, 2 June 1985, p. 2; Nisan, *Hamedinah Hayehudit Vehabe'ayah Ha'arvit*, pp. 119 and 200.
43 Quoted by Gide'on Levi, "Transfer of 100,000 without Anybody Saying a Single Word", *Haaretz*, 25 October 1988.
44 Melman and Raviv in *Davar*, 19 February 1988.
45 See Weitz's memorandum: "The Problem: The Refugees", dated 17 September 1967 in Weitz's papers (Rehovot: The Institute for Settlement Studies); see also article based on his memorandum in *Davar*, 29 September 1967.
46 This quote is found in the manuscript of Weitz's Diary in the Central Zionist Archives (Jerusalem) A246/7, entry for 20 December 1940, pp. 1090–1. The quote in the article in *Davar* is a slightly edited version of the entry in the diary. The *Davar* article is entitled "A Solution to the Refugee Problem: an Israeli State with a Small Arab Minority".
47 Katznelson was a co-founder and a leading ideologue of Mapai, the hard-core political component of the Labour Party.
48 Volcani was for many years a director of the Jewish National Fund and a member of the Executive Committee of the Histadrut.
49 Ussishkin was a key leader of the Zionist movement and the Jewish National Fund Board of Directors, while its chairmanship sat on his hands for nearly 20 years (1923–41).
50 Weitz hints here at the Jewish Agency Transfer Committee and schemes before 1948 and his own investigations in preparation for carrying out the transfer solution. See N. Masalha, *Expulsion of the Palestinians: The Concept of "Transfer" in Zionist Political Thought 1882–1948* (Washington DC: Institute for Palestine Studies, 1992), pp. 49–199.
51 In fact the figure of 15 per cent was referred to for the first time in the recommendations of the Israeli Government Transfer Committee – of which Weitz was a member – submitted to Prime Minister Ben-Gurion, on 26 October 1948. According to these recommendations, the Arabs should not exceed 15 per cent of the population of the mixed cities such as Haifa.
52 The number of the refugees on the West Bank registered with the United Nations Relief and Works Agency (UNRWA) in 1984 was 357,000. In the Gaza Strip an estimated two-thirds of the 700,000 inhabitants are refugees.
53 The Memorandum was not designed for publication but drafted for Ben-Gurion by the then Transfer Committee.
54 *Davar*, 29 September 1967.
55 Israeli Institute of Applied Social Research, "Israeli and Palestinian Public Opinion", p. 54, cited in D. McDowall, *Palestine and Israel: The Uprising and Beyond* (London: I. B. Tauris, 1989), p. 197. Dr Yaacov Cohen of the Hebrew University's Hillel Institution wrote an article in *Davar* on 4 October 1967 (p. 14) about the "dangerous nationalistic atmosphere" which has been created

in the wake of the 1967 war and asked "isn't it a fact that many Jews in Israel would welcome the emigration of the Israeli Arabs to Arab countries?"

56   M. Benvenisti, *Intimate Enemies* (London: University of California Press, 1995), p. 191.

57   See "Jerusalem Diary of Sister Marie-Thérèse" in *Cahiers du Témoignage Chrétien* (Paris), 27 July 1967; D. Hirst, *The Gun and the Olive Branch* (London: Faber and Faber, 1984), p. 225.

58   For further details, see Rashid Khalidi, "The Future of Arab Jerusalem", *British Journal of Middle Eastern Studies*, 19, no. 2 (1992), pp. 139–40; M. Dumper, *Islam and Israel: Muslim Religious Endowments and the Jewish State* (Washington DC: Institute for Palestine Studies, 1994), p. 116.

59   U. Benziman, *Yerushalayim: Ir Lelo Homah* (Tel Aviv: Schocken, 1973).

60   Ibid., pp. 37–8.

61   Yanai held important functions in the Haganah HQ; former First Commander of the Signal Corps and former Deputy Director-General of the Defence Ministry.

62   Benziman, *Yerushalayim*, p. 38.

63   Ibid., p. 40.

64   See Levi, "Transfer of 100,000 without Anybody Saying a Single Word"; and Yossi Melman and Dan Raviv in *Davar*, 19 February 1988, pp. 10–11.

65   Benziman, *Yerushalayim*, p. 41.

66   On the central role played by Kollek in the destruction of the quarter, see ibid., pp. 40–1.

67   Cited in M. Ben-Dov, M. Naor and Z. Aner, *The Western Wall* (Jerusalem: Ministry of Defence Publishing House, 1983), p. 163.

68   Benziman, *Yerushalayim*, p. 42.

69   Ibid., p. 43.

70   Ibid., pp. 45–6.

71   Ibid., p. 45.

72   Dumper, *Islam and Israel*, p. 116.

73   "Jerusalem Diary of Sister Marie-Thérèse" in *Cahiers du Témoignage Chrétien*.

74   See G. Aronson, *Israel, Palestinians and the Intifada* (London: Kegan Paul International, 1990), p. 19. For further discussion of Israel's settlement policies in occupied East Jerusalem, see Michael Dumper, "Israeli Settlement in the Old City of Jerusalem", *Journal of Palestine Studies*, 21, no. 4 (Summer 1992), pp. 32–53; Dumper, *Islam and Israel*, pp. 117–20; Michal Sela' in *Davar*, 30 December 1991, pp. 9–10; R. I. Friedman, *Zealots for Zion* (New York: Random House, 1992), pp. 96–100. According to Uzi Benziman, Shlomo Lahat and his assistant Yaacov Salman played a key role in the eviction of Arab residents from the Jewish quarter of the Old City of Jerusalem after June 1967; see Benziman, *Yerushalayim*, p. 45.

75   Quoted in David Sharrock (reporting from Jerusalem) in *The Guardian*, 1 January 1998, p. 9. Sharrock's report is based on *Haaretz*, 31 December 1997. See also *Haaretz*, 2 January 1998.

76   Cited by David Sharrock in *The Guardian*, 1 January 1998.

77   These figures were mentioned in a letter by the Inhabitants' Committee, cited in *Reconstruct Emmaus* (St Sulpice, Switzerland, Association for the Reconstruction of Emmaus, December 1987), p. 3

78   Cited in Ehud Maltz and Michal Sela' in *Kol Ha'ir*, 31 August 1984.

79 Cited in G. Dib and F. Jabber, *Israel's Violation of Human Rights in the Occupied Territories* (Beirut: Institute for Palestine Studies, 3rd edn., April 1970), p. xxi; Melman and Raviv in *Davar*, 19 February 1988, pp. 10–11.

80 See Levi, "Transfer of 100,000 Without Anybody Saying a Single Word"; and Melman and Raviv in *Davar*, 19 February 1988, pp. 10–11.

81 Cited in Husam Izzeddin, "A Tale of Three Villages", *Jerusalem Times*, 14 June 1996, p. 8.

82 Cited in Maltz and Sela' in *Kol Ha'ir*.

83 Cited by *Israel Imperial News*, London, March 1968. Kenan's report on the razing of Imwas, Yalu and Bayt Nuba was sent to all Knesset members. An English version of the report was also published in *Reconstruct Emmaus*, pp. 7–8.

84 "Jerusalem Diary of Sister Marie-Thérèse" in *Cahiers du Témoignage Chrétien*.

85 Levi, "Transfer of 100,000 without Anybody Saying a Single Word".

86 U. Narkiss, *The Liberation of Jerusalem* (London: Vallentine, Mitchell, 1983), p. 199.

87 Aronson, *Israel, Palestinians and the Intifada*, p. 19.

88 B. Beit-Hallahmi, *Original Sins: Reflections on the History of Zionism and Israel* (London: Pluto Press, 1992), pp. 95–6.

89 Ibid., p. 96.

90 Hirst, *The Gun and the Olive Branch*, p. 225; Dib and Jabber, *Israel's Violation of Human Rights in the Occupied Territories*, p. xxi.

91 See Yossi Melman and Dan Raviv, "Expelling Palestinians", *The Washington Post*, outlook, 7 February 1988. See also O. Lifschitz, *1967–1987: Kovshim Atzmam Lada'at* [Added title: *A Self-Defeating Conquest*] (Tel Aviv: Mapam and Al-Hamishmar, 1987), p. 77.

92 Cited in Maltz and Sela' in *Kol Ha'ir*.

93 These figures were cited by John Reddaway, Deputy Commissioner-General of UNRWA in *Daily Star* (Beirut), 21 July 1967. See also Ian Gilmour and Dennis Walters in *The Times*, 27 July 1967.

94 Based on personal communication by Dr Anis Al-Qasem, originally a resident of Qalqilyah. See also Dib and Jabber, *Israel's Violation of Human Rights in the Occupied Territories*, pp. 228 and 235.

95 See Maltz and Sela' in *Kol Ha'ir*.

96 "Jerusalem Diary of Sister Marie-Thérèse" in *Cahiers du Témoignage Chrétien*.

97 *The Times* (London), 30 November 1967; Dib and Jabber, *Israel's Violation of Human Rights in the Occupied Territories*, pp. 228 and 234–5.

98 Cited in the *Daily Star* (Beirut), 21 July 1967.

99 Cited in P. Cossali and C. Robson, *Stateless in Gaza* (London: Zed Books, 1986), p. 64. See also recollection by the 62-year-old Ibrahim, a construction worker from Gaza, in Lifschitz, *1967–1987*, pp. 77–8.

100 The list of universities which awarded him honorary doctorates include: Hebrew University of Jerusalem; Haifa University; Ben-Gurion University of the Negev; Bar-Ilan University; the Technion; Weizmann Institute of Science, Rehovot (Part of the Hebrew University); Georgetown University (Washington DC); University of Liberia; Yeshiva University, J.T.S.

101 Cited in Nisan, *Hamedinah Hayehudit Vehabe'ayah Ha'arvit*, p. 117.

102 Cited by Shmuel Meiri in *Ha'ir* (Tel Aviv), 8 November 1991, p. 13; *Kol Ha'ir*, 8 November 1991, p. 19.

103 Ibid.

104 Quoted in Levi, "Transfer of 100,000 without Anybody Saying a Single Word". Narkiss also talked about the eviction of "four villages in the Latrun area" and the "flight" of some 60,000 refugees from the three refugee camps near Jericho: 'Ayn Sultan, Nu'aymah, 'Aqbat Jabir.

105 "Jerusalem Diary of Sister Marie-Thérèse" in *Cahiers du Témoignage Chrétien.*

106 A. S. Becker, *Israel and the Palestinian Occupied Territories: Military–Political Issues in the Debate* (Santa Monica, Calif.: The Rand Corporation, December 1971), p. 11.

107 Ibid.

108 Both Milstein's and Pa'il's revelations are cited in *Kol Ha'ir*, 15 November 1991.

109 Ibid.

110 Harris, *Taking Root*, p. 9.

111 Cited in *Ha'ir*, 8 November 1991, p. 13.

112 Dodd and Barakat, *River Without Bridges*, p. 54.

113 Harris, *Taking Root*, p. 21. In October 1953, Unit 101, commanded by Ariel Sharon, attacked the village of Qibya in "reprisal" for the murder of a mother and two children in an Israeli settlement. Jordan had condemned the Arab perpetrators and offered its cooperation to track them down. UN military observers who arrived at the scene two hours after Sharon's commando had completed its operation described what they found: "Bullet-riddled bodies near the doorways and multiple bullet hits on the doors of the demolished houses indicated that the inhabitants had been forced to remain inside until their homes were blown up over them ... Witnesses were uniform in describing their experience as a night of horrors, during which Israeli soldiers moved about in their village blowing the buildings, firing into doorways and windows with automatic weapons and throwing grenades."

Cited in E. Hutchinson, *Violent Truce* (New York: Devin-Adair, 1956), pp. 152–8. Commander Hutchinson was an American UN observer. In the biographical sketches of his diary, Meir Har-Tzion describes the attack on Qibya, in which he took part, as follows: "They [members of Unit 101] stayed [in the village] for three hours, destroyed 42 houses and as a result 70 residents, most of whom hid in the houses, were killed" (M. Har-Tzion, *Perkei Yoman [Biographical Sketches and Selections from the Diary of Har-Tzion]* (Tel Aviv: Lavin-Epstein Publication, n.d.), p. 165. For further discussion of the Qibya episode, see B. Morris, *Israel's Border Wars, 1949–1956* (Oxford: Clarendon Press, 1993), pp. 225–62.

114 Harris, *Taking Root*, p. 22.

115 For Vilner's statement, see *Divrei Haknesset [Knesset Debates]*, Sitting 186 of the Sixth Knesset, Second Session, 21 June 1967, pp. 2384–5.

116 Ibid.

117 See *al-Ittihad* (Haifa), 6 August 1968.

118 See letter from the inhabitants of Imwas (Emmaus) to the Israeli authorities dated 17 March 1986 published in *al-Bayadir al-Siyasi*, 12 July 1986. On May 29 1987 a 20-minute film was shown on the Swiss Italian Television entitled: "Ritorno a Emmaus", showing the inhabitants of Imwas expressing their desire to return to their village. The film also showed two Israelis from the nearby Kibbutz Nahshon stating that they had refused to cultivate the lands of

Imwas. See *Reconstruct Emmaus*, pp. 4–5. For further details on the villagers' campaign, see Izzeddin, "A Tale of Three Villages".

119 Michael Adams, "The Road to Emmaus", *The Independent on Sunday*, 16 June 1991.

120 *The Guardian*, 19 February 1968.

121 McDowall, *Palestine and Israel*, pp. 204 and 302, n.109.

122 Cited in ibid., p. 302, n.109.

123 Quoted in Levi, "Transfer of 100,000".

124 Harris, *Taking Root*, pp. 15 and 17.

125 For further discussion of the 1948 exodus, see Masalha, *Expulsion of the Palestinians*, pp. 175–205.

126 Harris, *Taking Root*, pp. 15 and 17.

127 Ibid., pp. 9, 15 and 21.

128 Ibid., p. 21.

129 B. Morris, *1948 and After: Israel and the Palestinians* (Oxford: Clarendon Press, 1990), p. 2.

130 Cited in Shiloah, *Ashmat Yerushalayim*, pp. 53 and 281.

131 Levi, "Transfer of 100,000".

132 Benzimann, *Yerushalayim*, p. 45.

133 For further discussion, see A. Kapeliouk, *Israel: la fin des mythes* (Paris: Editions Albin Michel, 1975), pp. 28 and 183–222.

134 *Haaretz*, 4 April 1969, p. 15.

4

The Continuing Exodus – the Ongoing Expulsion of Palestinians from Jerusalem

Leah Tsemel

Introduction

It is no accident that the negotiations over Jerusalem were postponed to the last stage of the Israeli–Palestinian peace talks. The status of Jerusalem is one of the most sensitive issues in these negotiations, second only to the fate of the Palestinian refugees from the 1948 and 1967 Wars. Israel began to tighten its hold over Jerusalem long ago; the Palestinian National Authority, on the other hand, is not doing the best it can to prepare itself for the final status talks. Within the city, the Palestinian leaders are struggling without financial or political support to do what they can to preserve whatever is left of Palestinian Jerusalem. The Israeli attempt to ensure international recognition of its sovereignty has rendered Palestinians in East Jerusalem far more vulnerable in terms of their legal status than Palestinians living in other parts of the occupied territories. This paper seeks to draw attention to the steps taken by the Israeli government to achieve its goals. Looking at the geographic and demographic map of Jerusalem following 30 years of occupation, one wonders whether Israel had systematically planned throughout these years to displace Palestinians from Jerusalem so that if at some point in the future a settlement were to be negotiated about the status of the city, there would be a small Palestinian minority to be considered. If there were an Israeli conspiracy to marginalise the Palestinians in Jerusalem, it has certainly been well executed.

The Legal Status of Palestinian Jerusalemites

Israel's policy towards Jerusalem was made clear from the beginning of the occupation. On 25 June 1967, less than three weeks after Israeli forces took control of East Jerusalem, much of the Palestinian side was annexed through the application of three laws which

1. authorised the government to extend the law, jurisdiction and administration of the Israeli state to any area of Eretz Israel (The Land of Israel) designated by the Government by Order;[1]

2. empowered the Interior Minister to enlarge, by proclamation, the area of any municipality by the inclusion of an area designated by order under section 11b of the Law and Administration Law;[2]

3. provided that Jerusalem's holy sites be protected from desecration and other violations and "from anything likely to violate the freedom of access of the members of different religions to the places sacred to them or their feelings with regard to these places".[3]

Following the enactment of these laws, Israel annexed 72,000 *dunums* (four *dunums* equal one acre) of East Jerusalem, stretching from the village of Sur Baher in the south to Kalandia airport in the north. The annexation was accomplished by extending the jurisdiction of the Jewish municipality in West Jerusalem to encompass the new areas, which were then incorporated into the State of Israel. On the other hand, the 66,000 Palestinian inhabitants of this territory, who were registered in a census on 26 June 1967, were not granted citizenship but rather classified as "permanent residents of Israel". Israel portrayed this as a liberal measure aimed at reducing Israeli intervention in the lives of Palestinian Jerusalemites. At the same time, however, the legal separation of Palestinian Jerusalemites from other West Bank Palestinians, as well as from Israel, rendered these persons particularly vulnerable to future legal manipulation and drove a wedge between Palestinian Jerusalemites and the rest of the Palestinian community. These differences have become increasingly significant as Israel prepares for final status negotiations.

Permanent residency in Israel is regulated by the 1952 Law of Entry to Israel. This grants the same status to East Jerusalem Palestinians as to foreign citizens who have freely chosen to come to Israel and want to live in the country. The fact that the Palestinians did not enter Israel but that Israel took over their birthplace and areas of residency did not alter this ruling. The status of permanent residency differs substantially from citizenship. For the permanent resident, entry into and residency within Israel is a privilege, not a right, in stark contrast to the Israeli Law of Return, which guarantees Jews around the world an automatic right to Israeli citizenship. The resident is obliged to observe his financial, professional and social duties, whereas he enjoys only some of the rights of a full citizen, such as the right to live and work in Israel without the need to obtain special authorisation. He or she cannot take part in the election for the Knesset, the Israeli parliament.

Most importantly, permanent residency has a far less durable legal status than citizenship. Article 11a of Israel's Law of Entry empowers the Israeli authorities to revoke permanent residency if they believe the resident has changed his or her place of domicile and resides in another country. The authorities have typically considered any stay abroad by Jerusalem Palestinians of seven years or more for reasons other than education as proof of change of domicile. Since 1996, the West Bank is also regarded as an area outside Israel, and this has a devastating effect on Jerusalemites who have left Jerusalem, as shown later in this paper. The Israeli High Court of Justice (HCJ) has turned down the demand by Jerusalem Palestinians to be granted irrevocable "quasi-citizenship" status, arguing that this would discriminate against other permanent residents in Israel. Indeed, the High Court has even ruled that permanent residency can expire automatically under circumstances which are not listed in Regulation 11a. In a 1988 decision, Judge Barak made this ruling:

> A permanent residency permit – in contrast to citizenship – is a mixture of things. On the one hand, it has a constitutional aspect that establishes the right to permanent residency; on the other hand, it has a declarative aspect, which expresses the reality of the permanent residency. When this reality disappears, there is no longer anything to which the permit can adhere, and it is automatically revoked, without any necessity for formal revocation.[4]

In Israel, only citizens enjoy a practically unlimited right of return, despite the fact that the right of persons to leave and return to their country of origin is secured in the Universal Declaration of Human Rights (Article 13.2) and the International Covenant on Civil and Political Rights, which Israel has signed (Article 12.2, 12.4). Israel's position places Jerusalem Palestinians in an extremely difficult and uncertain legal situation, rendering them dependent on Israel's political considerations and goals.

Given these legal restrictions, the best strategy for Jerusalem Palestinians seeking to preserve their permanent residency status is to live continuously within Jerusalem's post-1967 municipal boundaries. But even those Palestinians willing to do so are not safe. Israel has adopted a policy of restricting the growth of Jerusalem's Palestinian population, deploying a mixture of bureaucratic obstacles and studied disinterest to make Palestinian life in Jerusalem difficult. Although Palestinians have faced numerous problems stemming from life under occupation collectively, Israel's attitude has been that Jerusalem Palestinians have to find their own individual solutions to their difficulties. This approach has left many Palestinians who wished to remain in Jerusalem with no alternative other than to leave the city. This, in turn, serves Israel's final goal: the reduction of the number of Palestinians living in Jerusalem.

The Palestinian Reality in Jerusalem

Typical of this drive to reduce the Palestinian population of Jerusalem was Moshe Dayan's policy of "open bridges", which was theoretically aimed at enabling Palestinians from East Jerusalem and the other occupied territories to maintain their family, business and social contacts with Jordan and other Arab states. The policy, however, also provided Israel with a useful excuse to avoid responsibility for dealing with Palestinian concerns. Young Palestinians looking for employment or postgraduate education, for example, could be directed to the surrounding Arab countries or even further abroad. For 28 years, Palestinians were "encouraged" to leave. The only stipulations were the different regulations concerning exit permits. As military ruler, Israel reserved the right to forbid some Palestinians to leave the occupied area because of security considerations. These restrictions, in turn, automatically placed a burden on every Palestinian, who was subject therefore to security screening before she or he was given the requested exit permit. Palestinians seeking to leave via the Jordanian border received an exit permit with a re-entry visa that had to be renewed after three years. Permits for exit via Israel's Ben-Gurion Airport, on the other hand, were valid for only one year. Palestinians who returned before the permit expired could regain their right of residency. For certain cases, or during periods of tension such as the Palestinian uprising – the *Intifada* – Israel granted Palestinians exit permits only if they agreed to stay abroad for at least nine months. In cases of suspected political or military resistance activities, Israeli authorities imposed a more draconian restriction, ordering the applicant to stay abroad continuously for three years. Among other considerations, the authorities hoped that the prolonged three-year stay would encourage those persons to settle abroad and lose their desire to return.

In Jerusalem, the high cost of living, the lack of sufficient housing, inadequate municipal services, problems with access to health insurance and shortage of municipally funded elementary schools have encouraged Palestinians to leave the city. Throughout the years of occupation, development within the annexed Palestinian areas was almost frozen. Most of the vacant land in East Jerusalem was either confiscated or designated "green" by the Israeli authorities and therefore could not be built on. In contrast to areas slated for Jewish development, the municipal authorities never prepared a master zoning plan for Palestinian areas in the city. Thus, as the Palestinian population grew, it was forced to look outside the city for land to build on. According to a 1997 report issued jointly by two Israel non-governmental organisations, B'Tselem and HaMoked, only 12 per cent of all the housing units built in Jerusalem since 1967 had been constructed for Palestinians. Many Palestinians moved to suburbs outside Jerusalem's official municipal borders, believing this would not risk their right to permanent residency in Jerusalem. Although the Israeli HCJ ruled in 1988 that anyone whose "centre of life" lies outside the city is liable to lose his or her status as a resident of the city, such a broad interpretation of the law was not commonly applied. Israeli authorities in fact gave the opposite impression, continuing to pay Palestinians living in the suburbs or even in the West Bank the entitlements they received beforehand from Israel National Insurance. According to different estimates there were approximately 70,000 Palestinians with Jerusalem identity cards residing in the occupied territories outside East Jerusalem. Nevertheless, these people were still considered Jerusalemites, and for 28 years they were not prevented from coming to and from Jerusalem.

Preparing the Ground for the Final Status Negotiations

Although the broader framework of occupation policies with regard to East Jerusalem has remained unchanged, a significant shift in Israeli policy could be seen as early as the beginning of the 1991 Arab–Israeli talks in Madrid. The military closure of the West Bank, introduced during the 1991 Gulf War, became a permanent feature in March 1993. The closure prevents Palestinians from access to Jerusalem for periods ranging from several days to a number of weeks. In addition to seriously infringing Palestinians' freedom of movement, the closure implies that access to Jerusalem is no longer a right to be taken for granted, but rather a privilege that can easily be withheld. The closure is, in fact, another method of separating East Jerusalem from the rest of the Palestinian territories and gradually eliminating the city's leading role as the West Bank's centre of commerce, culture, health and education.

Another measure adopted during the period leading up to the final status negotiations is the new policy of confiscating East Jerusalem identity cards and revoking permanent residency status. By broadly expanding the HCJ interpretation of the Entry to Israel Law, the Interior Minister has begun to revoke the permanent residence status of Palestinian Jerusalemites who have shifted their "centre of life" from "Israel" to the West Bank suburbs. Interestingly, where Palestinian residency is concerned, the Israeli authorities consider Palestinians living in the West Bank to be residing "outside of Israel". Jewish permanent residents living in Jewish settlements throughout the occupied territories, however, have nothing to fear.

In the past, the Israeli authorities lacked information about individual Palestinians from Jerusalem living beyond the city's municipal boundaries. Today, however, Israel has gained access to this crucial data through the registration lists for the elections to the Palestinian Legislative Council held in January 1996. Palestinian Jerusalemites living outside the city were required to register for the elections at their place of domicile in the West Bank or Gaza Strip. In Jerusalem, one could only vote in the post office. In addition, Palestinian candidates from Jerusalem had to prove that they had an alternative address in the West Bank before Israel would permit them to run for election.

The Palestinian authority, meanwhile, was obliged to transfer the election registry lists to the Israeli side for approval. In the euphoria surrounding the elections, the Israeli-imposed conditions failed sufficiently to set off alarm bells amongst Palestinians, who did not realise that the Israeli Interior Ministry would use the registration lists to hasten the process of determining who – in Israeli terms – is still entitled to residency rights inside the city. This assumption has been confirmed by the most recent report by the Israeli State Comptroller. According to her 1997 report, there were fewer than 170 cases of residency revocation between 1993 and 1995, but the figure increased to over 400 in 1996, after the newly elected Likud government came to power.

The Interior Ministry, however, never published an official notification of a change in its policy. It applied the new, unstated policy retroactively, revoking the residency of persons who had left the city under the old policy guidelines. The burden of proof that one's "centre of life" is actually in Jerusalem is placed on the Palestinians and not on the Ministry. Palestinians are required to bring proof of their continuous residence inside Jerusalem in the form of an apartment rental contract, gas and water bills, or letters attesting that their children study in Jerusalem schools. Since, according to the Israeli High Court, permanent residency automatically lapses with changes in one's place of domicile, the Interior Ministry is under no obligation to explain its decision-making process. For the very same reason it is impossible to appeal against the Ministry's decision. It deprives a resident of the right to argue his or her case to be heard in court, which should be a basic principle of natural justice as emphasised so often by the High Court.

As soon as the new policy was put into effect, entire families discovered, on going to the offices of the Interior Ministry in East Jerusalem, that they had been deleted from the computer system and classified as non-residents. Later, the Ministry sent these families a letter ordering them to leave Israel within 15 days because they had ceased to be permanent residents. The Ministry denied these Palestinians the benefits they had received until then as permanent residents, including the right to obtain national medical insurance, national security insurance (which includes child support), widows' pensions and disability insurance. These people found that they had all but ceased to exist: they could not open a bank account, send their children to Jerusalem's municipal schools, obtain a driving licence or sign a legal contract.

In a highly bureaucratised state such as Israel, where every public service or legal action requires the provision of an Israeli identity card number, a person whose residency is revoked cannot function. Many Palestinian Jerusalemites are now reluctant to approach the Interior Ministry because they fear the consequences of doing so. If the authorities can carry out their intention to issue new identity cards to Israeli citizens and permanent residents, the status of tens of thousands of Jerusalemites who have left Jerusalem in the past for work or education will be jeopardised.

This new Israeli policy also affects the issue of family unification. According to Israeli law, a resident of Jerusalem who is married to a person who is neither an Israeli citizen nor resident must apply for family unification in order to achieve the same status for the spouse. He or she applies to the Interior Ministry, which then grants or denies the request. The Ministry's decision typically takes several years, and during that time the couple is unable to live together in Jerusalem. The applicants, however, have to prove that their "centre of life" is in Jerusalem if they want to receive a unification permit. This leaves the couple with two alternatives: either to live separately in the hope that the request will finally be granted: or to leave the city in order to live together.

Ironically, Israel, which fought an international battle to gain recognition for the right of Soviet Jews to family unification, is limiting this very same right for Palestinians living inside its borders. In doing so, Israel violates international covenants and declarations. According to Article 27 of the Fourth Geneva Convention, for example, nations involved in a state of war or in a military occupation are obliged to respect family rights in all circumstances, including the right to live together.

Until 1994, requests by resident women on behalf of their non-resident husbands were automatically rejected by the Ministry, which argued that in Palestinian society it is the woman who follows the husband, and not the reverse. The new regulation which finally entitles women to family unification for their husbands meets international standards because even greater international involvement in Jerusalem affairs is expected once the final status negotiations begin. However, the right of family unification is less and less used because people fear losing their resident status when they are asked for proof of their permanent residency. According to the State Comptroller's report, only 940 such requests were made in 1996 – down from 3,400 in 1994, and 2,700 in 1995. Israel has acquired yet another tool to empty the city of its Palestinian inhabitants.

Conclusion

One of Israel's major achievements during the Oslo negotiations was to obtain the Palestine Liberation Organisation's (PLO) agreement to exclude any discussion of East Jerusalem and its Palestinian inhabitants. In doing so, the PLO has left Jerusalem's Palestinians without legal or political protection, forcing them either to forfeit their right to live in Jerusalem or to comply with pressure from the Israeli occupation by applying for Israeli citizenship. Whatever their individual choice, it will ultimately serve the Israeli aim of creating a small and controllable Palestinian minority in East Jerusalem. Once the final status negotiations begin, Israel can argue that due to the limited Palestinian presence in the city, the claim to Palestinian sovereignty in the city is baseless, and that the only issue to be negotiated should be limited minority rights for Jerusalem's remaining Palestinian neighbourhoods.

It is imperative to prevent Israel from completing its social, political and demographic transformation of Jerusalem. What is required is an immediate, concerted effort by local and international human rights organisations, political activists, the Palestinian Authority and Palestinian negotiators jointly to develop a realistic strategy to counter the new Israeli policy. The Palestinian Authority, as the political and diplomatic focal point of the Palestinian community, should play a key role in this effort. Activists must vigorously pressure the Authority to struggle against Israel's campaign to change Jerusalem's demographic make-up by protesting further against Israel's construction in East Jerusalem. Moreover, the Palestinian Authority must press Israel to freeze its policy of revoking the permanent residency status of Palestinian Jerusalemites. Time is working to the advantage of Israel; the final status negotiations should have begun in May 1996. There is little doubt that Israel will continue to ethnically cleanse Jerusalem of its Palestinians if the current policies against permanent residents meet with little or ineffective resistance.

NOTES

1 Law and Administration Ordinance Law, Amendment No. 11b, 5727/1967.
2 Municipalities Ordinance Law, Amendment No. 6, 5272/1967.
3 Protection of Holy Places Law, 5272/1967.
4 See Mubarak Awad, "Awad v. Yitzhak Shamir *et al.*", *Piskei Din* 42(2), pp. 424–35, 433.

PART II

SOLUTIONS:
THE RIGHT OF RETURN,
COMPENSATION AND
RECONCILIATION

5

The Right of Return in International Law

Anis Al-Qasem

The right of any individual to return to his country is such a natural right that it has always been taken for granted. No country has felt the need to pass legislation affirming, let alone conferring, this right. All efforts in that respect are directed towards excluding *aliens* from the exercise of this right. Immigration legislation, border controls, restrictions on entry, residence and acquisition of nationality through naturalisation apply to aliens, and not natives. Aliens may enjoy these rights only with the permission of the authorities of the country, and the permission is within the discretion of these authorities. Entry or residence, permanent or otherwise, is a privilege and not a right. These privileges cannot be enjoyed by a foreigner without permission from the authorities of the country concerned. Natives, however, are born with all these inalienable rights: the right to enter, to stay permanently, and to leave and return at will. No authority has the right to deny any of these rights.[1]

A person's country is his home and, like his home, his stay, departure and return are rights exercisable by him at will. On the other hand, he cannot force himself on the country of others, in the same way that he cannot force himself on the homes of others. By the same token, a person's return to his country is a return to his home, because he cannot reach his home without first returning to his country. For this reason, the right of return is exercisable in order to enable a native to return to what is his, particularly, his home, in addition to enabling him to exercise in his country the rights exercisable by his countrymen.

Thus, the right of return is not simply a right to return to one's country, but, on the personal level is also a right to return to one's town or village, to one's personal home and property, to one's community, with its culture and traditions, where one can resume normal life. The return is material, moral and cultural in a sense that one would not find in a foreign place. In our day, we have witnessed in Bosnia the return of people to their cities, villages, homes and communities from where they had been expelled or forced to leave by hostilities. Other parts of the same country may not qualify as "home"; the return must be to what was "home". The case was the same with the Rwandan refugees. They were returned not only to their own country, but also to the places they considered as their "homes" in that country. In both cases, the United Nations – and the European Union and the United States in the case of Bosnia – intervened to restore the situation to normality by enforcing the right of return.

Of necessity, the right to return and the right to stay that a native indigenous person enjoys in his country imply the right of permanent residence and vice versa. A native is not "resident" in his country in the sense that his stay is dependent upon the will of an authority that can grant it or revoke it. An indigenous person is in his country and has an inalienable right to be there by virtue of being indigenous. He does not need a residence permit and may not be prohibited from returning to live in his country simply because a permit has expired. The permit itself is in flagrant contravention of his native right to return and stay.

The right of return, by its very nature, embodies a permanent, inherent, unseverable relationship between a person and his country and the community which is native to that country. Nationality, as the legal expression of such belonging, is a fairly new phenomenon. Indigenousness, or nativeness, which is the natural expression of belonging to a country or a specific place on this planet, preceded the creation of states. When modern states were created, all persons native to the territory encompassed by the state became nationals by virtue of being such natives. Changes in legal sovereignty had and have no effect on the status of being a native, with all the rights that are consequential on that status, including the rights to live in the country, leave it and return to it. When new states emerged from colonialism or the partitioning of a territory, the natives of the territory of the new state became its nationals. That part of the country was their home, no matter who was in political control and no matter what changes in sovereignty might happen.

Jurisprudentially, the right involves the following elements:

1. The right to stay in one's country with no conditions reducing that right;

2. the right to leave it at will; and

3. the right to return to it at will.

These rights have their corresponding obligations on the authorities exercising power in the country of the person concerned. These obligations include the following:

1. not to place restrictions or require compliance with any formalities in connection with his stay in his country;[2]

2. not to deport, banish or expel him from it;[3]

3. not to impose conditions or place obstacles on his return or entry to it;[4] and

4. not to force him to return against his will.[5]

International Affirmation: The Universal Declaration of Human Rights

The right of return to one's country was highlighted through the plight of refugees in the event of armed conflict. The mass expulsions of populations during the First and Second World Wars and the problem of displaced persons have led to the inclusion of the right of return to one's country as a fundamental right in the Universal Declaration of Human Rights of 1948.[6] Article 13 (2) of the Declaration provides that: "Everyone has the right to leave any country, including his own, and to return to his country." This provision recognises the inherent relationship between a person and his country and confirms the right of return unconditionally. The exercise of the right is not made subject to any law the authority of the country may enact, or, as is often the case with other fundamental rights, the exercise of this right is to be in the manner prescribed by law. Under the Declaration, the right is absolute, and its exercise is at the will of the individual and not the authority in control of his country. If he is wanted for a criminal offence he has committed, or if he is a risk to national security, for example, he may be arrested on his entry for trial, but he cannot be denied entry.

Under Article 30 of the Declaration, states are prohibited from taking measures which may destroy any of the rights guaranteed under the Declaration, including, of course, the right of return. This Article provides: "Nothing in this Declaration may be interpreted as implying for any State, group or person any right to engage in any activity or to perform any act aimed at the destruction of any of the rights and freedoms set forth herein." Since the exercise of rights and their extent are frequently subjected, in one way or another, to national laws or administrative acts by the government or to judicial interpretation by courts of law, this provision operates as a restriction on the powers of states, groups and individuals by prohibiting any interpretation of the provisions of the Declaration as implying a right, in effect, to destroy these rights and freedoms. This is a basic constraint on the powers of a state, as well as its organs, such as the judiciary. The judiciary will be in violation of this provision if it sanctions an act of government aiming at the destruction of a right guaranteed by the Declaration.

The right of return to one's country is a right guaranteed under the Declaration. Article 30 prohibits acts of the state or its organs which aim at destroying this right.

The Declaration intentionally provided for the right of return to one's country, and not "one's country of nationality". The acquisition of the nationality of a country is subject to the nationality laws of that country and calls for some act of recognition by the competent authority of the state. Suppose a state is partitioned into two separate states, and nationals of the original state were abroad when the partition took place, and they wanted to return. The country of their nationality has disappeared on partition and two countries have come into being, each with its own nationality. Those abroad would no longer be nationals of a state on the day of partition. If the test is that of country of nationality, they would not be able to return to a country. However, it would be contrary to every principle to deny them the right of return to that part of the world which they considered as their country and home before partition. Thus, their country will be the new state where they lived before partition, and they will be entitled to return to that state.[7] Similarly, let us consider the example of an area annexed (lawfully or unlawfully) by a neighbouring state and individuals who habitually lived in that area but were outside it when the annexation took place. Their right of return to their home is exercisable in respect of the annexed area, despite the change of sovereignty and nationality. In situations of armed conflict, movement of population can take place out of fear, or because a party to the conflict commits atrocities to frighten the civilian population into flight, leaving their homes and properties behind. Their flight may take them to neighbouring countries to live as refugees. They are accepted as such, with the aim that they will return to their own country when the conflict becomes less acute. In the meantime, the conqueror passes a nationality law based on a date of residence, particularly chosen to be a date after the exodus of the inhabitants who have become refugees. According to this new nationality law, these refugees would have been deprived of the nationality of their country by arbitrary unlawful discriminatory legislation, and if the test of nationality is applied, they would have no right to return to their country because the country will no longer be the country of their nationality. Thus, by following a racist policy of discrimination, a regime will be allowed to deprive inhabitants of the country of their fundamental right of return to it, and force them to become or remain refugees or throw themselves at the mercy of the international community.

An example of this racist legislation of direct relevance to this paper is the Israeli Nationality Law of 1952. United Nations Resolution 181 (II) of 1947, which partitioned Palestine into an Arab and Jewish state with special status for the City of Jerusalem, dealt expressly with the question of nationality in the two states, particularly since, under the resolution, almost one half of the inhabitants of the new Jewish state would be Palestinian Arabs. Article 1 of Chapter 3 of the resolution provided that "Palestinian citizens residing in Palestine outside the City of Jerusalem, as well as Arabs and Jews who, not holding Palestinian citizenship, reside in Palestine outside the City of Jerusalem shall, upon recognition of independence, become citizens of the State in which they are resident and enjoy full civil and political rights."

By virtue of this provision, automatic nationality of the Arab or Jewish state would have been acquired not only by Palestinian citizens, but also by Arabs and Jews *resident* in Palestine, although they might not have been Palestinian citizens. This latter proviso was mainly intended to cover Jewish legal and illegal immigrants to Palestine during the

British Mandate who had not spent sufficient time in the country to acquire Palestinian nationality.

Before the official creation of Israel, the horrors of the armed conflict which followed the Partition Resolution of 1947 and the intentional expulsion through terror, such as the famous Deir Yassin massacre of 1948 committed by Jewish terrorist organisations against the civilian population of that village, thousands of Palestinians, resident in areas which became part of Israel, were forced to leave their homes and take refuge in neighbouring Arab states. In defiance of United Nations resolutions, Israel did not allow these refugees to return to their homes. Under the provision of the Partition Resolution on nationality quoted above, these refugees became *ipso facto* citizens of Israel. However, in 1952 Israel passed its Nationality Law and, as far as the Palestinians were concerned, granted citizenship only to those of them who were registered on 1 March 1952 as inhabitants under the Registration Ordinance of 1949, or in an area which became Israeli territory after the establishment of the state, from the day of the establishment of the state until the day the law came into force, or entered Israel legally during that period. Obviously, Palestinian refugees did not qualify under this law as Israeli citizens. This law, by departing from the United Nations resolution on nationality of the new Arab and Jewish states, through deliberate choice of date and criteria, was objective in appearance but was designed to exclude them. Many Palestinians who were in what became Israel whose registration was "missed" by the Israeli authorities were equally excluded from the application of the Nationality Law.[8]

If the test of nationality is to apply, a state, such as Israel, would be able, by passing a law, to deprive hundreds of thousands of their right to return to their country. It is for this and similar reasons that the Universal Declaration of Human Rights connected the right of return to one's country, the country where one had habitually lived in normal situations, and not the country of nationality.[9]

Article 12 (4) of the International Covenant on Civil and Political Rights of 1966[10] referred to the right of "entry". Again, the Covenant refers to one's "own country" and not "country of nationality". This provision stipulates: "No-one shall be arbitrarily deprived of the right to enter his own country." The right of entry is an exercise of the right of return. Thus, the two most important international instruments on fundamental human rights affirm the right of return to one's own country and not the country of nationality.

The Fourth Geneva Convention

The third international instrument which dealt with the subject was the Fourth Geneva Convention of 1949, which called it "repatriation".[11] In the same year, the United Nations General Assembly created the Office of the High Commissioner for Refugees.[12] These two instruments will be referred to in this essay only to the extent that they are relevant to the concept of the right of return.

The Fourth Geneva Convention on the Protection of Civilian Persons in Time of War (the Fourth Convention) does not simply affirm the right of return, nor is it limited in its application regarding repatriation to those civilians who were detained by the occupying power or those who, because of the hostilities, had left their place of residence. It went further by striking at the roots of one of the most ruthless causes of the problem: population transfers and deportation.

Article 49 (1) of the Convention provides as follows:

> Individual or mass forcible transfers, as well as deportations of protected persons from occupied territory to the territory of the Occupying Power or to that of any other country, occupied or not, are prohibited, regardless of their motive.

By virtue of this explicit provision, individual or mass forcible transfers or deportations of protected persons are prohibited, whatever the motive. These actions by an occupying power, when they are taken, are intended in many ways as a prelude to the denial of the right of return, once the transfer or deportation has taken place. By making transfer of population and deportation illegal, the Convention aims at providing protection to the right of individuals and communities to continue to live and stay in their homes and country despite occupation. Population transfer as well as transfer by the occupying power of its citizens to settle in occupied areas are crimes against humanity in violation of the Convention. So is forcible deportation of inhabitants from their country.

The Geneva Conventions did not create these rights: the right to repatriation, the right to stay in one's country and not be forcibly transferred from one's home, and the right not to be deported. The Conventions treated them as rights already in existence and recognised by international law.

The Fourth Geneva Convention is a special international instrument applicable to the special situations arising from a state of armed conflict and of occupation, and aims at the protection of the civilian population in those situations. As a special Convention, it takes precedence over other instruments in application to protected persons and their rights as set forth in the Convention. The enforcement of the Convention is not subject to national laws which might attempt to derogate the rights protected under the Convention. A state party is bound by the provisions of the Convention, and states which are not parties are bound by customary international law to protect and respect the rights protected by the Convention.

The Convention, like the Universal Declaration of Human Rights and the International Covenant on Civil and Political Rights, speaks of repatriation to one's own country, because it does not recognise population transfer or deportation. The *status quo ante* must be restored. De facto situations created by an occupying power are not recognised as capable of prejudicing those rights protected by the Convention.

This emphasis on "country" underlines, as stated earlier, the inherent inseparable connection between a person and his natural home, and is designed to meet exceptional circumstances which might delay or temporarily prevent the immediate exercise of the right of return.

The duration of occupancy is irrelevant; it is a state of *force majeure*. Continued occupation by force is illegal under modern international law and, in any event, it does not extinguish fundamental human rights, such as the right of return. A protected person who has been deported by an occupying power will not be able to return so long as the occupation continues. The same applies to refugees whom the occupying power prevents from return. Serious problems arise where there are mass expulsions of the population in the course of armed conflict by a belligerent who adopts and puts into effect deliberate policies that undermine the possibility of return of those who were expelled. Apart from denying the right itself, such policies may include confiscation of property,[13] or destruction of homes, or even of complete villages,[14] and the settling of citizens of the occupying power in the confiscated properties or in the villages. The aim of such policies is to create facts on the ground as obstacles in the way of the exercise of the right of return. Appeals are then made to pragmatism as the solution. Appeals of this kind are both unlawful and dangerous. They are unlawful because they recognise and give effect to acts which in themselves are unlawful and in flagrant violation of international law with malice aforethought. They are dangerous because they undermine recognition and enforcement of fundamental human rights on the grounds of expediency. Once that treacherous road is trodden, precedents are created for further erosion of human rights.

The proposition that the Fourth Geneva Convention was intended for application to short periods of occupation is fallacious. It finds no support in the Convention itself, or in its basic aims. The Convention is designed to protect the rights of persons under occupation, and not the unlawful acts of the occupier. Occupation may last for a long period, despite resistance, for reasons utterly unconnected with the wishes or capabilities of the people suffering under occupation. And it is the aim of the Convention to protect the rights of these people, no matter how long the occupation may last.

Long occupation will certainly have a serious impact on the lives of refugees who have been expelled from their country. Life has to go on and some may be forced by circumstances to acquire a foreign nationality in order to be able to maintain a family and provide it with some decent living. Acquisition of a foreign nationality in these circumstances is not an exercise of free will to abandon one's belongings to or his rights in his country. When the possibility of return arises, such people are entitled to exercise their right of return, should they decide to do so. Change of nationality under these circumstances of duress and necessity does not destroy the right, and is not an expression of the will to give up that right. Only when a person is free to exercise it does his decision, whatever it may be, become an expression of his free will.

Consequently, the rule under international law, customary and conventional, is that a person who has become a refugee in consequence of an armed conflict has the inalienable, unconditional right to return to his home in his country. This right is an individual right, exercisable by the person concerned, and the authorities in control of his country are under an obligation to permit his return. It is within this framework that the right of the Palestinian refugees to return to their homes in their country, as confirmed by the UN General Assembly, should be viewed.

The Law of Return

In 1950, Israel passed the Law of Return. Its first Article provided that "Every Jew has the right to immigrate to this country." Under Article 3 (a): "A Jew who comes to Israel and subsequently expresses his desire to settle may, whilst still in Israel, receive an immigrant's certificate."

Under this law, only Jews, whether they had or had not lived in Palestine before the creation in it of Israel, have the right to immigrate and settle there by the simple choice of the applicant. However, Palestinians who had their homes, land and property and who for generations had lived in what became Israel, are not given the right to return. One would have thought that, in compliance with the United Nations Partition Plan, the Universal Declaration of Human Rights and the Fourth Geneva Convention, to which Israel is a party, Palestinians would have been given at least a similar opportunity.

Thus, whether through the Law of Nationality, the Law of Return or the policies of confiscation of property and destruction of homes and villages, Israel has deliberately taken a position of denial to Palestinians of the right of return to their homes in Israel.

The Right of the Palestinians to Return

During the hostilities that erupted after the adoption of the General Assembly of the United Nations of the Partition Plan of Palestine (Resolution 181 of 29 November 1947), tens of thousands of Palestinian civilians were forced to leave their country. The myth that persisted for decades that they left voluntarily in response to calls by Arab leaders has been exploded, and is now utterly discredited. Israeli terror, purposely exercised to drive them out, is now fully and conclusively documented.[15] In their panic, the refugees left everything they owned behind. Palestinian "abandoned property was one of the greatest contributions toward making Israel a viable state".[16] While Israel was exploiting the property of the Palestinian refugees to build

[132]

itself as a viable state, the refugees themselves were thrown upon the charity of the world to live in refugee camps in neighbouring Arab countries.

The plight of the refugees was brought to the attention of the United Nations by Count Bernadotte, the UN Mediator who was later assassinated by members of the Zionist terrorist organisation, the Stern Gang, on 17 September 1948.[17]

In his Progress Report, submitted one day before his tragic assassination, Bernadotte dealt, *inter alia*, with the question of Palestinian refugees, significantly under the heading of "Right of Repatriation": "The right of innocent people, uprooted from their homes by present terror and ravages of war, to return to their homes, should be affirmed and made effective, with assurance of adequate compensation for the property of those who may choose not to return."

It is to be noted that Count Bernadotte's evidence was that the uprooting was caused by "*present terror and ravages of war*". The "present" was the period preceding and contemporaneous with the writing of his report in 1948. The source of terror on the Palestinians was Israeli, and no other. To him, the right of return needed only affirmation and implementation, not recognition or creation as a new right. In line with this, he made the following specific recommendation to the United Nations:

> The right of the Arab refugees to return to their homes in Jewish-controlled territory at the earliest possible date should be affirmed by the United Nations, and their repatriation, resettlement and economic and social rehabilitation, and payment of adequate compensation for the property of those choosing not to return, should be supervised and assisted by the United Nations Conciliation Commission . . .[18]

The recommendation of Count Bernadotte to the United Nations was that the refugees should be repatriated to "*their homes in Jewish-controlled*" territory. The operative part is "their homes" in implementation of the right of return. It is of no significance for the exercise of that right that the homes were in Jewish-controlled territory. Such control could not, in law, deprive them of their homes or of their right to return to them. The choice is for the refugees themselves to make.

The General Assembly of the United Nations, on the basis of that report, adopted Resolution 194 (III) on 11 December 1948. On the question of the refugees, the General Assembly

> *Resolves* that the refugees wishing to return to their homes and live at peace with their neighbours should be permitted to do so at the earliest practicable date, and that compensation should be paid for the property of those choosing not to return and for the loss of or damage to property which, under principles of international law or in equity, should be made good by the Governments or authorities responsible.

The important points to note in this resolution can be summarised as follows:

1. The resolution divides the refugees into two categories: (a) those wishing to return and (b) those choosing "not to return". The exercise of the right is left, in conformity with its nature, entirely to the choice of each individual refugee.

2. The return is to "their homes", that is, each refugee is to return to his home, whether that home is in the Jewish-controlled area or outside it. It is not a return to the area outside Israel if the home of the refugee was in the area of Palestine now called Israel or under Israeli control.

3. It is not required of a returning refugee to accept Israeli nationality or of Israel to grant him that nationality. However, those Palestinians whose homes were within the area designated as the Jewish State in the Partition Resolution were deemed by the resolution to have become Israeli citizens. Consequently, at least these will have the right to that citizenship.

4. The returning refugee must be willing "to live at peace with [his] neighbour". A declaration by the individual refugee to that effect should be sufficient to satisfy this requirement, because after his return he becomes subject to the law in force and will be personally responsible for his acts. It cannot, and should not, be assumed that a returning refugee would not be willing to live at peace with his neighbours, and therefore deny him the right to return on that basis. There are Palestinians inside Israel who are

living at peace with their Jewish neighbours, and there is no reason to assume that the returning refugees will not do so.

5. The return of those wishing to return must, according to the resolution, be "at the earliest practicable date". After about 50 years, that date has still to arrive.

6. Returning refugees must, in pursuance of the resolution, be compensated for the loss of or damage to their property.

7. Refugees "not wishing to return" should be compensated for the value of the property abandoned by them.

8. The compensation, according to the resolution, is payable by the government or authorities responsible for the damage or seizure of the property.

Under the resolution, compensation is payable to both categories. The Conciliation Commission for Palestine, created by the United Nations to bring about a peaceful resolution of the problem and which was composed of the United States, France and Turkey, gave the following interpretation of the provision on compensation:

> The General Assembly has laid down the principle of the right of the refugees to exercise a free choice between returning to their homes and being compensated for the loss of or damage to their property on the one hand, or, on the other, of not returning to their homes and being adequately compensated for the value of the property abandoned by them.[19]

According to this interpretation of the resolution, the refugees, not Israel, have the right to exercise a free choice between returning and not returning to their homes. The first category will be compensated for the loss of or damage to their property, while the second will be adequately compensated for the value of the property abandoned by them.

The efforts of the Conciliation Commission to implement Resolution 194 (III) were doomed to failure because of Israel's refusal to comply. Nevertheless, the General Assembly of the United Nations, in a number of resolutions, continued affirming the right of the refugees to return and calling upon Israel to facilitate the return of those wishing to do so. Resolution 194 (III) has remained operative and in force.

Another wave of refugees accompanied the 1967 War when the question was put once more before the General Assembly, as well as the Security Council. By Resolution 237 of 14 June 1967, the Security Council called upon Israel to facilitate the return of those displaced by the 1967 War. By Resolution 2452A of 19 December 1968, the General Assembly called upon Israel to take "effective and immediate steps for the return without delay" of those who became refugees, some of whom for the second time, as a result of the 1967 hostilities. More and more resolutions were adopted, but Israel remained adamant in its refusal to implement them.

Another category of refugees is rarely mentioned: the internal Palestinian refugees. This category is composed of Israeli Palestinians, who are in Israel and were there before its creation, but who were denied return to their homes and villages inside Israel. These Israeli nationals of Palestinian origin are forced to seek homes and livelihood outside their villages. They are denied the right to return to their villages and lead a normal life, although they are Israeli nationals. This is one of the glaring examples of Israeli racist ideology and policies. Israel is a party to the United Nations Covenant on Civil and Political Rights which prohibits such discrimination. But again, Israel is allowed to violate its treaty obligations without any serious criticism or action by the United Nations or the other parties to the Covenant. Israel is also in violation of the United Nations Convention of the Elimination of All Forms of Racial Discrimination and the United Nations Declaration on the same subject.

Another wave of Palestinian refugees is now in the making: the Palestinian inhabitants of the city of Jerusalem. The Israeli government classifies them as "residents" and, as expected, the Israeli Supreme Court has been ready to provide the "legal" cover. It treats them as aliens, like transient labourers or tourists on short visits, not as people who have lived in their own country for generations.[20] Refusal of or delay in the renewal of "residence" exposes these "residents" to expulsion. It should be recalled that the Security Council has repeatedly declared Israel's annexation of Jerusalem illegal and has requested Israel to repeal, annul and desist from such measures and from introducing any demographic changes. The Jerusalemites are a direct responsibility of the Security Council. The protection of their rights and status is the responsibility of the Council and the United

Nations, whose partition resolution placed Jerusalem outside both the proposed Jewish and Arab states. Nevertheless, the Council has remained ineffective.

Remedies

The problem of the refugees, of all categories, has remained unresolved. Relief has been provided to them through the United Nations Relief and Works Agency (UNRWA). But the budget of the agency is hardly sufficient to meet the minimum needs of the refugees, and has been facing one crisis after another. Attempts at repatriation have failed because of Israeli intransigence. Similarly, attempts at resettlement have failed because of resistance by refugees and host countries alike, both of whom insist on the right of return. There is a real deadlock: Israel's persistent refusal to comply with international legality and the binding resolutions of the United Nations, and Palestinian insistence on the exercise of their inalienable right to return to their country. With this deadlock, the suffering of the refugees continues while their homes and properties are increasingly incorporated into Israeli life and economy, with no return for the refugees themselves.

The solution to the problem lies in Israel's implementation of the United Nations resolutions on the question and the main obstacle has been the American veto which has been used to protect Israeli violations. In recent years, in the wake of the Gulf War, the world has been a witness to the double standards being applied by the United States (and Great Britain) regarding the implementation of United Nations resolutions. The United States, as sole superpower, is in open and persistent support of Security Council resolutions on Iraq to the extent of waging unilateral war on Iraq, while it is against even condemnation of Israel for its continuous violation of Security Council resolutions on Jerusalem and UN Resolution 194 (III) on the right of return of Palestinian refugees. This policy has seriously undermined US credibility, not only in the Arab world, and has left the problem of the refugees without the active support of the Security Council.

Attempts at Enforcing the Right of Return through Israeli Courts

As stated above, one category of Palestinian refugees denied the right of return are those Palestinian Israeli citizens who cannot go back to their homes and villages inside Israel. Normally, a citizen whose rights have been violated resorts to the courts of his country for the recovery of his right, and will expect the courts to recognise that right and the authorities to respect the court decision and enforce it. He will also expect the rule of equality before the law of all citizens to apply to him, without any discrimination based on race or ethnic origin. Israel has presented itself to the world as the only democracy in the Middle East where the rule of law is fully observed. In the circumstances, one would have expected that these Israeli citizens would have no problem in returning to their homes and villages, even without the need to resort to the courts to enforce their right. However, despite the passage of 50 years, Israel still refuses to allow them to return to their villages and property, which are still there, in the hope that, with the passage of time and the force of circumstance, the will to return will be frustrated and the new generation will lose interest and remain settled in other areas. Nevertheless, attempts through Israeli courts have been made, and I shall now refer to a few examples which are fully documented.

In *Jamal Aslan et al.* v *The Military Governor of Galilee*,[21] the villagers of Ghabisiya in North Galilee (inside Israel) were ordered, in February 1950, to leave their village by the Israeli military governor, and their village was declared a closed area. A year after their expulsion, the villagers submitted a complaint to the Israeli Supreme Court requesting repeal of the military governor's orders and that they be allowed to return to their village. The Supreme Court judged that the declaration of an area as "closed" was a "legal act". However, it could not be considered effective "unless the declaration had been published in the *Official Gazette*". In view of the fact that there had been no official announcement for Ghabisiya, the villagers should be returned to their homes.

Nevertheless, the villagers were not allowed to return. Instead, the military governor published the order in the *Official Gazette*. When the villagers went back to the Supreme Court complaining that they were not allowed to return, the Court did not hold the authorities in contempt. Instead, it ruled that villagers who had not returned home before the order could still not return – except, of course, with the written permission of the authorities. In other words, the order, once published, was given an effect which it never had to deny the right of return, previously agreed as enforceable. It was irresponsible of the Court to assume that the villagers would be able to return before the publication of the order, while the military governor was in control of their village and their movements.

The second case I would like to refer to is that of the village of Ikrit, described by the editor of *The Palestine Yearbook of International Law* as "perhaps one of the longest legal battles ever known".[22] In this case, on 5 November 1949, the villagers were ordered to leave their homes "for two weeks" until "military operations in the area were concluded". Their attempts to return peacefully were unsuccessful, and they applied to the Supreme Court. On 31 July 1951, the Court ordered the Israeli authorities to allow the villagers to return to their village. The Israeli authorities refused to implement that decision and declared the area closed. The villagers appealed against this action. On the date fixed for hearing the appeal, which was Christmas Day 1952, the Israeli army gave the villagers, who were all Christians, a Christmas present: it blew up all of the houses in the village.[23] Until this very day, despite their successive attempts to invoke the rule of law in Israel, the villagers have not been successful in returning to their homes.[24]

However, Israel cannot be taken as an authoritative example of how the judicial and executive authorities of a democracy should behave in their treatment of this basic right. In Israel, where a matter concerns Palestinians, be they Israeli citizens or not, such rights are rarely viewed, even by the judiciary, as an issue to be determined according to law. The courts, especially the Supreme Court, have proved themselves ready to accommodate the illegal acts of the executive and offer such acts a cynical and often transparent cloak of legality. Political considerations seem decisive, and the law becomes subservient to the ideology of the state and its political objectives.

Through the High Commissioner for Refugees

The main duty of the High Commissioner for Refugees is to achieve repatriation of refugees to their home country, and not to seek their resettlement in another country. However, the High Commissioner can seek the return only of those refugees within his jurisdiction and his functions are exercised through diplomacy. In other words, agreement of the power in control of the territory is necessary, and without that agreement the High Commissioner can only exercise moral persuasion and submit his report to the United Nations.[25] From the beginning of the problem, the Palestinian refugees were put outside the jurisdiction of the High Commissioner, as UNRWA was created to attend to their needs.

Through the United Nations

UN Resolution 194 (III) on the right of the Palestinian refugees to return established a Conciliation Commission for Palestine. In general, the Commission was given the functions which had been entrusted to the murdered UN Mediator for Palestine, Count Bernadotte. The General Assembly, in paragraph 11 of the Resolution, instructed the Commission in the following manner:

> [The General Assembly] *Instructs* the Conciliation Commission to facilitate the repatriation, resettlement and economic and social rehabilitation of the refugees and the payment of compensation, and to maintain close relations with the Director of the United Nations Relief and Works Agency for Palestine Refugees and, through him, with the appropriate organs and agencies of the United Nations.

Commenting on this paragraph, two distinguished scholars on the question of Palestine observe that: "The conciliatory wording of the entire resolution [194 (III)] was apparently based on the assumption that the Government of Israel would cooperate in good faith with the Conciliation Commission and take all possible steps in the implementation of the present resolution."[26] The assumption has proved to be misplaced. Israel did not respond to this conciliatory wording and the Commission failed in its efforts. This failure has been noted by the General Assembly of the United Nations in operative paragraph 1 of Resolution 2452B, in which the General Assembly

> *Notes with deep regret* that repatriation or compensation of the refugees as provided for in paragraph 11 of General Assembly Resolution 194 (III) has not been effected, that no substantial

progress has been made in the programme endorsed in paragraph 2 of Resolution 513 (VI) for the reintegration either by repatriation or resettlement and that, therefore, the situation of the refugees continues to be a matter of serious concern.

Paragraph 4 of the same resolution requested the Commission to continue its "efforts towards the implementation of [Resolution 194 (III)]". No action was taken by the United Nations to implement its resolutions.

This issue is of vital importance to the international community and the peoples of the world. The problem is not political. It is a problem of the enforcement of a basic, inalienable right: the right of everyone to return to his country. Moreover, it is a right protected by one of the most solemn international conventions, the Fourth Geneva Convention. Dangerous precedents are being created through failure to enforce this Convention and the right of return. A number of states, including the United States, have made observance of human rights an important element of their foreign policy. Yet, when the question concerns Israeli violations of a fundamental right, such as the right of return, the opposite policy is adopted. Human rights should not be a political game. Respect for human dignity and fundamental rights are basic to the United Nations system and the world order based on its Charter. In response to this, the United Nations has been instrumental in the decolonising process and in the conclusion of international conventions for the protection of human rights and the establishment of international bodies to supervise their implementation. Only the rights of the Palestinian people have, so far, been excluded from this arena.

The 1967 War led to the famous Security Council Resolution No. 242. The last item in the resolution simply provided for a settlement of the refugee problem. The resolution, which was intended to be a statement of principles governing the solution of the Arab–Israeli problem, failed to refer to the right of return as the solution to the refugee problem.

The United Nations is taking an increasing role in refugee problems as part of its general concern for world peace and security. The Security Council is the United Nations organ empowered under the Charter to take binding decisions and enforce such decisions.

However, the Security Council has not shown a consistency in the implementation of its decisions. In particular, while the Council has consistently condemned Israeli violations of the Geneva Conventions, including the forcible deportation of Palestinians, no action is taken to enforce the Security Council resolutions on Palestine, and the resolution on the right of return. On the other hand, the United Nations has played an important role in enforcing the right of the Bosnians to return to their homes, to the extent of stationing UN forces (led by the US) for that purpose. The same is being done in connection with the present refugee crisis in Rwanda/Zaire. Unfortunately, the Security Council cannot be relied upon to act objectively for the enforcement of the Fourth Geneva Convention and Israel and the United States must bear the responsibility for this. The use, or threat of use, of the veto to defeat the objectives of the Fourth Geneva Convention is utterly irresponsible and no political considerations can provide a proper justification.

Through the Parties to the Geneva Conventions

Article 2 of each of the four Geneva Conventions places a treaty obligation on the parties not only to respect, but also to "ensure respect" for the provisions of the Conventions. When a party to one of the four Conventions violates its provisions, one would expect action by the other parties to ensure respect of the provisions in pursuance of their obligation under the Conventions. The Conventions are the cornerstone of international humanitarian law, and acquiescence in their violation undermines the sanctity of these basic Conventions. All of these deal with the question of repatriation, and place this obligation even beyond the reach of renunciation. The parties, however, do not seem to have the political will to ensure respect for the Conventions, at least as far as the Palestinians are concerned.

The Oslo Agreement

One of the direct, but not declared, consequences of the Gulf War of 1990 was the attempt to resolve the Palestinian–Israeli problem. However, instead of adopting the same policy of enforcing the rules of international legality through the Security Council, a system of negotiations between the parties was resorted to under the joint auspices of the United States and Russia. One of the main objectives of this procedure, as clearly demonstrated by the United States whenever the question was later brought before the Security Council and the General Assembly of the United Nations, was to exclude the role of the United Nations in contributing to the solution. If the two parties to the conflict settle their differences amicably and lay down principles and procedures for its settlement, the United Nations, it could be argued, would have no role other than to call on the parties to abide by their agreement.

The result of these direct negotiations, conducted in complete secrecy, was the Oslo Declaration of Principles of 13 September 1993. The Palestinian negotiators were not equal to the task and lacked the expertise, particularly in legal matters, to negotiate and conclude this vital agreement. No Palestinian legal experts participated or were consulted before its conclusion. The result was an agreement which involved Israel in decisions that should have been an exclusive Palestinian prerogative (for example, the future of the Palestinian territories and their people). The negotiations, as judged from the Declaration, were not directed towards an agenda of terminating Israeli occupation in accordance with international law.

As regards the question of refugees, the Declaration failed to make any reference to the right of return. Instead, the refugees were divided into two categories: the 1967 refugees and the earlier refugees. In both cases, the solution required the agreement of Israel.[27]

Refugees and Displaced Persons
Article 8 of the Declaration states:

1. Recognising the massive human problems caused to both parties by the conflict in the Middle East, as well as the contribution made by them towards the alleviation of human suffering, the parties will seek to further alleviate those problems arising on a bilateral level.

2. Recognising that the above human problems caused by the conflict in the Middle East cannot be fully resolved on a bilateral

level, the parties will seek to resolve them in appropriate forums, in accordance with international law, including the following:

(i) in the case of displaced persons, in a quadripartite committee together with Egypt and the Palestinians;

(ii) in the case of refugees,
- a) in the framework of the Multilateral Working Group on refugees;
- b) in negotiations, in a framework to be agreed, bilateral or otherwise, in conjunction with and at the same time as the permanent status negotiations pertaining to the territories referred to in Article 3 of this Treaty;

(iii) through the implementation of agreed United Nations programmes and other agreed international economic programmes concerning refugees and displaced persons, including assistance to their settlement.

The foregoing provision dealt with the refugee problem as a "human problem" and not as a problem of the failure to permit the refugees to exercise their right to return to their country, or a problem of implementation of that right. Israel's responsibility, even to compensate the refugees for their property which it has expropriated or utilised as "absentee property", is not referred to. In any event, the solution of the refugee problem is left to the final status negotiations without any commitment on the part of Israel, in the same manner as other important issues, such as Jerusalem, the settlements, borders and security (Article V (3)). The parties did not provide for any agreed principles or rules that are to govern those negotiations. In this case, it would be proper for the Palestinian side to insist on the application of the principles of international and humanitarian law governing refugees. These principles, as shown above, affirm the right of repatriation or the right of return. General Assembly resolutions are a specific application of those principles to the case of Palestinian refugees.

The Declaration of Principles was, however, more specific about the 1967 refugees, who are described as "displaced persons". Many of them are second-time refugees, displaced from the first refugee camps. Article XII, dealing with "Liaison and Cooperation with Jordan and Egypt", establishes a Continuing Committee which, according to this

Article, "will decide by agreement on the modalities of admission of persons displaced from the West Bank and Gaza Strip in 1967, together with necessary measures to prevent disruption and disorder".

The agreement of the parties, under this provision, is required for "the modalities" of admission. The right of return *per se* is accepted for all those wishing to return, and only the mechanics of such return are to be discussed and agreed upon.

In law, there is no difference between those displaced in 1947–8 and those displaced in 1967, and the General Assembly and Security Council of the United Nations have dealt with them on the same basis. Both have the right of return if they wish. Consequently, the acceptance of that right in the Oslo Declaration of Principles for the 1967 refugees must be taken as an acceptance of the same right for the earlier refugees, and only the modalities need to be agreed upon. Obviously, this was not the Israeli intention.

It is common knowledge that no progress whatsoever has been made by the Continuing Committee so far and the problem has remained. Since the 1967 refugees are entitled to return to the West Bank and the Gaza Strip, one doubts the wisdom of the Palestinian negotiators in involving Israel at all. The cooperation of Egypt and Jordan may be required because of the presence of these refugees in their territories, but Israel should have no say whatsoever in the matter if the Palestinian Authority decides to implement United Nations resolutions calling for the return of these refugees to their homes. Israel, as an occupying power, is under an obligation by virtue of the Fourth Geneva Convention to permit their repatriation.[28]

Resolution 194 has thus remained unimplemented and the current deadlocked negotiations make a solution less attainable. In my view, the time has come for the refugees themselves to make their voice heard more effectively. They should organise themselves into a pressure group, acting on the Palestinian leadership and the international community. The Palestinian leadership must be reminded constantly of the urgency of finding a solution to the satisfaction of the refugees themselves. Israel and the international community must be made aware of the fact that the problem has not disappeared and that it is very much alive. Without such a movement by the refugees themselves, the question will remain on the back burner or become permanently marginalised.

NOTES

1 The fact that, under national legislation, natives may be jailed, thereby losing the freedom to leave and return to their country, has no effect on this basic position.

2 When Israel occupied and later annexed East Jerusalem in the wake of the 1967 War, it treated the Palestinian inhabitants of the city as "residents" and issued them with resident permits which were subject to renewal at the discretion of the Israeli authorities. Any Palestinian inhabitant whose residence permit expired would automatically lose his right to stay in the city. Many Palestinian Jerusalemites who happened to be abroad either for study or work lost, in the eyes of the Israeli authorities, their right to return to their home town, Jerusalem, if their residence permit had expired while they were abroad. Israeli embassies were not keen on renewing those permits – nor, of course, were the Israeli authorities. Recently, the Netanyahu government has adopted a policy of not renewing the permits of even those Palestinians who remained in Jerusalem, and the issue has become one of the burning issues of the flagging peace process. Even the US Secretary of State has asked Israel to reconsider its policy in this respect. The obvious objective is to empty the city of its Palestinian inhabitants. What is amazing to a student of law is that, once more, the Israeli Supreme Court has sided with the government. Nowhere has there been a supreme court more ready to provide legalistic support, in flagrant violation of fundamental human rights, to the policies of the government than in Israel.

3 During the British Mandate over Palestine, which lasted from 1922 to 1948, the British government, in violation of this principle, banished Palestinian leaders who opposed the government's policies on Jewish immigration to Palestine and its suppression of the national rights of the Palestinian people in their own country to British colonies, especially the Seychelles. This was done in order to facilitate the creation in Palestine of a Jewish national home. Israel adopted the policy of expulsion of Palestinians to neighbouring Arab countries after its occupation of Palestinian territories in 1967. The Security Council has frequently condemned such activity as illegal.

4 Under the Israeli occupation of the Palestinian territories of the Gaza Strip and the West Bank, Palestinians who wished to travel abroad for study or work were issued by the occupying authority with travel permits which stipulated conditions of no return before a fixed period. A Palestinian could not return home before the expiry of that period, and had to obtain renewal of the permit to be able to stay and return. Many lost their status as inhabitants of their homeland because of failure to renew, not always without intentional Israeli bureaucratic delay. Israeli "legal" tricks to empty the land of its people deserve a special study in the abuse of the exercise of power and the administration of law.

5 The question of extradition of criminals is an exception. However, such exception is carefully regulated by law and/or extradition treaties. The

legislation of some countries prohibits the extradition of its nationals to face trial in other countries.

6 Adopted and proclaimed by the United Nations General Assembly Resolution 217A (III) of 10 December 1948.

7 Such a situation arose when Palestine was divided and the West Bank became part of Jordan, in the wake of the 1948 Arab–Israeli War. Palestinians who habitually resided in the West Bank and who happened to be abroad at the time, like the writer, were able to return to the West Bank because that was the part of Palestine which was their home before partition.

8 For a more detailed consideration of this law, see Don Peretz, *Israel and the Palestinian Arabs* (Washington DC: The Middle East Institute, 1958), pp. 121–6.

9 Israelis are particularly troubled by this provision of the Universal Declaration of Human Rights and, whenever they can, they try to advocate the theory of return to one's country of nationality in order to deprive Palestinian refugees of their right to return to their homes and properties in that part of Palestine which has become Israel. Such an attempt took place, for example, at a conference of lawyers and judges organised in Washington in 1975 by the Peace Through the Law Organisation. The attempt failed.

10 Adopted and opened for signature, ratification and accession by United Nations General Assembly Resolution 2200A (XXI) of 16 December 1966, and brought into force on 23 March 1976.

11 The four Geneva Conventions are: (1) the Geneva Convention for the Amelioration of the Conditions of the Wounded and Sick in Armed Forces in the Field; (2) the Geneva Convention for the Amelioration of the Conditions of Wounded, Sick and Shipwrecked Members of Armed Forces at Sea; (3) the Geneva Convention relating to the Treatment of Prisoners of War; and (4) the Geneva Convention relating to the Protection of Civil Persons in Time of War. The four conventions were approved on 12 August 1949.

12 Resolution 319 (IV) of 3 December 1949, followed by Resolution 428 (V) of 14 December 1950. The first resolution established the Office as of 1 January 1951, while the latter promulgated the Statute of the Office of the United Nations High Commissioner for Refugees.

13 Such as the Israeli Absentee Property Law of 1950, under which the Israeli authorities took over the property of Palestinian "absentees" and the never-ending confiscation of Palestinian property for the establishment of Israeli settlements.

14 Israeli destruction of Palestinian villages, on whose sites many Israeli kibbutzim are established, has aimed, in part, at eliminating villages to which Palestinian refugees may have wanted to return.

15 Staff Officer Yigal Yadin recalled that he prepared the nucleus of Plan Delta in 1944, which was later implemented with the "main Arab villages" as its key targets. Former Foreign Minister Moshe Sharett stated, "The most spectacular event in the contemporary history of Palestine – more spectacular in a sense than the creation of the Jewish state – is the wholesale evacuation of its Arab population", and that "the most vexing problem of the Jewish state" was resolved by expelling the Palestinians. M. Palumbo, *The Palestinian Catastrophe* (London: Quartet Books, 1987), pp. 145, 204; and Editorial, *Return Review*

(The Palestine Return Centre, vol. 2, issue 3, December 1997). As noted above, the right of return is enjoyable by any person who has left his country, for whatever cause. It is irrelevant whether the Palestinian refugees left voluntarily because of fear or actual terror or, as has been alleged by Israel, in response to calls by Arab leaders.

16 Peretz, *Israel and the Palestinian Arab*, p. 143. It is instructive to read at least Chapter VIII, "Israel's Initial Absentee Property Policy" on early estimates of the extent and value of Palestinian property, and Israeli policies, particularly through its definition of "abandoned" and "absentee" in order to justify its seizure and exploitation of Palestinian property.

17 It is tragic that this great Swedish humanitarian who had done so much to help many Jews escape Nazi gas chambers should be the victim of an assassination by Jewish hands, while he was again trying to do justice to the Palestinian victims of Israel.

18 This Commission was created by the United Nations.

19 *Historical Survey of Efforts of the UN Conciliation Commission for Palestine to Secure the Implementation of Paragraph 11 of G.A. Resolution 194 (III)*, para. 38; UN Document A/AC.25/W.81/Rev.2 at 20–21.

20 This aspect is dealt with by Leah Tsemel in Chapter 4 of this book. This problem is one of the causes of the stalled peace talks. Israel is again violating Security Council resolutions on Jerusalem which called on Israel to make no changes in the demographic composition of the city.

21 Judgements of the Supreme Court of Israel, vol. 6: 284, Appeal 220/51; and vol. 9: 689, Appeals 288/51, 33/52, quoted in Sabri Jiryis, *The Arabs in Israel* (New York Monthly Review Press, 1976), pp. 89–90.

22 The three judgements of the Israeli Supreme Court are reproduced in an English translation in vol. II (1985) of the *Yearbook*, pp. 119–50. For background, see Jiryis, *The Arabs*, pp. 91–2.

23 In other countries, these actions of the executive would be treated as contempt of court. It is basic to the rule of law that the decisions of the courts are respected and executed.

24 Later judgements of the Court in this case confirmed the expulsion order and provided the "legal" grounds for the expulsion.

25 The Palestinian refugees are not within the jurisdiction of the High Commissioner. A special United Nations agency (UNRWA) was created to attend to their needs. It was unlike the Office of the High Commissioner in that repatriation of the refugees was not a part of its mandate. The mandate was given to the UN Conciliation Commission, which was a complete failure and eventually vanished from the scene.

26 W. Thomas Mallinson and Sally V. Mallinson, *The Palestine Problem in International Law and World Order* (Harlow: Longman, 1986), p. 179.

27 The full text of the Declaration is published in Eugene Cotran and Chibli Mallat (eds.), *Yearbook of Islamic and Middle Eastern Law* (The Hague: Kluwer Law International, 1994), vol. 1.

28 A constant feature of Israeli adherence to international instruments on human rights is the failure to abide by the obligations undertaken. Israel is a party to the Geneva Conventions, the International Convention on the Elimination of

all Forms of Racial Discrimination and the International Covenant on Civil and Political Rights and has been in violation of these instruments in so far as they affect the rights of the Palestinian people. It adhered to the Statute of the International Court of Justice, yet it placed too many reservations to make such adherence of any value at all regarding its disputes with the Palestinians and its neighbours.

6

The Right of Displaced Palestinians to Return to Home Areas in Israel

John Quigley

One of the major tragedies of the long-standing dispute over Palestine is the exodus of Palestinians that occurred in 1948. The overwhelming majority of the Palestinians living in the territory that became Israel were displaced at that time, fleeing in most instances with only what they could carry. The exodus was orchestrated by the military units that established Israel, the leadership of the Israeli statehood movement viewing a large population of Palestinians as incompatible with their aspiration for a Jewish state. Elsewhere, this writer has explored these events in some detail, tracing the legal and factual basis of Israel's responsibility for the exodus.[1]

Regardless of the circumstances of the exodus, however, that is, even if the exodus is not deemed to have been coerced, the Palestinians displaced in the wartime circumstances of 1948 may enjoy a right to return to their home areas, and in particular to their home areas in what became Israel. Palestinians as individuals, and the various political parties representing the Palestinians, insist on a right of return. Ever since the exodus occurred, the international community has urged Israel to repatriate the displaced Palestinians.

The issue of the displaced Palestinians will be on the agenda of anticipated Israeli–Palestinian negotiations aimed at resolving the major outstanding issues between these two parties. Israel denies any obligation to repatriate. The fact that the issue is to be the subject of negotiation, perhaps at an early date, calls for clarity. If there is a right for the displaced Palestinians to return to their home areas, then that right must be respected.

A Right of Return

The subject of international population displacement and the right of displaced persons to return has received considerable attention in recent years. The momentous events befalling Eastern Europe since 1990 have brought population evacuations. Inhabitants have fled their home areas, often in fear of their lives. In some cases they have been physically removed by an opposing military force.

In trying to settle such situations, the international community has insisted on the right of the displaced to return. The United Nations High Commissioner for Refugees has taken an active role in encouraging governments to repatriate the displaced. The United Nations Security Council has routinely demanded that governments permit the return of the displaced. When a civil war in Abkhazia, part of former Soviet Georgia, generated an outflow of refugees, the Security Council affirmed the right of "refugees and displaced persons to return to their homes".[2]

In the Balkan conflict, the Security Council has taken the same view. Regarding displaced Bosnians, the Council resolved that "all displaced persons have the right to return in peace to their former homes".[3] Regarding Serbs displaced from their home areas in Croatia, the Council demanded that Croatia

> in conformity with internationally recognised standards . . . respect fully the rights of the local Serb population including their rights to remain, leave or return in safety . . . [and] create conditions conducive to the return of those persons who have left their homes.[4]

In earlier conflicts as well, the United Nations insisted on the repatriation of the displaced. When warfare in Namibia, then still under South Africa, led to an exodus, the Council called on South Africa to "accord unconditionally to all Namibians currently in exile for political reasons full facilities for return to their country".[5] Similarly, when Turkey's intervention in Cyprus in 1974 saw thousands of Greek Cypriots fleeing from northern Cyprus to the south, out of an area in which a new Turkish state was soon proclaimed, the UN General Assembly "call[ed] for respect of the human rights of all Cypriots and the institution of urgent measures for the voluntary return of the refugees to their homes in safety".[6]

The United Nations took the same position regarding Palestinians displaced during the 1948 hostilities that led to the establishment of Israel in what had been Mandate Palestine. Its first major step was to appoint a mediator for the Palestine conflict, Count Folke Bernadotte. During the summer of 1948, Bernadotte focused considerable attention on the displacement issue. He viewed repatriation as an urgent matter, given the large numbers displaced, and the desperate situation of many of them in the states of refuge. Without success he urged the authorities of the new Israeli state to repatriate.[7]

On the basis of Bernadotte's recommendation that repatriation was needed, the General Assembly took up the issue, along with other issues involved in the Palestine conflict. Soon afterwards, the Assembly adopted Resolution 194, in which it addressed all major aspects of the Palestine conflict. In a provision of this resolution on the displaced Palestinians, the Assembly resolved

> that the refugees wishing to return to their homes and live at peace with their neighbours should be permitted to do so at the earliest practicable date, and that compensation should be paid for the property of those choosing not to return and for loss of or damage to property which, under principles of international law or in equity, should be made good by the Governments or authorities responsible.[8]

To implement its resolution, the General Assembly set up what it called the Palestine Conciliation Commission, composed of representatives from Turkey, France and the United States.[9] The three-member commission asked Israel to implement the General Assembly's call for the repatriation of the displaced Palestinians.[10] The United States, in particular, used both public and private diplomacy to press Israel to repatriate.[11] Israel admitted 8,000 Palestinians on the basis of reuniting split families,[12] and offered to admit 100,000 more, but when UN officials pressed Israel to admit a larger number it withdrew that offer.[13]

Israel took the position that it is not legally obliged to repatriate the displaced Palestinians. It has disputed the existence of a norm of international law that would require it to repatriate. However, such a norm seems to be comfortably embedded in the legal regime that has developed in the international community to deal with internationally displaced persons.

A state's obligation to admit its nationals into its territory developed as a corollary to the right of states to expel those who do not hold its nationality. The obligation to admit one's nationals is said to be "an inherent duty of States resulting from the conception of nationality".[14] If, as is true, states are not required to allow aliens to remain permanently, then the state of origin must be obliged to accept them back.

Return when Sovereignty Changes

In the case of a person displaced from territory that has come under new sovereignty, a state's obligation to admit applies even if the state does not recognise the person as a national.

> A state may not refuse to receive into its territory a person, upon his expulsion by or exclusion from the territory of another state, if such person is a national of the first state or if such person was formerly its national and lost its nationality without having or acquiring the nationality of any other state.[15]

A state may not force another state to accept a person by revoking nationality, or by refusing to acknowledge the nationality of a person displaced from what has become its territory.[16] Occasionally, this obligation has been violated, particularly by states that, like Israel, seek to exclude persons of a given ethnic group. The UN High Commissioner for Refugees has described the plight in recent years of

> ethnic minority groups who do not receive the citizenship of the place with which they are most closely connected. In some cases, ethnic minorities have been severely uprooted from their place of habitual residence, states arguing that as those concerned are not citizens, they have no right of residency . . .[17]

The United Nations has strenuously objected to such non-recognition by insisting on the right of return of the displaced. European institutions have also recognised a right of persons to domicile in their home areas, despite any change of sovereignty. Thus, in the context of changing borders in the territory of the former

Soviet Union, European institutions have insisted that newly formed states grant nationality to all permanent residents, even if the newly formed state would prefer to exclude persons of certain ethnic groups.

A treaty within the Council of Europe requires a state newly assuming sovereignty to refrain from making racial or ethnic distinctions in according nationality, and to take account of the habitual residence and place of birth of persons affected.[18] The provision mandating use of these factors must be applied, according to an official commentary, "in the light of the presumption under international law that the population follows the change of sovereignty over the territory in matters of nationality".[19] The International Law Commission has taken the same position in a draft treaty on nationality in the event of a change of sovereignty.[20]

A recent example of recognition of a right of return in such circumstances is Ukraine's repatriation to Crimea of the Tatar population of Crimea that was forced out by the government of the USSR during the Second World War. At the time of the displacement, Crimea was part of Russia. Since 1953, however, it has been part of Ukraine. The government of Ukraine facilitated the return of the Tatars despite the fact that the Tatars were not Ukrainians at the time of their displacement.

The principle found in the law is that inhabitants of a territory have a right to nationality even if the territory changes hands. Thus, a new sovereign must grant nationality to them. Even without some affirmative act to do this, inhabitants are assumed to carry the nationality of the new sovereign, at least so long as they do not in some fashion reject it. This approach was accepted by an Israeli court in a case involving not Palestinian Arabs, but Jews. Until 1952, Israel had no nationality in law. Yet the courts had to decide cases between 1948 and 1952, and the nationality of litigants might be at issue. In a 1951 case, the district court in Tel Aviv surveyed international law authorities and concluded that inhabitants of the territory that became Israel automatically became Israelis, even in the absence of any legislation defining an Israeli nationality. The court stated that: "in the case of transfer of a portion of the territory of a State to another State, every individual and inhabitant of the ceding State becomes automatically a national of the receiving State". Applying this principle, the court said that all persons resident in the territory that became

Israel as of the date of declaration of Israel's statehood automatically became Israeli nationals.[21]

The Tel Aviv court did not have to address the question of the nationality of persons temporarily absent when the new state enters sovereignty, as would have been the situation of the several hundred thousand Palestinians displaced prior to the date of Israel's declaration of statehood. International law authorities make it clear, however, that even residents who are temporarily absent on the date of transfer of sovereignty assume the nationality of the new sovereign. When, for example, the United States acquired Puerto Rico from Spain, it established a procedure to register as US nationals "native inhabitants of Puerto Rico temporarily sojourning abroad".[22]

Return as a Right of the Individual

International institutions have deemed return to be a matter of right running to the individual displaced person. They have based this view on norms of law, and have relied not only on the traditional law relating to a state's obligation to admit nationals, but on human rights as well. Human rights instruments guarantee a right of return to the displaced.[23] According to the Universal Declaration of Human Rights, "Everyone has the right to leave any country, including his own, and to return to his country."[24] The International Covenant on Civil and Political Rights specifies that "no one shall be arbitrarily deprived of the right to enter his own country".[25] The International Convention on the Elimination of All Forms of Racial Discrimination says that a state may not deny, on racial or ethnic grounds, the opportunity "to return to one's country".[26] Israel is a party to both these treaties.

As for the displaced Palestinians, the United Nations, as indicated, called on Israel to repatriate them. That call was in keeping with the generally recognised obligation of states to repatriate nationals, an obligation that applied to a new state that might not recognise as nationals a population group to whom it refused repatriation.

Analysts arguing in favour of Israel's position that no right of return exists in international law have cited various aspects of the above-quoted 1948 resolution of the General Assembly, in an effort to show that the General Assembly did not view return as a matter of right. Some said that the General Assembly called for repatriation only in the context of an eventual overall settlement, and therefore that it imposed no independent obligation to repatriate.[27]

The General Assembly, however, rejected such an interpretation. In the General Assembly's First Committee, a draft of what became Resolution 194 was introduced by the United Kingdom.[28] Guatemala suggested that Israel should be required to repatriate only upon an overall settlement, and so it proposed amending the paragraph on repatriation by adding the words "after the proclamation of peace by the contending parties in Palestine, including the Arab states".[29] In floor debate, Israel supported the Guatemalan amendment,[30] but the United States opposed, arguing that the displaced Palestinians "should not be made pawns in the negotiations for a final settlement".[31] The proposed Guatemalan amendment was defeated, by 37 votes to seven, with five abstentions.[32] Thus, the General Assembly considered and rejected the idea that return might lawfully be delayed pending peace agreements.

Some analysts have argued that by calling for the repatriation of displaced Palestinians "wishing to . . . live at peace with their neighbours", the General Assembly limited the return of Palestinians so inclined and thus fell short of recognising a right of return for all of them.[33] This conclusion is also unwarranted. Returning Palestinians would be living under Israeli rule, even though they overwhelmingly objected to the creation of a Jewish state in Palestine. The phrase "wishing to live at peace" provided a way to refer to those Palestinians who were disposed to return even if it meant living under Israeli sovereignty.

In any event, in later resolutions calling for repatriation of the Palestinians, the General Assembly clearly viewed any Palestinian wishing to return as having a right to do so. In one later resolution, it referred to "the inalienable right of the Palestinians to return to their homes and property from which they have been displaced and uprooted".[34]

Other commentators have focused on the word "should" in Resolution 194, arguing that the General Assembly did not view Israel as legally required to repatriate but was merely asking it to do so as a measure that would promote an overall settlement. Thus, it was said that the General Assembly did not recognise a right for the Palestinians to return.[35]

When the resolution was debated in the General Assembly, the delegate of the United Kingdom, the resolution's drafter, called the provision on displaced persons a "precise directive", a characterisation that makes sense only if it is a call for repatriation.[36] In the United Nations debate, only Israel questioned whether repatriation was a matter of right.[37] Delegates of other states indicated their view that Israel was required to repatriate. Thus, the United States said that "those who wished should be returned to their homes",[38] China referred to "the rights of the Arab refugees to return to their homes",[39] and Colombia said that the displaced Palestinians "should have the right to choose between receiving compensation or returning to their homes".[40]

Later United Nations resolutions, like the one quoted above, referred to return for the displaced Palestinians as an issue of legal right. Secretary-General U Thant referred to the displaced Palestinians' "natural right to be in their homeland".[41] The United Nations Commission on Human Rights found a "right of the Palestinians to return to their homeland Palestine and their property, from which they have been uprooted by force".[42]

In its Resolution 194, the General Assembly was focusing on displaced Palestinians as individuals. Consistent with the right of return existing in international law, it viewed them as being entitled, as individuals, to be repatriated by Israel if they so desired. Beginning in the 1970s, the UN General Assembly viewed the Palestinians as enjoying a right of self-determination in Palestine. It viewed them as entitled to return on that basis as well.[43]

Some analysts have taken this later position as a repudiation by the United Nations of its view that Palestinians as individuals are entitled to return to the territory that became Israel. Thus, one analyst states that in the UN view, if Palestinian self-determination is exercised in the West Bank and Gaza Strip, this would substitute for repatriation to Israel.[44]

These analysts misread the United Nations position. During the years in which it began to refer to Palestinian self-determination, the General Assembly continued to refer back to Resolution 194 and to call on Israel to implement the return for which it called in Resolution 194. In 1974, for example, the Assembly resolved

that the enjoyment by the Palestinian Arab refugees of their right
to return to their homes and property, recognised by the General
Assembly in Resolution 194 (III) of 11 December 1948, which
has been repeatedly reaffirmed by the Assembly since that date, is
indispensable for the achievement of a just settlement of the
refugee problem and for the exercise by the people of Palestine of
its right to self-determination.[45]

The General Assembly has not deviated from its view that individual
Palestinians are entitled to return to their home areas, even if those
areas lie in territory that became Israel. As indicated, that is the
only view that is consistent with the matter as viewed in international
law.

Return as an individual right may seem incompatible with
the manner in which the issue of the displaced Palestinians is to be
addressed. Under the Oslo Accords, the matter is to be negotiated
between Israel and the Palestine Liberation Organisation. The 1993
Declaration of Principles between these two parties, the first of the
Oslo Accords, specifically calls for them to deal with this issue along
with a number of others that they have agreed must be resolved. If
return is to be negotiated in this fashion, then it must seem that the
right is of a collective character only.

Such a conclusion would not, however, be proper. Many issues
involving human rights are resolved between governments via negotiation. That fact does not, however, negate the character of the rights as
appertaining to the individual. States in their negotiations are required
to respect human rights. The United Nations High Commissioner for
Human Rights, Mary Robinson, addressing the topic of the anticipated
Israeli–PLO negotiations at a conference in Gaza city in December 1997,
stressed that in resolving the issues affecting their two constituencies, the
two parties must observe human rights. They are not free to dispense
with rights by way of political accommodation.

Changed Character of the Home Area

From another perspective, considerations of a practical character have
been raised to question whether an individual right of return is
feasible for situations like that of the displaced Palestinians, where the

displacement involves large numbers of persons and where the displacement continues over a period of decades.

One such issue is that of the areas to which the displaced might return. Many of the localities from which Palestinians were displaced in what is now Israel have changed in character since 1948. What in 1948 was a rural village may today be a block of apartments inhabited by suburban commuters. Such transformations may make it difficult to conceptualise a "return". In such situations, it may not be possible to restore the displaced to the environment from which they departed. It may not be feasible to recreate a rural community where one no longer exists. But what is required under the right of return is, first, admission to the state's territory for purposes of residence, and second, conferment of nationality, such that the person is entitled to the rights enjoyed by others there. As for restoring the displaced to a specific location, this should be done if feasible. If the locality has so changed in character that this cannot be done, then some approximation of restoring the person to the situation they left may be found.

The experience of the Crimean Tatars provides some clues as to how such a return might be managed. Both groups were displaced during the 1940s and with the Tatars, as with the displaced Palestinians, many of their home areas have changed radically in character. Returning Tatars have been accommodated in areas close to their former homes, but in most instances not in the precise location of their former homes.

Furthermore, even if the property of a displaced family remains intact, it may now be occupied by others. In such a situation, restoring a displaced family to a specific house or property may necessitate evicting the more recent occupants. This has been a difficult problem to resolve in recent instances of return of the displaced. In the former Yugoslavia, the principle of return to specific houses was recognised. The Dayton Agreement on Bosnia, for example, provides: "All refugees and displaced persons have the right freely to return to their homes of origin."[46] However, some local authorities – for example, in Serb areas of Bosnia – have refused returning Muslims repossession of their homes and have let the more recent Serb occupants remain. A similar phenomenon is observed in Croatia, where returning Serbs have been unsuccessful in many instances in gaining occupancy of their former homes.

In Rwanda, the same issue has arisen, as Hutus returning from several years of exile in neighbouring states have, in many instances, found their homes inhabited by Tutsis, who themselves had been displaced years earlier and had returned in the wake of the Tutsi military movement that took power in the country in 1994. In Rwanda, the principle of restoring the returning Hutus to their property has been recognised, and for the most part implemented.

Despite the practical difficulties, the right of the original inhabitants to their homes needs to be respected. Persons coming into occupancy of housing abandoned in wartime circumstances know that they are taking property that has an owner, even if the government grants them what appear to be full property rights.

The Security Council has taken the clear view that a government may not set up obstacles that make it difficult for returnees to reoccupy their lands and property. After it called on Abkhaz authorities to repatriate Georgians, it subsequently resolved that it remained "deeply concerned at the continued obstruction of the return of the refugees and displaced persons by the Abkhaz authorities".[47] When Croat authorities set time limits for returning Serbs to reclaim their lands, the Council reacted sharply, demanding that Croatia "respect fully the rights of the local Serb population including their right to remain or return in safety", and calling on Croatia "to lift any time limits placed upon the return of refugees to Croatia to reclaim their property".[48]

The significant general point here is that a right of return is not defeated by the fact that the area from which a person was displaced has changed in character. Reasonable accommodation must be made between the returnees and the current inhabitants.

Duration of a Right of Return

A second consideration of a practical nature is that of the time period over which a right of return may exist. The right attaches to those individuals who depart, as well as to their progeny born abroad. However, the question arises as to whether, if the displacement continues for a period of decades, the right of return remains, or whether it expires at some point in time.

The answer given by the law here is that the right continues until such time as a displaced individual voluntarily abandons the attachment to the home area. Thus, if a displaced individual decides to reside permanently in a new state and naturalises there, the right to return to the state encompassing the home area is lost. This might occur, for example, if a refugee child marries a national of a host state, decides to lead his or her life there, and gains the nationality of that state.

It may occur, however, that a displaced person acquires the nationality of a new state in circumstances that do not reflect a voluntary abandonment of the attachment to the home area. An example is the Palestinians displaced in 1948 from areas that became part of Israel and who took refuge in the West Bank of the Jordan River. These Palestinians were extended nationality by Jordan, as part of Jordan's annexation of the West Bank in 1950.

Jordan's extension of nationality to these Palestinians did not, however, affect Jordan's claim against Israel for the repatriation of these Palestinians. Jordan, as the host state for these displaced persons, continued to insist on Israel's obligation to repatriate. Jordan did not cease participating in the United Nations' demand on Israel to repatriate in accordance with Resolution 194. Jordan's grant of nationality was, moreover, of a conditional character. In approving the annexation of the West Bank, Jordan's parliament indicated:

> Arab rights in Palestine shall be protected. Those rights shall be defended with all possible legal means and this unity [of the West Bank with the other territory of Jordan] shall in no way be connected with the final settlement of Palestine's just cause within the limits of national hopes, Arab cooperation and international justice.[49]

Jordan thus viewed its annexation as being subject to the West Bank ultimately becoming part of a Palestine state. An analyst writing in 1970 said of this situation "that the Palestinians are only *provisionally* placed under Jordanian sovereignty".[50] When a Palestinian independent state was declared by the Palestine National Council in Algiers in 1988, Jordan renounced this provisional sovereignty, King Hussein announcing: "We respect the wish of the PLO for an independent Palestinian state."[51] Jordan then phased out Jordanian nationality for West Bank Palestinians.

There may, to be sure, be cases of some difficulty, in which there might be legitimate controversy as to whether a particular displaced Palestinian has abandoned the connection to the home area by virtue of gaining nationality elsewhere. The existence of what may be certain hard cases does not, however, negate the basic right of return.

Resettlement as an Alternative to Repatriation

A final consideration of a practical nature is that resettlement of the displaced in their state of refuge, or elsewhere, may in some situations seem more feasible than returning them to their home area. It has been suggested by some that it may make more sense for many of the displaced Palestinians to be accepted on a permanent basis by the states of refuge than to be repatriated by Israel. Thus, some analysts have said that the neighbouring Arab states that house large numbers of Palestinian refugees should be required to regularise their status, grant them nationality, and accept them in a permanent fashion.[52] Apart from Jordan, these states have not accorded nationality to displaced Palestinians.

That the Arab states should accept the displaced Palestinians on a permanent basis has been urged by Israel since its inception. In 1948 its Foreign Minister told the United Nations that "[Israel] believed that serious thought should be given to the resettling of the Arab refugees in neighbouring territories".[53] Some encouragement to this approach was provided by the United Nations during the 1950s and 1960s, when the General Assembly in fact asked the Arab states to resettle displaced Palestinians.[54] This approach was interpreted by some as reflecting a United Nations view that resettlement was just as appropriate as repatriation.

> Subsequent resolutions [i.e. subsequent to Resolution 194] . . . indicated the understanding . . . that unrestricted repatriation of refugees was neither a feasible option nor the preferred one. At the same time that it repeatedly reaffirmed Resolution 194 (III), the General Assembly advocated programs that would include the resettlement of the refugees in Arab countries.[55]

"For many years following the adoption of Resolution 194 in 1948", wrote another analyst, "the focus of General Assembly attention with respect to the Palestinian problem drifted from repatriation toward resettlement as a solution."[56]

However, contrary to these views, the United Nations' call on the Arab states to resettle did not bespeak an abandonment of the international effort to gain the repatriation of the displaced Palestinians, or a repudiation of their right of return. The Palestine Conciliation Commission said that

> it would be necessary to take into account the possibility that not all the refugees would decide to return to their homes. The Commission believed, therefore, that the Arab States should agree in principle to the resettlement of those refugees who did not desire to return to their homes.[57]

The call was thus to resettle those wishing to remain in the state of refuge and did not in any way diminish the obligation on Israel to repatriate. The General Assembly was concerned as well that the United Nations might run out of funds to maintain the displaced Palestinians in refugee camps and hoped that the Arab host states would assume some of the financial burden. Thus, in a 1950 resolution, the General Assembly stated that it

> Considers that, without prejudice to the provisions of paragraph 11 of General Assembly Resolution 194 (III) of 11 December 1948, the reintegration of the refugees into the economic life of the Near East, either by repatriation or resettlement, is essential for the time when international assistance is no longer available, and for the realization of conditions of peace and stability in the area.[58]

Thus, resettlement was viewed as a way of shifting the financial burden but was not a negation of the right of return.

Security Council Resolution 242

It has also been suggested that the United Nations abandoned the notion of repatriation following the adoption by the Security Council in 1967 of its Resolution 242, a resolution that the PLO and Israel have agreed should be the basis for their negotiations on the issues outstanding between them. Resolution 242 calls for the "just settlement of the refugee problem".[59] According to one view,

The weakness of the claim to a legal right of return and repossession is reinforced by United Nations resolutions on the settlement of the refugee problem in the Middle East. Security Council Resolution 242 . . . calls for "a just settlement of the refugee problem."[60]

These analysts continue: "The acceptance of Resolution 242 in the [Israeli–PLO] accords seems to reject a general right of return and repossession."[61]

Resolution 242 cannot, however, be taken in this way. It dealt with the issue of the displaced Palestinians in the most general terms, merely advocating a "just settlement of the refugee problem". Given that Resolution 242 was not more specific, what was meant by "just" must be the solution that had been sought by the United Nations since 1948 – namely, repatriation. Thus, in regard to the "just settlement" language in Resolution 242 the following argument has been put forward:

There are no elements of such a just settlement stated in the resolution and the only authoritative principles adopted by the United Nations on this subject remain the General Assembly resolutions which have been considered above [General Assembly Resolution 194 and its progeny].[62]

Clearly, the United Nations viewed repatriation of the displaced Palestinians as a necessary ingredient in any peace arrangement. The issue of repatriation had been aired at a UN-sponsored conference on the Palestine issue in 1949. Mark Ethridge, the US member of the Palestine Conciliation Commission, informed the State Department that at that conference, "Commission members, particularly US Rep, have consistently pointed out to Prime Minister, Foreign Minister, and Israeli delegation that the key to peace is some Israeli concession on refugees."[63] "[T]here was broad agreement", one analyst of UN activity on Palestine has written, "that the return of the Palestinians was a necessary ingredient in any peace plan."[64]

At the 1949 conference, Commissioner Ethridge, frustrated by the failure of his efforts to convince Israel to repatriate, said that Israel's "attitude toward [the Palestinian] refugees is morally reprehensible . . . Her position as conqueror demanding more does not make for peace."[65]

That statement is as true today as it was in 1949. A true peace cannot be negotiated without providing for the return of the displaced Palestinians. Given that repatriation is required by law, it is necessary that the matter be dealt with appropriately in any Israeli–Palestinian agreement. In any event, the right of return exists even apart from what such an agreement might provide. If an agreement fails to provide for the return of some or all of the displaced Palestinians, they will none the less have a valid claim to repatriation by Israel, a claim that they will be free to pursue before appropriate human rights institutions.

The displacement of the Palestinians in 1948 is one of the most visible and disastrous consequences of the events of that year. The refugee issue has haunted the United Nations ever since. No true peace will come to the region until there is implementation of the right of return of the displaced Palestinians.

NOTES

1 John Quigley, "Displaced Palestinians and a Right of Return", *Harvard International Law Journal*, vol. 39, no. 1 (1998).
2 Security Council Resolution 876, UN Document S/RES/876 (1993).
3 Security Council Resolution 779, UN Document S/RES/779 (1992).
4 Security Council Resolution 1009, UN Document S/RES/1009 (1995).
5 Security Council Resolution 385, UN Security Council Official Records, 31st Sess., *Resolutions and Decisions* 8, UN Document S/INF/32 (1977).
6 General Assembly Resolution 37/253, UN General Assembly Official Records, 37th Sess., Supp. (No. 51) at 48, UN Document A/37/51 (1953).
7 *Progress Report of the United Nations Mediator on Palestine*, UN General Assembly Official Records, 3rd Sess., Supp. (No. 11), UN Document A/648 (1948).
8 General Assembly Resolution 194, para.11, UN General Assembly Official Records, 3rd Sess., *Resolutions* 21, UN Document A/810 (1948).
9 *1948–49 Year Book of the United Nations* p. 176.
10 *The Ambassador in France (Bruce) to the Secretary of State*, Top Secret, 12 June 1949, 1949(6) *Foreign Relations of the United States* 1124.
11 *Major-General John H. Hildring to Secretary of State*, 25 July 1949, 1949(6) *Foreign Relations of the United States* 1249, 1250.
12 Kurt Rene Radley, "The Palestinian Refugees: The Right to Return in International Law", *American Journal of International Law*, vol. 72, p. 603, n. 66 (1978).

13 Henry Cattan, *The Palestine Question* (London and New York: Croom Helm, 1988), p. 65; Ilan Pappe, *The Making of the Arab–Israeli Conflict 1947–1951* (London and New York: I.B. Tauris, 1992), p. 231; Mark Tessler, *A History of the Israeli–Palestinian Conflict* (Bloomington: Indiana University Press, 1994), p. 314.

14 P. Weiss, *Nationality and Statelessness in International Law* (Alphen aan den Rijn, Neth., and Germantown, Md., USA: Sijthoff and Noordhof, 1979).

15 Research in International Law, Harvard School, *Nationality, Responsibility of States, Territorial Waters: Drafts of Conventions Prepared in Anticipation of the First Conference on the Codification of International Law, The Hague, 1930*, The Law of Nationality, arts. 20, 23 *American Journal of International Law* 13, 16 (Supp. 1929).

16 Richard Plender, *International Migration Law* (Leiden: Sijthoff, 1972), p. 87.

17 "Comment: UNHCR and Issues Related to Nationality", *Refugee Survey Quarterly* (UNHCR Center for Documentation on Refugees), vol. 14, no. 3, (1995), pp. 91, 96.

18 Draft European Convention on Nationality, art. 18, in *Draft European Convention on Nationality and Its Explanatory Report*, Strasbourg, May 14, 1997, Council of Europe Document DIR/JUR (97) 6 (1997).

19 *Id.* at 34.

20 See Draft Articles 4, 20, 22 and 24 in *Draft Report of the International Law Commission*, 49th Session (Mrs Z. Galicki, Rapporteur), UN Document A/CN.4/L. 539/Add.1 (1997).

21 *A.B. v. M.B.*, District Court, Tel Aviv, 6 April 1951, 17 *International Law Reports* 110, 111 (1956).

22 J. B. Moore (ed.), *Digest of International Law* (Washington DC: U.S. Government Printing Office, 1906), vol. 3, p. 315.

23 Hurst Hannum, *The Right to Leave and Return in International Law and Practice* (Dordrecht and Boston: M. Nijthoff, 1987), pp. 56–9.

24 *Universal Declaration of Human Rights*, General Assembly Resolution 217A, art. 13, para. 2, UN Document A/810, at 71 (1948).

25 *International Covenant on Civil and Political Rights*, 999 UN Treaty Series 171, art. 12, para. 4.

26 *International Convention on the Elimination of All Forms of Racial Discrimination*, art. 5(d) (ii), 660 UN Treaty Series 195.

27 Ruth Lapidoth, "The Right of Return in International Law, with Special Reference to the Palestinian Refugees", Israel Year Book on Human Rights, vol. 16, 1986, article begins page 103; Radley, "The Palestinian Refugees, p. 602.

28 UN General Assembly Official Records, 3rd Sess., Part I, *Annexes to the Summary Records of Meetings* 61, UN Document A/C.1/394.Rev.2 (1948).

29 UN General Assembly Official Records, 3rd Sess., Part I, *Annexes to the Summary Records of Meetings* 69, UN Document A/C.1/398.Rev.2 (1948).

30 UN General Assembly Official Records, 3rd Sess., Part I, C.1, *Summary Records of Meetings 21 September–8 December 1948* 906, UN Document A/C.1/SR.226 (1948) (Mr Eban, Israel).

31 UN General Assembly Official Records, 3rd Sess., Part I, C.1, *Summary Records of Meetings 21 September–8 December 1948* 909, UN Document A/C.1/SR.226 (1948) (Mr Rusk, USA).

32 UN General Assembly Official Records, 3rd Sess., Part I, C.1, *Summary Records of Meetings 21 September–8 December 1948* 912, UN Document A/C.1/SR.226 (1948).
33 Radley, "The Palestinian Refugees", p. 602.
34 General Assembly Resolution 3236, para. 2, UN General Assembly Official Records, 29th Sess., Supp. (No. 31) at 4, UN Document A/9631 (1974).
35 Lapidoth, "The Right of Return in International Law", p. 116; Radley, "The Palestinian Refugees", p. 601; Donna E. Arzt, "Palestinian Refugees: The Human Dimension of the Middle East Peace Process", 1995 *Proceedings of the American Society of International Law*, 372.
36 UN General Assembly Official Records, 3rd Sess., 184th plen. mtg. at 948, UN Document A/PV.184 (1948) (Mr McNeil, UK).
37 UN General Assembly Official Records, 3rd Sess., Part I, C.1, *Summary of Records of Meetings 21 September–8 December 1948* 724, UN Document A/C.1/SR.200 (1948) (Mr Shertok, Israel).
38 UN General Assembly Official Records, 3rd Sess., Part I, C.1, *Summary of Records of Meetings 21 September–8 December 1948* 683, UN Document A/C.1/SR.205 (1948) (Mr Jessup, USA).
39 *Id.* at 686 (Mr Liu Chieh, China).
40 UN General Assembly Official Records, 3rd Sess., Part I, C.1, *Summary Records of Meetings 21 September–8 December 1948* 724, UN Document A/C.1/SR.209 (1948) (Mr Urdaneta Arbelaez, Colombia).
41 *Introduction to the Annual Report of the Secretary General on the Work of the Organization, UN General Assembly Official Records*, 22nd Sess., Supp. (No. 1A) at 7, UN Document A/6701/Add.1 (1967).
42 UN Commission on Human Rights, Resolution 1987/4, *Situation in Occupied Palestine*, art. 2, 28th mtg., Feb. 19, 1987, *Economic and Social Council Official Records*, 43rd Sess., Supp. (No. 5) at 20, UN Document E/1987/18, chap. 2, sec.A (1987).
43 General Assembly Resolution 3236, para. 2, UN General Assembly Official Records, 29th Sess., Supp. (No. 31) at 4, UN Document A/9631 (1974).
44 Donna E. Arzt, *Refugees into Citizens: Palestinians and the End of the Arab–Israeli Conflict* (New York: New York Council on Foreign Relations, 1997), p. 25.
45 General Assembly Resolution 3089(D), UN General Assembly Official Records, 28th Sess., Supp. (No. 30) at 27, UN Document A/9030 (1974).
46 *General Framework for Peace in Bosnia and Herzegovina: Annex 7: Refugees and Displaced Persons*, art. 1, 14 Dec., 1995 (Dayton agreement), reprinted in *International Legal Materials*, 75, 136 (1996), p. 35.
47 Statement of Security Council President Juan Somavia, UN Document S/PRST/1996/20, quoted in "'Substantive progress' towards conflict settlement urged", *UN Chronicle*, vol. 45, no. 2 (1996), p. 33.
48 Security Council Resolution 1019, UN Document S/RES/1019 (1995).
49 "Decision of the Council of Representatives and the Council of Notables in Joint Session on April 24, 1950, Concerning the Union of Eastern and Western Jordan" in Helen Miller Davis, *Constitutions, Electoral Law, Treaties of States in the Near and Middle East*, 2nd edn. (Durham, North Carolina: Duke University Press, 1953), p. 265; also in Albion Ross, "Amman Parliament Vote Unites Arab Palestine and Transjordan", *New York Times*, 25 April, 1950, at A1.

50 G. Feuer, *Les Accords Passés par les Gouvernements Jordanien et Libanais avec les Organisations Palestiniennes* (1968–1970), vol. 16: *Annuaire Français de droit international* (1970), p. 189.

51 John Kifner, "Hussein surrenders claims on West Bank to the PLO", *New York Times*, 1 August 1988, at A1.

52 Arzt, *Refugees into Citizens*, p. 25.

53 UN General Assembly Official Records, 3rd Sess., Part I, C.1, *Summary Records of Meetings 21 September–8 December 1948* 724, UN Document A/C.1/SR.200 (1948) (Mr Shertok, Israel).

54 General Assembly Resolution 513, UN General Assembly Official Records, 6th Sess., Supp. (No. 20) at 12, UN Document A/2119 (1951).

55 Eyal Benvenisti and Eyal Zamir, "Private Claims to Property Rights in the Future Israeli-Palestinian Settlement", *American Journal of International Law*, vol. 89 (1995), pp. 295, 326.

56 Radley, "The Palestinian Refugees", p. 603–4.

57 *General Progress Report and Supplementary Report of the United Nations Conciliation Commission for Palestine*, UN General Assembly Official Records, 5th Sess., Supp. (No. 18) at 12, UN Document A/1367/Rev.1 (1951).

58 General Assembly Resolution 393, UN General Assembly Official Records, 5th Sess., Supp. (No. 20) at 22, UN Document A/1775 (1950).

59 Security Council Resolution 242, UN Security Council Official Records, 22nd Sess., *Resolutions* 8, UN Document S/INF/22/Rev.2 (1968).

60 Benvenisti and Zamir, "Private Claims to Property Rights", p. 326.

61 Ibid., p. 329.

62 Thomas Mallison and Sally V. Mallison, *The Palestine Problem in International Law and World Order* (Harlow: Longman, 1986), p. 188.

63 *The Ambassador in France (Bruce) to the Secretary of State*, Top Secret, 12 June, 1949, 1949(6) *Foreign Relations of the United States* 1124.

64 Tessler, *History of the Israeli–Palestinian Conflict*, p. 311.

65 *The Ambassador in France (Bruce) to the Secretary of State*, Top Secret, 12 June 1949, 1949(6) *Foreign Relations of the United States*, 1124, 1125.

7

The Feasibility of the Right
of Return

Salman Abu-Sitta

The conflict between Israel, the Palestinians and the Arab world is
the consequence of the creation of the Israeli state, its conquest of
Palestine in 1948 and the expulsion of the indigenous population.
The struggle today is, therefore, about land and the people expelled
from it. Furthermore, the old arguments that it was Arab governments
who ordered the refugees to leave in what was, for Israel a "war of
independence" can no longer be sustained against the growing body
of revisionist scholarship.

Half a century later, there are some 4,600,000 refugees, expelled
from 532 localities in Palestine. After 50 years of strife, it is abundantly
clear that there can be no peace without their rights being acknowledged and that they only wish to return to Palestine. This simple reality
has not been obliterated by the self-serving myths that have been
created to justify their continued exclusion from their homes – whether
Golda Meir's notorious claim that there is no such thing as the
Palestinians, or the equally blatant claim of "a land without a people
for a people without a land". One of the persistent myths is that the
return of Palestinian refugees is impractical because their country is
now full of new immigrants, their villages are destroyed and the original
property boundaries can no longer be defined. This view is advanced
by Israel and is adopted by many who might well agree that the
Palestinian right of return is perfectly legal, but cannot be implemented
in practice because of the problems involved. As will be discussed
below, such a view is not correct.

The Dimensions of *al-Nakba* (the Catastrophe)

Any discussion of this issue must begin by establishing what was actually
involved in *al-Nakba*, the catastrophe in which the Palestinians were

originally expelled. Between 1920 and 1948, the number of Jews in Palestine rose from 61,000 to 604,000, of which only 150,000 were born in Palestine. The rest were immigrants, mostly of military age; some were veterans of the Second World War, having fought in the British army during the war. In 1948, the 1,441,000 Palestinian Arabs formed an absolute majority of the population.[1] As a result of Israeli aggression in 1948, 805,000 Palestinians (84 per cent of the indigenous Arab inhabitants of Palestine) were expelled and the refugees lost homes, property and land in 532 localities.[2] Thus, the refugee problem was born. By 1994, their numbers had grown to 4,476,000, 30 per cent of whom still live in the West Bank and Gaza and 53 per cent in neighbouring Arab countries. In total, 83 per cent of the refugees – and 88 per cent of all Palestinians – are still in Palestine, or live within 100 miles of its borders. The rest are located in the Gulf, Europe and the Americas.

Israel had taken control of a total of 20,325 square kilometres of land – or 78 per cent of Mandate Palestine: 1,682 square kilometres (8 per cent of present-day Israel) was land under Jewish control prior to the 1948 War; 1,465 square kilometres (7 per cent) was Palestinian land whose inhabitants stayed in Israel, and 17,178 square kilometres (85 per cent) was land which belonged to Palestinians who now became refugees.[3] Thus, fully 92 per cent of contemporary Israel is made up of Palestinian land. Despite sustained attempts by the Israeli authorities to obfuscate the reality of this dispossession, recent analysis of Israeli archives, such as the excellent studies by Morris, Pappe, Flapan and Finkelstein, have confirmed the original claims of the refugees. Even while Palestine was still under the British Mandate, 213 localities (43 per cent of those eventually captured) were overrun and depopulated by Zionist forces. Between 15 May and 11 June 1948, the period in which Arab forces entered Palestine to prevent the Zionist takeover, we find that 291 localities (59 per cent) were depopulated. The Arab intervention not only failed to restore the refugees to their homes, but also failed to rescue the remaining one-third of the Palestinian population.

There is one other striking feature of this Palestinian exodus. A comparison of the depopulation date of each village captured with the dates of Israeli military operations shows that practically no exodus took place outside periods of hostilities, however brief the lull in the fighting. That, after all, would have been an ideal opportunity for the villagers to leave, since the threat to their lives and property would still have been present but sufficiently removed to make a safe departure possible, if that had been what they wanted. The fact is they did not leave. The correlation between their departure and Israeli assaults is compelling, demonstrating that, in every case, their departure had been forced on them by military action.

The impact of the massacres on this process of forced migration was considerable. The massacre in the village of Deir Yassin is an infamous example, but the massacre in Dawamiyya is the largest and most brutal. About 500 people were butchered by the units of the Israeli 89th Battalion (the 8th Brigade) on the afternoon of 29 October 1948. A total of 33 massacres have been reported during major Israeli operations between April and October 1948, and these were clearly used as military instruments to accelerate the exodus. Accounts of the expulsions have revealed that, when expelled, villagers moved to a nearby safe place or stayed with relatives, awaiting an opportunity to return. Many circulated around their villages, but those who were seen trying to return were shot on the spot as infiltrators. Soon after, their houses were destroyed and their harvest burnt to prevent their return. With the exception of those inhabitants of coastal towns who left by sea and those who were forced to march away, most refugees lingered around their villages, trying in vain to return before they ended up in a place of refuge.

In short, the claim that the refugees left their homes on the orders of Arab governments and not through Israeli expulsion and military assaults, has no basis.[4] A corollary of this claim has been that the Arab governments, not Israel, are responsible for the refugees and that they must resettle them in their countries at their expense. This, equally, has no basis. Return therefore becomes a viable means of resolving the problem within the context of the current peace process in the Middle East, particularly since the original expulsions resulted from acts of war. Analysis of the archival material shows that 23 per cent of the evacuated villages had been depopulated due to expulsion by Jewish forces, 51 per cent by military assault, and 9 per cent by imminent attack. Eighty-three per cent of the villages were depopulated as a result of Zionist military attacks. Psychological warfare was responsible for 9 per cent of the villages evacuated, while the population of 1 per cent of villages involved left of their own accord, and 7 per cent for unknown reasons.[5] In effect, therefore, the depopulation of the refugees was the direct result of an all-out war against them.[6]

Any question of return, however, raises a series of genuine problems. One which deserves careful attention is the practical issue of identification: namely that today, villages have been destroyed and the associated land boundaries are unrecognisable.[7] In fact, this is not the case and return to the sites from which they were expelled would be quite possible for the majority of refugees and their descendants, although, of course, extensive reconstruction would be necessary.[8] With the exception of the central district of Israel, relatively few village sites are occupied by modern construction. Most kibbutzim buildings are installed away from old village sites. It is also claimed that land boundaries have disappeared and are impossible to determine today. In fact, detailed maps of Palestine and Israel, which are available, assisted by the modern technology used by Israel to lease the land of refugees, are quite sufficient to determine old and new boundaries. It can thus be demonstrated that all boundaries and ownerships have been well-recorded and can be identified.[9] Indeed, not only are villages retained in the collective memory of refugees and their children, but their original images have been preserved for posterity through the British aerial survey of 1945–6.

Resettlement Schemes

Israel and its supporters have proposed many schemes to dispose of the refugee problem for ever. As Masalha[10] has clearly demonstrated, the origin of the idea of resettlement is to be found in the Zionist policy of "transfer" (expulsion). After 1948, Zionist supporters in the West – Sybilla Thicknesse,[11] for example – suggested the resettlement of refugees in Syria and Iraq (but not Lebanon), possibly with UNRWA as an instrument of resettlement. After 1967, pro-Israeli authors proposed a plethora of resettlement schemes. Don Peretz, who writes frequently on the subject, endorses solutions which allow a limited return of the refugees to a Palestinian entity, but not to their original homes. He also considers limited compensation for lost property to be offset against the unrelated and exaggerated claims of Jews who left Arab countries to settle on Palestinian land. Mark Heller also proposes resettlement elsewhere and a limited return (750,000 out of the eligible 2,700,000), again to a nominal state, not to their homes.

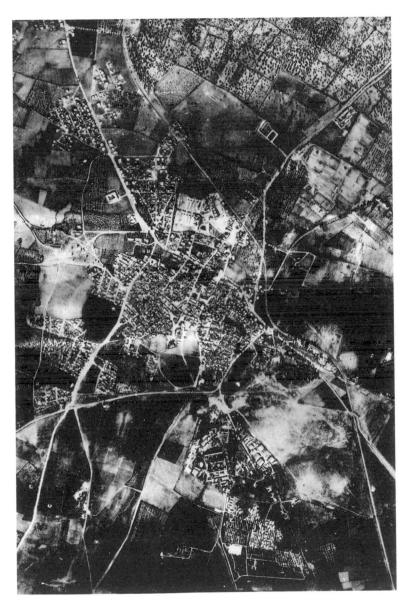

AERIAL PHOTOGRAPH 7.1
© Crown Copyright/MOD

Ramleh, one of 13 depopulated towns. Together with its twin, Lydda, their inhabitants, numbering 60,000, have been expelled by the direct orders of Rabin on 11 July 1948. They were forced to march in the searing heat, children and old men falling by the wayside. Under heavy Jewish mortar bombardment, Haifa and Jaffa inhabitants left in overloaded small boats, amid screams and search for lost family members. Many of the boats sank.

AERIAL PHOTOGRAPH 7.2
© Crown Copyright/MOD

Bureir, one of 419 depopulated villages. Bureir was occupied before the entry of the Arab regular forces and was the scene of a massacre on 12 May 1948.

AERIAL PHOTOGRAPH 7.3
© Crown Copyright/MOD

Al Ma'in, one of 99 tribal lands (14 May 1948). Although in the Negev, it was fully cultivated, as can be seen. Total cultivated land in Beer Sheba was greater than it is today. Negev is underpopulated today.

AERIAL PHOTOGRAPH 7.4
© Crown Copyright/MOD

Deir Yassin, one of 419 fully depopulated villages, in addition to the refugees from 662 secondary localities. Deir Yassin was the site of the infamous massacre on 9 April 1948. Twenty-five massacres were committed during the expulsion of the Palestinians in 1948.

AERIAL PHOTOGRAPH 7.5
© Crown Copyright/MOD

Emmaus, mentioned in the Gospel of St Luke as the place where Jesus appeared after the crucifixion. Emmaus was destroyed and the inhabitants were expelled on Rabin's orders in 1967, in continuation of the 'Transfer' policy followed since 1948.

Zureik[12] presented a comprehensive review of resettlement plans and other refugee issues. He describes in particular the semi-official proposal made by Shlomo Gazit. Gazit insists on the finality of the solution, the renunciation of the right of return, the dismantling of UNRWA and the abolition of the special status of refugees. As a reward, Gazit wants Israel to issue a moral-psychological acknowledgement recognising the suffering of the Palestinians over the past 50 years. To avoid admitting Israeli responsibility, this acknowledgement should form part of a UN resolution abolishing the Right of Return enshrined in Resolution 194, paragraph 11.

The Palestinian writer, Ahmed Khalidi,[13] has picked up the thread by suggesting a trade-off between this formal acknowledgement and the admission by the Palestinians that the implementation of the right of return is impossible. However, his has been a lone voice amongst Palestinian refugees which has received no support whatsoever. Arzt,[14] in a much publicised report, suggests the permanent dispersal of the Palestinians through their resettlement wherever they wish, except in their original homes. As a palliative, she also proposes that Palestinians maintain their link as a people by holding some kind of Palestinian identity papers, provided that they drop their claim to their land. In such an event, Israel would be able to retain their land legally.

As an act of generosity, Israel would, however, allow back 75,000 persons, after rigorous vetting and within a limited period. Translated into 1948 figures, this means 8,000 original refugees – a fraction of the 300,000 figure proposed by President Truman in 1949 as a price for admitting Israel into the UN. Finally, Israel was admitted to the UN following the promise made by Moshe Sharett, Israel's representative in the UN, that it would allow the return of 100,000 persons – a promise he never fulfilled.

None of these schemes has had the slightest chance of being accepted by the Palestinians, and alternatives must therefore be found.

The Return Plan

An alternative proposal must counter the common argument that, in practice, Israel is now fully populated and return of the Palestinian refugees is no longer a practical possibility. The proposal outlined below is designed to demonstrate that this fear is unfounded and that the return of the refugees is possible with no appreciable dislocation of Jewish residents.

Israel is divided into 41 "natural regions" (see Map 7.1).

The first eight of these natural regions[15] have an area of 1,683 square kilometres (8 per cent of Israel). This is where the majority of Israelis (2,924,000 or 68 per cent of the Jewish-Israeli population) live – Area A. It is remarkably similar in size, but not exactly in location, to the area in which Jews lived in pre-1948 Palestine. This population concentration emphasises the traditional pattern of Jewish life, in close proximity to one another and in pursuit of occupations such as commerce and industry. Fifty years of Israeli conquest and expansion have not convinced the majority of Israelis to abandon traditional habits.[16] The next five natural regions[17] – Area B – have an area of 1,318 square kilometres (7 per cent of Israel) in which 419,000 Israelis (10 per cent of the Jewish population) live. By coincidence, the size of this area is close to that of the land of the Palestinians who remained in Israel. In short, 78 per cent of Jewish-Israelis in Israel live on 15 per cent of the land area. This leaves Area C (17,325 square kilometres, 85 per cent of Israel). This area is remarkably similar in size and location, but not exactly identical, to the land from which the Palestinian refugees were driven. Who lives there now? About 800,000 urban Israeli Jews, 154,000 rural Israeli Jews and 465,000 Israeli Palestinians. In effect, 154,000 Israeli Jews cultivate the land of 4,476,000 refugees who are prevented from returning to it. In the proposed return plan, refugees will be able to return to their original homes in the majority of cases, or to be relocated close to their original homes in most other cases. The original Palestine sub-district boundaries are close to those used by Israel today; namely Safad, Tiberias, Nazareth, Baysan, Acre, Haifa, Jaffa, Gaza, Ramleh and Beer Sheba. The largest differences occur in sub-districts that were divided by the 1949 Armistice Line. It will therefore be possible to relate the refugees' return to Israel's own administrative districts. In the large Beer Sheba sub-district, refugees would be distributed in the plan according to their original population density – high in the north and low in the south.[18] With the return of the refugees, the overall population density will be 482 persons per square kilometre, instead of the present level of 261 persons per square kilometre, which is still an acceptable figure. The figure should also be compared with current levels of population density in areas under the

Area A
(Jewish Concentration)

Area B
(Mixed Population)

Area C
Sparsely Populated
(Future Palestinian Concentration)

WEST
BANK

JERUSALEM

GAZA
STRIP

MAP 7.1
Population Concentration in the Proposed Return Plan

control of the Palestine National Authority (PNA). The present population density in the Gaza Strip is 4,400 and in the West Bank 880 persons per square kilometre. In the return plan (see Table 7.1), Area A will remain largely Jewish (76 per cent Jews), Area B will be mixed, and Area C will be largely Palestinian (81 per cent).

Some practical adjustments, however, would be desirable. In the densely populated Area A, rural Palestinians (about 900,000) should be relocated to Areas B and C. Conversely, 154,000 rural Jews should be relocated from Area C to Area A, after their leases end, to allow Palestinian farmers to recover their land. This disparity in the numbers of the relocated population, although unfair to Palestinians, is advisable in that it would enhance the homogeneity of population. Given the special status of Jerusalem, no relocation would be applied.

With the return of the refugees, the population density in the Jewish Area A will change only slightly, while it would increase three-fold in the Palestinian Area C, to 246 compared to the present 82 persons per square kilometre. Ramleh-Lydda and Khadera areas will have higher population densities, but this would be balanced by merging them into the Triangle, which already has a significant Palestinian population. It is expected that natural population movement and economic forces would eventually lead to a voluntary and more balanced distribution.

A more detailed examination of the Southern District (the Palestinian Gaza and Beer Sheba sub-districts) shows that only 78,000 rural Jews live in 14,107 square kilometres. Their relocation to the north, if they wish, should not cause any hardship. Of the remaining 555,000 urban Jews, 63 per cent live in three Palestinian towns – Beer Sheba, Ashdod and Majdal-Ashqelon and a further 24 per cent live in three new towns – Qiryat Gat (Iraq Manshiya), Elat (Um Rashrash) and Dimona (Rujm el Belewi). The activities carried out in these towns – shipping, transport, industry and education – are beneficial to the district and should continue. It is ironic that these new towns, with populations ranging from 26,000 to 42,000, are equivalent in size to, or smaller than, a typical refugee camp such as Jabaliya Camp in Gaza, which has a population of 40,000. In short, the return of the Palestinians to their land and the pursuit of their traditional occupation in agriculture should not cause major disruption, either to the Jewish-Israeli population or to their economic activities.

TABLE 7.1
Summary of the Return Plan

Land	Palestine 1948			Israel					
	Area (sq. km)	Designation	Description	Area (sq. km)	Jews[d] (000s)	Palestinians[e] (000s)	Jewish (%)	Present density (p/sq. km)	New density
Jewish-controlled land	1,682[a]	A	Largely Jewish	1,683	3,078	991	76	1,934	2,418
Remaining Palestinians' land	1,465[b]	B	Mixed	1,318	419	1,037	29	482	1,106
Expelled Palestinians' land	17,178[c]	C	Largely Palestinian	17,324	803	3,460	19	82	246
Total Israel	20,325			20,325	4,300	5,488	44	261	482

Sources and notes: (a) Hadawi, Appendix VI, p. 230 (endnote 3). This area includes public land, concessions and other transfers. The area duly registered is about half, or 3.6% of Palestine. *A Survey of Palestine* (see endnote 1) gives a figure of 1,392 sq. km (correcting for Turkish *dunums*). Leading Zionist proponents of the transfer policy, Y. Weitz and A. Granott, put the area at 1,731 sq. km and 1,588 sq. km, respectively; see Weitz's memorandum, "The Problem: The Refugees" (Rehovot: The Institute of Settlement Studies, 1967) and Granott's *The Land System in Palestine, History and Structure* (London: Eyre and Spottiswoode, 1952).

(b) Hadawi, Appendix VII, p. 242.

(c) Based on compilation of individual village ownership; see Abu-Sitta (endnote 2). Also Hadawi, Appendix VII, pp. 247, 248.

(d) No change from 1994 figures, although some may emigrate – typically 17%.

(e) Existing (1994) and returning refugees (4,476 million), although some may not return but still hold the right to return.

In the Northern District (3,325 square kilometres) there is a similar pattern, although not so clear cut. Of 134,000 rural Jews, only 76,000 would need to be offered voluntary relocation. Urban Jewish residents in the district form 71 per cent of the total Jewish population. About 90 per cent of them live in just nine towns, three of which were originally Palestinian (Acre, Tiberias, Shefa Amr). The largest town in the district (Nazareth, population 54,000) is today totally Palestinian. Apart from Nazareth, the remaining towns are, once again, similar in size to a typical refugee camp.

Although Haifa and the Central districts are densely populated Jewish areas, the presence of Palestinians in these districts is significant, forming 26 per cent and 9 per cent of the number of Jews in each district respectively. In these districts, there are 13 purely Palestinian towns, each with a population in excess of 10,000.[19]

What is clear from these figures is that there is already a substantial Palestinian presence throughout Israel. Thus, the return of the refugees would not be a novelty, nor as catastrophic as some suggest. Although the relationship between the two peoples has not been easy in the past, the fact is that Palestinians and Jews have lived together for the last 50 years without major problems – not to mention the centuries of Arab and Jewish harmony before Zionism appeared in Palestine. The return of the refugees would be consistent with existing concentrations of Jews and Palestinians in contemporary Israel and with their respective occupation patterns. The return would not cause significant dislocation of the Jewish population, for there would be minor voluntary relocation.

The proposed plan represents a maximalist scenario in which *all* refugees return and *all* Jewish Israelis stay. Palestinians must have the right to return, whether they actually return or not. Israel gave Jews everywhere the right to come to live in Israel, but only one-third of world Jewry have exercised this option. Many who do, eventually emigrate (17 to 20 per cent). But even in the maximalist case, only 154,000 Jews would face relocation elsewhere in Israel to allow 4,476,000 refugees to return to their homes. This is a very small concession to achieve real peace and to end a state of hostility that has existed for 50 years.

Agriculture and the Palestinian Return

One of the main tenets of Zionism was the return to the land – the abandonment of traditional occupations in finance and commerce in order to become farmers. Communal colonies, the kibbutzim, were set up in pre-1948 Palestine to turn the vision into practice and their members formed the Zionist elite and the backbone of Israel's army. They enjoyed political dominance and unparalleled advantages. Post-1948 immigrants rejected the Zionist agrarian vision.[20] Although they were given land, many of the new farmers drifted to the urban environment. In the 1980s, agricultural labour decreased from 6.4 per cent to 4.7 per cent of the labour force,[21] as agriculture itself faced economic crisis. Dozens of agricultural projects were abandoned, for only 26 per cent of kibbutzim were viable, using 60 per cent of all irrigation water and land, and producing 75 per cent of all production. One problem was that three-quarters of the rural population did not engage in agriculture.[22] Even in the Negev, the Zionist dream of making the desert bloom with consequent major population settlement did not materialise. In 1987, the Jewish rural population in the central and southern Negev was only 7,000, while that in the more fertile northern Negev was just 25,000.[23] These figures did not change, since outward migration balanced the newcomers.[24]

The contribution of agriculture to Israel's GDP decreased from 7.9 per cent in 1983 to 2.4 per cent in 1993.[25] Today it accounts for only 4 per cent of exports as Israel's economy moves towards industrialised manufactured exports instead of continuing its traditional dependence on agricultural exports. To increase the economic value of agricultural exports, Israel plans to reduce the area of low-value crops such as cotton, citrus, avocado and wheat, in favour of speciality crops such as flowers, spices and herbs.[26]

The Palestinians, however, have been farmers for centuries. As successive British government reports during the Mandate show, every possible plot of land was cultivated. In the south, wheat was extensively grown where annual rainfall was just above 200 mm, and barley when the rainfall was above 100 mm. Productivity was low because of the subsistence nature of the agricultural sector and because of a lack of capital. The system is still viable today – Gazan agricultural exports compete in price with comparable Israeli produce.

It would thus contribute effectively to the overall economy if the refugees were to return and resume their traditional activities.

Water: the Key to Resettlement

If the country's population were to be doubled through the process of return, water resources in Israel might come under pressure. Israel has in the past used about 80 per cent of the water resources it controls for agriculture, although this proportion is now falling. More important is the issue of cost, for water for agricultural use has been heavily subsidised. Subsidised water, at between 5.85 and 12.5 cents per cubic metre (compared to 50 cents for domestic use), was provided for agricultural use.[27] The average cost of water provision was between 30 and 36 cents per cubic metre, while for arid areas, desalination costs run as high as $1.6 per cubic metre – 16 times the costs to the Israeli farmer.[28] Moreover, this exploitation of resources is far in excess of safe yield limits. Serious undermining of aquifers has been observed in the Coastal Plain and near Tiberias.[29] Fresh water from Yarmouk is pumped into Lake Tiberias, thus rendering the water of the lower Jordan River, which is accessible to Jordan as well, unsuitable for irrigation. The salinity of Gaza water is responsible for declining levels of agricultural output, and water pollution has caused widespread health problems. The issue of water access has been a factor in the 1967 War and the 1982 invasion of Lebanon, and has been seen as a potential source of future conflict.[30] Water consumption in Israel grew from 350 million cubic metres per year in 1948 to 1,000 million cubic metres per year in 1956. By 1990, consumption had increased to 2,020 million cubic metres per year, of which 1,471 million cubic metres per year was water taken from sources located in Arab territory.[31] In the next 20 years, Israel plans to increase its consumption to 3,000 million cubic metres per year, despite the danger of conflict that this might provoke.[32] It is clear that a regional agreement over water use will be necessary if conflict is to be avoided, and this would also have to form part of any Palestinian resettlement plan.

Table 7.2 demonstrates three scenarios for water use. Scenario 1, which describes the current situation, shows that Israeli consumption of 1,300 million cubic metres per year goes to agriculture, 133 million

TABLE 7.2
New Water Requirement with and without the Return Plan

Case no.	Case	Year	Israeli Jews (000s)	Russians (000s)	Israeli Palestinians (000s)	Israeli total (000s)	Palestinian refugees (000s)	Municipal use Mm³/year	Industrial use Mm³/year	Agricultural use Mm³/year	Total consumption Mm³/year
1	Actual case	1995	4,058	562	1,096	5,716	0	594	133	1,300	2,028
2	All refugees return; Russian immigration ceases	2020	5,888	739	2,032	8,659	9,726	1,103	343	1,300	2,746
3	No refugees return; 1.5 million Russians immigrate	Net population increase after 1995, % p.a.	1.50%	1.10%	2.50%		3.00%				

Notes: Israel's municipal consumption is 104 m³/person/year (1986 figure) and should be reduced to 60 m³/person/year as in Jordan. The present West Bank consumption is as low as 37.5 m³/person/year because of the occupation. In case 2, municipal consumption will have to be fixed at 60 m³/person/year for all the population. In case 3, the level of municipal consumption will remain at 104 m³/person/year.

Israel's industrial growth was 2.92% p.a. from 1958 to 1986; the same rate is assumed in the table with 25% added for Palestinian use.

Between 1951 and 1955 Israel's agriculture used an extravagant amount of water, 860 m³/*dunum*, while between 1986 and 1990 this fell to 500. Agricultural use cut-off at 1400 Mm³/year is assumed as agriculture must be industrialised thereafter.

cubic metres per year to industrial use, and 594 million cubic metres per year for municipal (domestic) use. Israel's municipal consumption is extremely high at 104 cubic metres per person, per year (285 litres per person, per day), as compared to Jordan's (60) and the West Bank's (37.5). This level would clearly have to be reduced under any form of regional cooperation.[33]

If agricultural consumption is maintained at 1,300 million cubic metres per year, two additional future scenarios emerge. In the first, all Palestinian refugees return, but Russian immigration ceases and municipal use is fixed at 60 cubic metres per person, per year for all the population. In the second scenario, no refugees return and an additional 1.5 million Russians emigrate to Israel, with Israeli municipal water use remaining at 104 cubic metres per person, per year. Both scenarios require roughly the same amount of water, about 2,700 million cubic metres per year, which is the maximum amount of water which may be extracted for Israel/Palestine from its territory and the immediately adjacent region.

The first of these scenarios would be feasible through regional agreement for water resource use. This would allow the refugees to return, although agricultural water use would have to be cut back to meet WHO standards of supply. Case 3 is not possible without a new war to acquire more Arab land and water and, at the same time, a policy of keeping the refugees away from their homes. The consequences of either allowing the refugees to return or admitting more Russians are therefore obvious. There are no water resources available at present for both cases. The second will not be politically acceptable to Israel's neighbours, whose cooperation will be essential if Israel is to acquire access to sufficient water without renewed hostilities. A solution to the refugees' problem will be vital if the coming water crisis is to be resolved, and Israel will therefore have to contemplate modifying its own immigration policies, particularly towards Russia. If, however, Israel continues to insist on the sole control of land and water and to plan for expansion (on the belligerent principle that water cannot be a consequence of peace while in fact it is a condition for peace),[34] then true peace seems impossible to achieve. The key to any solution will be the unrestricted return of Palestinian refugees.

Return in Practice

The problems of the logistics of return are not insuperable. After all, between 1949 and 1951, Israel admitted over 650,000 Jews during a period of ongoing hostilities. In the 1990s, Israel admitted a similar number of Russian Jews without any noticeable disruption. The vast majority of Palestinian refugees, furthermore, are close at hand – in Lebanon, Syria and Jordan, or in Gaza and the West Bank. They know where to go; their village sites are mostly vacant. They know who they are; a typical village consists of four to five *hamula*s (extended families) which are still intact. Complete records of about 700,000 families and five million individual files still exist, and the construction of new homes could be achieved in record time. UNRWA has a wealth of experience in this regard and is run by a Palestinian staff of 21,000. Thousands of qualified Palestinian workers, engineers and planners have similar experience. The task of reconstruction and rehabilitation is in principle quite manageable; for instance, the logistical exercise for Operation Desert Storm in 1990 ensured that half a million soldiers were moved, fed and housed in a matter of a few weeks.

Protection of Property Rights

To protect the property rights of refugees during the transitional period of refugee resettlement, it will be necessary to form a Palestine land authority (PLA).[35] This will have a mandate to represent the property rights of Palestinians wherever they may be; to document, recover, hold, protect, maintain and develop Palestinian property and act as custodian of all Palestinian property, until individual owners are determined and property is returned to them. The PLA would be an independent authority, cooperating with the Palestine National Council (PNC) and relevant UN or other agencies, which should remain in existence until all its functions have been fulfilled. It would be democratically controlled by a general assembly to consist of approximately 1,500 members, representing 532 depopulated localities, at the rate of three persons per locality. These representatives could be elected or appointed from *mukhtar*s, chief landowners and leading personalities. The total area of Palestinian land in question would be the sum of village and town lands, including common and public land *minus* land under Jewish ownership in 1948. The latter is very well-defined, as Zionist immigrants and corporations insisted on proof of land purchased or acquired in Palestine.

Initially, village land would be held collectively, through the PLA, in the form of shares assigned to each village. The areas of village lands are well-defined and the total land owned by each village is therefore indisputable. The village unit, with its monolithic, historical, cultural and blood-ties continuity, remains the best instrument for repatriation and rehabilitation. Individual ownership would then be assigned. The UN Conciliation Commission for Palestine (CCP) has 450,000 records of registered individual ownership. These records, however, represent only 5,194 square kilometres[36] out of the total of 17,178 square kilometres of Palestinian refugee land. The balance was unregistered as a result of the hasty departure of the Mandate government, but its ownership was recognised. Custom and inheritance laws may be applied for these cases within the context of the village unit. The legal transfer of property held by Israeli bodies is straightforward. The 49-year land leases held by the kibbutzim are due to expire in 1998. The deeds can be transferred to the legal owners through the PLA by the Israeli Custodian of Absentee Property. The Israeli Development Authority will then become redundant and the Israel Land Administration should hand over the documentation. There should be no cases of dispute between individual Jews and Palestinians, since practically all Jews who have benefited from Palestinian land since 1948 have no personal title deeds.[37] UNRWA would continue to function until all refugees were adequately and safely repatriated. UNRWA would then turn into a development authority under the United Nations Development Programme (UNDP). The return plan would be carried out under the guardianship of the CCP, which would ensure the physical and legal well-being of the returnees. All returning Palestinians would be issued with certificates of Palestinian Identity – converted from the present UNRWA refugee IDs, together with new certificates for about 1,241,000 (1994) refugees who are not registered – in addition to, and regardless of, any other citizenship (including Israeli) they may have. They would enjoy full civil and religious rights within Israel, although their political rights would depend on their country of citizenship. They would, however, have the right to obtain citizenship without discrimination on any grounds.

The Future

The proposed plan of return certainly runs counter to schemes of resettlement preferred by Israel. It is, however, in line with the rights and wishes of five million refugees whose voice is rarely heard. It is abundantly clear that, of the parties in the Arab–Israeli conflict, Palestinians are the only ones who have nowhere else to go, or that they wish to go, except to Palestine. Demographically, their return would cause minimal voluntary relocation of Israelis and no transfer of populations. It could be done, and would inevitably contribute towards permanent peace.

The Palestinians have no moral or legal obligation to accommodate Israelis at their own expense. By any standards, Israel has such an obligation – to correct the monumental injustice it has committed. Yet, the refugees' return has no implications for Israel's sovereignty. It has nothing to do with whether the Oslo Accords succeed or fail. It has nothing to do with settlements, boundaries, or even Jerusalem. The problems facing the proposal are, of course, clear. Israel will not allow it, at least at present, and can prevent it from taking place. Israel's justification for this denial would be the need to protect its security and preserve its nature as a Jewish state.

However, Israeli Palestinians comprise 18 per cent of the population of Israel and 45 per cent of them are less than 20 years old, compared with 29 per cent of the Jewish population. This young community will eventually become a majority within the state if present trends continue – perhaps even within the next two decades. Israel would then have little choice but to accept them as full members of its polity, since subjugation or transfer would no longer be an internationally acceptable option. In that case, Israelis should, perhaps, face reality and accept full partnership with Palestinians by allowing the refugees to return. It is the inevitable, democratic solution, even if it overturns the assumptions of Zionism which have ruled Israel for the past 50 years. Many Israelis themselves are already questioning the usefulness of Zionism in the fragmented mosaic that is Israel today.

NOTES

1 Figures for Jews born in Palestine are estimated from the natural increase of those resident in Palestine in 1920. In 1995, 4,388,000 Jews lived in Israel alongside 1,011,000 Palestinians. A further 4,646,000 were the descendants of those originally expelled. Since 1980, Palestinians resident and exiled have outnumbered Israelis despite unrestricted immigration for the latter. For pre-1948 Jews and Palestinians, see *A Survey of Palestine for the Anglo-American Committee of Inquiry* (Washington DC: Institute for Palestine Studies, 1991) vol. 1, Chapter VI, p. 140 and Appendix I, p. 841. For Palestinians in Israel/Palestine (67 per cent of the total), see J. Abu-Lughod, "The Demographic Transformation of Palestine" in Ibrahim Abu-Lughod (ed.), *The Transformation of Palestine* (Evanston, Ill.: Northwestern University Press, 1971), Table 3, p. 160. For post-1948 Israeli figures, see *Statistic Abstracts of Israel*, CBS, no. 46, 1995, Table 2.27 and others.

2 See S. H. Abu-Sitta, 'The Right of Return, Sacred, Legal and Possible' [in Arabic], *Al-Mustaqbal al-Arabi*, Beirut, vol. 9, no. 208, June 1996, pp. 4–38, for the list of the depopulated localities comprising 13 towns, 420 villages and 99 tribes. This list is based on Benny Morris, *The Birth of the Palestinian Refugee Problem 1947–1949* (Cambridge University Press, 1987) and W. Khalidi, *All that Remains: the Palestinian Villages Occupied and Depopulated by Israel in 1948* (Washington DC: Institute of Palestine Studies, reprint 1987) in addition to Beer Sheba Sub-District, the details of which have been published here for the first time. Population estimates for 1948 have been based on the village statistics of 1945. This paper also contains analysis of the depopulated villages, their population size and land area, when the inhabitants left and why they did so, together with the incidence of massacres.

3 See Sami Hadawi, *Palestinian Rights and Losses in 1948* (London: Saqi Books, 1988) Appendix V, p. 224, Appendix VI, p. 230, Appendix VIII, p. 247; and Abu-Sitta, 'The Right of Return', Table 3. Note that half of the Palestinian land owned by Palestinians who remained in Israel has been expropriated by the Israeli state, although its owners are Israeli citizens, the so-called "present absentees".

4 See the well-known works by Morris (1987, 1990) for a new look at the now-declassified Israeli files. For the myth of Arab orders to leave, see W. Khalidi, "Plan Dalet: Master Plan for the conquest of Palestine", *Journal of Palestine Studies*, vol. XVII, no. 1, Autumn 1988, pp. 3–70. For further discussion of Morris's research, see Finkelstein. For a new review by Israeli authors of Israel's responsibility, see Pappe, Segev, Flapan. For a review of UN archives, see Palumbo. For a database analysis of all depopulated villages, see Abu-Sitta. (Reference details of the above works are given in the Bibliography.)

5 This analysis is an extension of Morris's work in *Birth of the Palestinian Refugee Problem* (1987) using the same criteria, to cover 532 localities. See Abu-Sitta, "The Right of Return".

6 For a field survey of physical and cultural destruction of the Palestinian presence in Israel, see G. Falah, "The 1948 Israeli–Palestinian War and its Aftermath", *Annals of the Association of American Geographers*, 86(2), 1996, pp. 256–85.

7 See for example, Don Peretz, who, in *Palestinians, Refugees and the Middle East Peace Process* (Washington DC: US Institute of Peace Press, 1993), argues that the return is "neither feasible nor practical" (p. 72) and that "conditions have so changed . . ." (p. 73), so as not to permit return. See also the comments by Elie Sanbar, the chief Palestinian delegate in the multilateral talks on refugees, who claims that the Palestinian delegation was given "the practical difficulties" as a pretext for no return (interview in *Al-Hayat*, London, 18 and 19 December 1996, p. 18).

8 Original depopulated Palestinian towns (Jaffa, Acre, Beer Sheba) have been left unrepaired since their Palestinian populations departed. Palestinians who remained in Israel have been prevented from maintaining or upgrading their own property, except by special permission, which is difficult to obtain. Israel destroyed most villages immediately after the expulsion of their inhabitants. In a field survey of 418 villages, Falah ("The 1948 Israeli–Palestinian War and its Aftermath") found roughly 67.2 per cent of the villages involved were totally destroyed, 17.7 per cent partially destroyed, but 12.5 per cent partially habitable.

9 Palestine is a well-documented country. The first scientifically-prepared map was prepared by Jacotin in 1799, during Napoleon's campaign. In 1872–7, the Palestine Exploration Fund surveyed Palestine and produced 26 sheets with 15,000 names (none of them Jewish) under 46 designations. The Government of Palestine (1920–48) produced maps of Palestine (1:100,000, 1:20,000, 1:12,500 down to 1:1,250 series). It also kept Land Registry records, from which the United Nations Conciliation Commission on Palestine produced the Landowners Index, available on microfilm. Israel used and updated the above maps for lease of land to the kibbutzim. Geographical Information System (GIS) can recreate past, present and forecast future conditions of land and people.

10 See Nur Masalha, *Expulsion of the Palestinians: The Concept of Transfer in Zionist Political Thought, 1882–1948* (Washington DC: Institute of Palestine Studies, 1992) and *A Land without a People: Israel, Transfer and the Palestinians* (London: Faber and Faber, 1997).

11 Sybilla Gratiana Thicknesse, *Arab Refugees: a Survey of Resettlement Possibilities* (London and New York: Royal Institute of International Affairs, 1949) vol. viii, p. 68.

12 See Elia Zureik, *Palestinian Refugees and the Peace Process* (Washington DC: Institute for Palestine Studies, 1996).

13 See his article in the *International Herald Tribune*, 12 February 1997.

14 Donna Arzt's report (see Bibliography) suggests a permanent solution for the Palestinian refugee problem, although it contains errors of fact. In the permanent "transfer" plan, Table 4.1, p. 88, Arzt quotes US Bureau estimates for the year 2005, cited in Peretz, p. 16, which omits Palestinians in Europe and the Americas. Yet Arzt conveniently halves the figure of "other Mideast States" to include "non-Mideast States". Arzt's table for 1995 is equally inaccurate. Furthermore, her tables for total Palestinians underestimate the figure by about one million persons (1995 estimate: 7,025,000 minimum − 7,590,000 maximum). The substance of Arzt's plan is to resettle the refugees mostly wherever they are, with transfer for 1,800,000 persons, half to Europe and the Americas and the other half to the West Bank. Most of the latter are "Displaced

Persons" anyway. They would normally have returned, had Israel not kept the West Bank under occupation. Half of Gaza's refugees will have to endure another transfer somewhere else while a negligible number will return to their homes in Israel if they satisfy the strict rules already in force since 1950.

15 These are: Tel Aviv, the Judean hills, Haifa, Petah Tiqwa, Sharon, Rishon Le Zion, Southern Sharon and Rehovot. The highest present population density is 6,711 (Tel Aviv) and the lowest 767 (Sharon) persons per square kilometre.

16 See, for example, Arnon Sofer, "Geography and Demography in Eretz-Israel 2000" [translated into Arabic], *Journal of Palestine Studies*, no. 1, Winter 1990, pp. 117–35 and 126. Many others have lamented the concentration of Jews in such localised areas as a danger to Israel which should be solved by "transfer" (expulsion) of the Arabs (in Israel) to prevent them living in sparsely populated areas. Michael Romann argues that Jewish demographic patterns have put a limit on the ability to attain maximum territorial control of Arab land (*Middle Eastern Studies*, 26(3), July 1990, pp. 371–82). Recent information (*The Sunday Times*, 9 February 1997, p. 17) about a plan to build 40 islands offshore is an indication that the pattern of dense coastal urban settlement will continue.

17 These are: Lod, Hadera, Yizra'el, Nazareth, Kinerot (Tiberias). The highest present density is 883 (Nazareth) and the lowest 189 (Yizra'el) persons per square kilometre.

18 Ninety per cent of the returnees are to be distributed over the three most northern regions, Gerar, Besor and Be'er Sheva (Beer Sheba), and ten per cent in the remainder of Beer Sheba Sub-District. This is consistent with their residence patterns in 1948.

19 These are, in descending order of population, from a maximum of 30,000 to a minimum of 10,000: Umm al-Fahm, Bag'a al Gharbiyya, Judeida, Daliet al-Karmel, Tayibe, Tire, Tirat Karmel, Kafar Qasem, Kafar Qara, Arrabe, Ar'ara, Qalanswe, Ramleh (mixed). (Israel Central Bureau of Statistics T.2.16.)

20 Yair Aharoni, *The Israeli Economy: Dreams and Realities* (London: Routledge, 1991), p. 200.

21 Ibid., p. 134, Table 3.8. In 1989, employed persons in agriculture, forestry and fishing numbered just 69,000.

22 Ibid., pp. 208–13.

23 See Elisha Efrat, *Geography and Politics in Israel since 1967* (London: Frank Cass, 1988) who discusses the failure in Negev at length (pp. 182–5). His figure for Beer Sheba bedouins is underestimated.

24 In the Southern District, those who entered and left respectively (in thousands) in the years indicated are: 1965: 22.6/20.6; 1970: 15.2/14.3; 1980: 15.5/16.9; 1990: 23.5/24.9 (Israel Central Bureau of Statistics, T. 2.19.)

25 1993 figures from Aharoni, *The Israeli Economy*, p. 200. Figures for 1993 are from *The Statistical Abstract of Israel*, T. 6–7 (1994).

26 Daniel Hillel, *Rivers of Eden: The Struggle for Water and the Quest for Peace in the Middle East* (Oxford University Press, 1994), p. 227.

27 Ibid., p. 228; Efrat, *Geography and Politics*, p. 211.

28 See Dabbagh et al., "Desalination an Emergent Option" in Peter Rogers and Peter Lydon (eds.), *Water in the Arab World: Perspectives and Prognoses* (Harvard University Press, 1994), p. 228, Tables 3 and 4.

29 Miriam R. Lowi, *Water and Power: The Politics of a Scarce Resource in the Jordan River Basin* (Cambridge University Press, 1993), p. 151.

30 See for example Davis *et al.*, p. 40.

31 These figures are compiled from Lowi, Hillel, Davis, Kahhala, Eisa, Masri, Bakour and Kolars in Rogers and Lydon (eds.), *Water in the Arab World*, p. 131.

32 For the damage to and the illegal exploitation of the Occupied Territories' water resources, see UN report, UNA/AC. 183 (02) W21, p. 6, p. 66, respectively. This report also quotes claims, (p. 10) that Israel "controls more than 2,300 mcm [million cubic metres] of the Arab world water resources".

33 The reduced figure of 60 m³/year (164 litres/day) is still larger than most Arab countries other than the Gulf. The reduction can be achieved by applying disciplined and serious policies of water economy, as was the case in Tunis which reduced its municipal consumption from 44 to 30 m³/year. See Dabbagh *et al.*, p. 5. None the less, WHO standards recommend levels above this.

34 This statement represents the Likud position given by Ploss and Rubenstein; quoted in Rogers and Lydon (eds.) *Water in the Arab World*, p. 60.

35 This idea is not without some precedent. The UN discussed in its early deliberations the appointment of "an administrator for refugee property". See A/AC.25/W.81/Rev.2, p. 73.

36 Or 5,194,091 *dunums* (1 *dunum* = 1,000 sq.m) estimated as the *registered individual* Arab property in Israel (RP/1), excluding "unsettled title", common and public Aran property and the whole of Beer Sheba Sub-District (12,577,000 d). See the CCP land expert report by Jarvis, UN A/AC.25/W.84, 28 April 1964.

37 After the conquest of Palestine in 1948, Israel passed a series of laws, described by Peretz as "a sort of legal fiction". A Custodian of Absentee Property was appointed, who in turn transferred this property to a "Development Authority". The latter was empowered to sell, buy, lease, develop or cultivate the absentees' property, provided that such transactions are restricted to Jewish entities only. In pre-1948 Palestine, land held by the Jewish National Fund (JNF) was declared to be "in the name of the Jewish People everywhere in perpetuity". With the vast land gains acquired in 1948, a dispute arose between the JNF and Israel's government about its control. The latter claimed that such land should be registered in its name as the reward for "the triumph of the Hagana and the flight of the Arabs". It was finally agreed that the JNF would be allowed to increase its holdings and all Palestinian land be administered by the Israel Land Administration (ILA) according to JNF rules. The JNF stated in 1949 that, "of the entire area of the State of Israel [20,325 sq.km], about 300 sq. km are state domains. The JNF and private Jewish owners possess under 2,000 sq. km [1,682 sq. km]. Almost all the rest [i.e. 88 per cent] belongs in law [*sic*] to Arab owners, many of whom left the country . . ." All the Palestinian land is now run in custody by the ILA (until the owners return). For a comprehensive description of JNF activities, see Walter Lehn and Uri Davis, *The Jewish National Fund* (London: Kegan Paul International, 1988), particularly pp. 108, 114 and 132.

8

The Question of Compensation and Reparations

Ghada Karmi

It is a remarkable fact that 50 years after the original loss of their homeland, property and belongings, the Palestinians have received virtually nothing in compensation. This is even more remarkable when viewed against the background of current campaigns to compensate victims of other conflicts. In 1997, an international three-day conference took place in London under the auspices of the British government. The aim of this conference was to discuss the question of compensation for Jewish victims of Nazism and their quest for a return of money and possessions which they claim belonged to them at the time of the Second World War. The impetus for the conference was the international row over monies held by Switzerland which had originated during the Nazi era. It is instructive in the context of the present paper briefly to review the background to this "Nazi gold" and the actions taken to rectify past mistakes on the part of European governments in respect of it. A striking contrast emerges between the moral attitudes and practical steps taken towards resolving this issue and those towards rectifying outstanding Palestinian losses from 1948 onwards.

It is said that during the war, Swiss banks became the repository for gold and currency deposited by the Nazis and believed to be Jewish in origin. At the same time, many Jews opened bank accounts there to safeguard their money. Many of them perished in the Holocaust and these accounts have lain dormant ever since. In addition, gold looted by the Nazis from European central banks was also deposited in Switzerland. This and previous Nazi deposits of gold and currency were all pooled together to form the so-called "Nazi gold" which led to the convening of the London conference. US intelligence reports have suggested that this gold amounted to $400 million at the time of the war. In 1946, the Swiss returned $60 million to the Allies and in

1962, they paid a further SwF10 million towards the victims fund, but they kept the rest. Today, 5.5 tonnes of this gold is estimated to be the rightful property of Holocaust victims,[1] and Switzerland is also being asked to release monies held in private accounts to the Jewish wartime depositors or their heirs.

When the issue was first raised in 1995 – actually by a Swiss MP who suggested that her government should return dormant bank accounts belonging to Holocaust victims – the Swiss government was evasive and uncooperative. However, Jewish groups took up the issue and subsequently, under enormous pressure from America, Britain, France and several international Jewish organisations, the Swiss agreed to set up a $71 million compensation fund for Holocaust victims, which was later increased to $155 million,[2] and also to support an inquiry into the origins of Nazi gold. No fewer than 15 committees or investigations were set up to research Swiss wartime activities, including research by the US State Department, the US Senate and US Congress Banking Committee and the British Foreign Office.[3] "This is not a question of monetary compensation", said Henri Hajdenberg, President of the Council of French Jewish Institutions in February 1997: "It is a moral issue where the truth must be known so that we can make peace with the past."[4] Just before the opening of the London conference on "Nazi Gold" in November 1997, the British Foreign Secretary Robin Cook stated: "Nothing can compensate for what happened in the Holocaust. But the international community can now take practical action, and as we enter the 21st century, to display humanity and understanding to those who suffered . . .[5]

If Switzerland and other European states which also hold money and property allegedly belonging to Jews from the time of the Second World War eventually return these to their rightful owners, we must remember that this will not have been the first time that the Jewish victims of Nazism have been compensated. After the war, the newly formed Federal German Republic was required to pay compensation for the crimes inflicted on the Jews by Hitler's Third Reich. In 1945, Chaim Weizmann, on behalf of the Jewish Agency, had claimed compensation from Germany for the physical extermination of Jews, the confiscation of their possessions and the destruction of their religious and cultural heritage. He estimated Jewish material losses at the time to be an astronomical £2 billion,[6] and suggested that the money should be given to the representatives of world Jewry and some of it used for the settlement of Jewish Holocaust survivors in Palestine. In 1950, Israel, as the new representative of the Jewish people, claimed for compensation against West Germany. The Israelis considered that Germany owed the Jews a moral debt of which material compensation was only one factor.

Accordingly, in 1952, the Luxembourg Agreement between Israel, a number of Jewish organisations and the Federal Republic of Germany was signed. The Germans agreed to pay DM3,000 million to the State of Israel and DM450 million to the Jewish organisations – payment to be made firstly in goods over a period of 14 years, as the German post-war economy was in poor condition.[7] The payment to Israel was made "in recognition of its needs to settle Jews who had suffered from Nazism". In the Restitution Agreement of 1952, Germany was also required by the three occupying powers to return lost property belonging to the victims or to pay them its replacement value. It was at this time that the concept of *Wiedergutmachung* (meaning to make good again) was introduced by the Germans to describe the compensation they were offering the Jews by way of making amends for the crimes committed under the Nazi regime. Applications for restitution were invited from victims or their relatives and by 1984, more than 734,900 claims had been submitted of which 734,700 – that is, all but 200 – had been settled.[8] The total amount paid out for restitution of lost property was in excess of DM4,250 million, although the sum initially set aside for this purpose had been DM1,500 million.

Up to 1984, the total amount paid out in compensation by Germany to the State of Israel and to Jews inside and outside the country was DM85,800 million (not including other economic, military and diplomatic aid which Germany provided to Israel over the period).[9] One interesting feature of the German compensation programme was its inclusion of social and psychological damage as justifiable categories for compensation. Thus, compensation covered "loss of freedom, income, professional and financial advancement, health and tranquillity". It also included those, such as artists and scholars, whose work had been persecuted by the Nazis and had consequently suffered. Finally, compensation was payable to the relatives of deceased victims. Between 1953 and 1983, 4,393,365 compensation claims under these various categories were made and 99.9 per cent had been settled by the latter date at a cost of DM56,200 million. Ninety per cent of the claimants were Jews and of these, 40 per cent lived in Israel, 20 per cent in West Germany and 40 per cent in other countries.[10]

Compensation and the Palestinian Case

With these data in mind, we should now ask what, by comparison, has been done to compensate the Palestinians for the loss of their lives, their land, homes, property, income, professional advancement, health and tranquillity. How have these victims of the victims, so to speak, been dealt with after they were evicted from their land in 1948 and in 1967, and where is the Palestinian equivalent of *Wiedergutmachung*? Since the Lausanne conference of 1949, not one international conference has been held to discuss the issue, and no world leader has expressed any moral regret for what happened to the Palestinians. Rarely has any linkage been made between the Nazi persecution of Jews and the dispossession of Palestinians, although the two events are clearly connected. When Israel came to negotiate its reparations agreement with Germany in 1952, the Arab states proposed that refugee compensation should be deducted from any payments made to Israel. The Arab League attempted to persuade Germany to delay such payment until Israel had agreed to compensate the refugees, but neither was willing to accept this condition.[11] The German connection has been raised again much more recently by Israel's former Director of Military Intelligence on the West Bank, Shlomo Gazit. Writing in 1995, he suggested that if the German government pays former East Germany's share of reparations to the Jewish victims of Nazism, then part of that money could go towards compensating the Palestinians.[12]

Even so, it will be said that the two situations are not comparable, since nothing can approach in magnitude the genocidal horror of the Holocaust. Indeed, Gazit points out that his proposal for channelling German money into Palestinian compensation might arouse hostile reactions from Holocaust survivors on the grounds that it would implicitly equate the Holocaust with the refugee problem. Of course, it has partly been this sensitivity to the Holocaust which has prevented any proper discussion of Israeli responsibility for the Palestinian tragedy. Yet, the two issues are connected, not least because Palestine became the refuge for the victims of Nazism, and its people displaced to make room for them. Indeed the compensation payments which were explicitly made to Israel for resettling the victims in the new state are a formal recognition of this fact. For the Palestinians, too, the issue is a moral one – of which material compensation is but one aspect. The essence of the Palestinian grievance is not only that they lost their homeland, but that the perpetrators have consistently refused to make reparation or even to acknowledge their responsibility in the matter.

If we review Israeli reactions to the "problem of the refugees", as it came to be known, we see a consistent thread of denial and evasion and attempts to foist the responsibility onto others. From 1949 onwards, Israel has constantly rejected a return of the refugees and sought to resolve the issue by calling on the host societies in which they reside to integrate them. The Israeli line has been to assert that, on the one hand, the Arabs left under orders from their leaders, and on the other, that their exodus was part of what happens in the course of wars. Both of these allegations have been shown to be baseless,[13] and even then, international law is quite clear on the right of anyone who leaves his home for whatever reason to return to it. The Universal Declaration of Human Rights, to which Israel became a signatory, states that "everyone has the right to leave any country, including his own, and to return to that country" and that "no one shall be arbitrarily deprived of his property".

At the same time, Israel has avoided making any meaningful restitution or compensation for the losses incurred by the displaced Palestinians. In 1949, an offer was made by the Israeli government of a single compensation payment for refugee property in rural areas, for undamaged urban property and for Palestinian bank accounts left behind. However, this payment would only be made in the context of an overall settlement of the Arab–Israeli conflict. No compensation would be made for state land or to refugees on an individual basis. Speaking in a Knesset debate on the issue in 1951, Moshe Sharett made clear that any offer of compensation to be made by Israel was predicated on several assumptions. First, that the abandoned Arab property was a legacy of the war of 1948–9, which had been forced on Israel. The war had resulted in damage to Israel and loss of life and hence had impaired its ability to pay. Second, Israel would look to the international community for help in making any such payment. Third, the payment would be final and Israel could not be subject to further demands thereafter. Fourth, that the Israeli compensation paid would be deducted from frozen assets belonging to Iraqi Jews who had settled in Israel. And fifth, and most importantly, that fulfilment of its obligations in the matter of compensation would free Israel from any obligation towards refugee repatriation.[14]

However, in 1949, absentee property was released on a small scale to refugees who had never left Israel. This amounted to 100,000 *dunums* of land which was returned to 5,000 families.[15] In other cases, families were not allowed to return to their original homes but were resettled in other villages, which the government promoted as a positive step in the process of solving the problem of displaced persons in Israel. In 1953, 2,000 urban dwellings were returned to "absentee" Arab owners, and in the same year, the Land Acquisition Law was passed. This promised to pay compensation for 300,000 *dunums* of land belonging to Israeli citizens who were Arabs, but no provisions were to be made for land belonging to Arab refugees who had left the country.

For these, in 1950 Israel proposed a resettlement scheme to be administered by the recently established United Nations Relief and Works Agency (UNRWA) with a so-called "reintegration fund". Israel offered the sum of one million Israeli pounds to this fund as the first instalment of its compensation for abandoned property.[16] Soon after, however, it was arguing that it would have to curtail its payment because of the need to rehabilitate Iraqi Jews who had arrived in Israel and, by 1951, it cited the Egyptian closure of the Suez Canal and the Arab economic boycott as further obstacles to its ability to pay.[17] The Conciliation Commission for Palestine (CCP), originally set up in 1949 by the UN to oversee the repatriation of refugees and their compensation, recognised Israel's difficulties in meeting its financial obligations and stated that it would require help to do so. In 1955, the American Secretary of State, John Foster Dulles, offered US assistance in funding the compensation costs through an international loan to Israel. The CCP urged the Israelis to take up the offer, but the latter replied that nothing could be done outside the general context of Arab–Israeli relations and a removal of the Arab economic blockade of Israel. As a result, nothing came of the American proposal, nor indeed of any other.[18]

From the 1950s onwards, the Israeli position was that Israel would be willing to contribute to any fund which would resettle the Palestinian refugees, provided this took place outside Israel and provided that its share of the costs was small. To this day, the Israelis have remained willing to contribute towards an international fund for the refugees with the lion's share to be contributed by the rich Arab states and the West.[19] They have even suggested that the Palestine National Authority, recently installed, should direct part of its aid package towards such a fund. From the mid-1950s onwards, they started increasingly to tie any offer of compensation they made to the right of compensation for Jews who had left their homes in Arab countries, especially Iraq, to settle in Israel. This became a convenient weapon to use in their war against compensating the Palestinians. But of course this is a spurious excuse, since the case between Israel and the Palestinians has nothing whatever to do with cases which Israel may have with other countries.

However, one financial settlement did meet with some success. In 1953, the Israeli government, under the urging of the CCP, reluctantly agreed to a gradual release of Palestinian bank accounts and deposits held in Barclays and Ottoman Banks which had been frozen by the Israelis in 1948. Subsequently and until 1953, they were held under the jurisdiction of Israel's Custodian of Absentee Property. These bank accounts, including safe deposit boxes and bonds, and owned by 10,000 Palestinians, were estimated by the Arab League to amount to £6 million Sterling.[20] The CCP found the bank accounts to number 6,500 with a total value of P£4 million.[21] The Israeli government put up numerous obstacles to the release of these funds which was considered in any case to be a concession on Israel's part. There were demands for the release of frozen Jewish accounts in Arab banks and for reciprocal action on the part of the Arab states to resettle the refugees.[22] In 1954, Barclays Bank agreed to make a Sterling loan to the Israeli government to enable it to liquidate all the outstanding accounts owing to the refugees. As a result of this and six years of laborious negotiations on the part of the CCP, £2,633,175 – that is, 87 per cent of the value of the accounts – had been released by 1957.[23] Israel charged a levy of 10 per cent on each refugee account, as part of its compulsory National Loan imposed on all bank accounts in Israel, as well as administrative handling costs. By 1965, 143 safe deposit boxes, 274 bonds and 323 Palestine government bearer bonds had been released, but the balance still remained in Israel.[24] Although the sums involved are apparently much smaller, it is interesting to contrast the silence over this situation with the vociferous outrage expressed at Switzerland's retention of wartime Jewish investors' monies in its banks.

From the 1950s until the Madrid Peace Conference in 1991, shortly to be followed by the signing of the Oslo Accords in 1993, nothing further was offered or accomplished on the issue of compensation for the Palestinians. It is especially striking that nothing was said about Palestinian losses incurred as a result of the war of 1967. Jewish settlements established on Arab land in Jerusalem, the West Bank and Gaza after 1967 should properly form the subjects of restitution or compensation, even though the task to attain these will be formidably difficult.[25] In the wake of the 1967 occupation, the Israeli government took considerable precautions to prevent Palestinians from claiming rights of land ownership. The land registration scheme instituted by the Jordanians after 1948 had mapped and registered land ownership in the West Bank. But it was incomplete and up to half the land was still not registered by 1967. The Israelis hindered all further attempts to register land ownership and land transfers and declared much of the area "state land". Because of the confused tenure situation, many Arab land sales have taken place since then with forged documents and consequent loss to the owners, or have become the subjects of inheritance and border disputes. Unravelling this maze may prove insuperably difficult and even then, Israel will try to downplay the value of Palestinian assets and also wish to turn the matter over to the international community for funding and resolution.

The peace process brought back the contentious issue of the refugees, since the Oslo Accords required that this be discussed during the final status talks. Within the framework of the peace process, Israel reluctantly agreed to accept applications from 5,000 Palestinians displaced in 1967 – to be admitted over a period of three years and only as part of a family reunion scheme. These numbers are of course extremely small by comparison to the total 1967 displaced population, and the 1948 displaced Palestinians feature nowhere. The Israeli position remains adamant on rejecting the return of these refugees, still insisting that they are resettled in their countries of present residence or elsewhere, but not on any account in Israel. Meanwhile, and not surprisingly, the multilateral Working Group on refugees, set up after the Madrid Conference, has made little progress. Since the election of the present Israeli government, it has not met at all.

One may cite a much more recent example of Israel's attitude towards compensation than the refugee cases of 1948 and 1967. Following the outbreak of the *Intifada* in 1987, Palestinians injured by the Israeli army made claims for compensation. In most cases they were immediately rejected, although later allowance was made for certain individual "humanitarian" cases. The late Yitzhak Rabin, Prime Minister at the time when the claims were first made, was determined to find some legal means by which to stop the Palestinians from applying for compensation. Rabin's successor, Shimon Peres, was convinced that nothing should be paid to the Palestinians on the basis that the *Intifada* had been started by them with the aim of destroying Israel. As he said in 1996: "We have asked for no compensation for our victims of the Intifada, what about our injured and our dead? Who will pay for them?"[26]

By the beginning of 1997, 4,754 Palestinian claims had been submitted to the Israeli Ministry of Justice at an estimated cost of 900 million shekels. The Defence Ministry was able to raise 63 million shekels of this sum, but in order to avoid paying the rest of the money, the Ministry of Justice announced on 19 February that it had submitted for government approval a new law which would define the *Intifada* as a war. According to Israeli law, no compensation is payable for damages incurred during war. In particular, no compensation is forthcoming in cases of damage incurred during aggressive operations against the Israeli Defence Forces (IDF) or committed by someone previously implicated in acts of terrorism. Specific conditions were added to the new law – namely that no act which had been committed by soldiers in defence of their lives could be considered for compensation. The Israel newspaper *Haaretz* pointed out that if the law were passed, it would lead to the courts applying criteria for compensation to those living in the occupied territories different from those applying to Israeli citizens.[27] The paper went on to say that Israel, which had avoided paying compensation for the sufferings of the Palestinians in 1948, was unlikely to do so now for the victims of the *Intifada*. Both the ruling Likud Party and the Labour Party, which had initiated the search for a legal loophole out of the obligation to pay compensation in the first place, voted for the new legislation's first reading in the Knesset. It has still to pass a second and third reading before it becomes law.

At the same time, it is to be noted that the legal justification for the Jewish settlement established inside the city of Hebron after the 1967 Arab–Israeli War was the claim that the land taken by the government had previously been Jewish owned.[28] This refers to the fact that the Jewish community which had lived in Hebron until 1935 had owned several buildings in the commercial part of the city as well as a small amount of agricultural land outside. Hence, the Israeli government claimed that it was merely restoring Jewish possessions to their rightful owners. However, the area of Hebron they have taken over is many times the original size of these Jewish holdings and the people who presently claim them are not legally entitled to do so (since they are neither the heirs nor descendants of those Jews), showing once more that Israel remains assiduous in its search for restitution for itself, while remaining oblivious to Palestinian claims.

The Legal Basis for Compensation

What is the legal case for Palestinian compensation? Basically, this has two aspects. First, the legality vested in UN resolutions and international agreements and second, reference to historical precedents. The most important amongst the latter is the example of German restitution made under the auspices of the Allies following the Second World War in the Paris Conference of 1945 and Agreement of 1946, to which allusion has already been made. However, there have been other historical precedents, of which we may mention the treaties enacted between Spain and France in 1678 and the Treaty of London of 1839, whereby the independence and neutrality of Belgium was agreed.[29] In both of these treaties, provision was made for restitution to those who, as a result of war or sequestration, had lost effects, moveables and immoveables. The Treaty of Sèvres, signed with Turkey after the First World War, required the Turks to pay compensation to Armenians who had fled from Turkey. The relevant article reads as follows:

> The Turkish government solemnly undertakes to facilitate to the greatest possible extent the return to their homes and re-establishment in their businesses of the Turkish subjects of

non–Turkish race who have been forcibly driven from their homes ... it recognises that any immoveable or moveable property of the said Turkish subjects or the communities to which they belong, which can be recovered, must be restored to them as soon as possible.

In the event, the Treaty of Sèvres was not ratified by Turkey, but it established the principle of repatriation and restitution for those who had fled their homes because of fear of persecution. In 1923, the land dispute between Hungary and Romania came before the League of Nations. This involved the loss of Hungarian property in land transferred from Hungary to Romania and was finally resolved in 1930 by payment of compensation to the Hungarians. More recently, the case of India–Pakistan after partition in 1948 provides a particularly apt precedent. In the riots which followed partition, an estimated 11 million people on both sides fled their homes. As a result, the Indian and Pakistani governments set up machinery to assess the damage and extent of moveable and immoveable property belonging to the displaced persons, and custodians were appointed to look after the property while claims were processed. Through an Indian–Pakistani agreement signed between the two countries in August 1948, it was agreed that reparation would be made by the government of each side to those who had been forced to flee from its territory.[30] Most recently, there have been the compensation agreements for displaced persons in the Bosnian conflict.

However, the most important legal basis for the Palestinian case remains the UN and its resolutions, and of these the single most significant resolution is UN General Assembly Resolution 194. First passed in December 1948, it has been reiterated every year since then and remains unimplemented to this day. Paragraph 11 of this resolution states:

The General Assembly . . . resolves that the refugees wishing to return to their homes and live at peace with their neighbours should be permitted to do so at the earliest practicable date, and that compensation should be paid for the property of those choosing not to return and for loss of or damage to the property which, under principles of international law or in equity, should be made good by the government or authorities responsible.

There are several things to note here. The payment of compensation in the resolution has two aspects: first, as payment in lieu of return, and second as compensation for those wishing to return. In other words, the issue of return and compensation are not mutually exclusive. The "loss of or damage" phrase in the paragraph refers not to war damages, but to destruction and plunder which occurred without military necessity. This is in line with the Hague Convention of 1907, another important instrument of international law which is relevant here. The Convention explicitly prohibited the destruction or seizure of enemy property unless such destruction or seizure were necessities of war, and stipulated that a belligerent party which violates the provisions shall be liable to pay compensation.[31] It is quite clear that the wholesale Zionist seizure of land and property in Palestine did not take place because, to quote the Hague Convention, they were "imperatively demanded by the necessities of war". Actually, in 1948, the Israelis passed a number of laws purporting to legalise this seizure: the Abandoned Areas Ordinance, the Absentee Property Regulations, and the Emergency Cultivation of Waste Lands Regulations. These regulations empowered the Israelis to declare a conquered Palestine area as "abandoned" and therefore available to become their possessions. The euphemistically entitled Israeli Custodian of Absentee Property put the situation like this:

> The Arabs abandoned great quantities of property in hundreds and thousands of dwellings, shops, storehouses and workshops. They also left produce in fields and fruit in orchards and vineyards, placing the fighting and victorious community before serious material temptation.[32]

The Israelis justified this legislation on the basis of precedent in the agreements reached between India and Pakistan following partition.[33] The 1947 partition of India had resulted in an exchange of populations with the loss of large areas of land and property owned by each side. The governments of India and Pakistan, when faced with the need to resettle their respective refugees, had been forced to do so in the abandoned property of each side. They had each appointed Custodians of Muslim, Hindu and Sikh property to supervise the task. The Israelis argued that they were in a similar situation, since they had had to accept a large influx of Jewish refugees who needed resettlement.

Between the middle of 1948 and the end of 1951, 684,000 Jews came into Israel from Europe and the Arab countries, all of whom had to be housed and supported. Precedents other than the situation in India/Pakistan also justified the Israeli position, they argued. These were the population transfers which had taken place between Turkey and Greece, between Turkey and Romania, and between Romania and Bulgaria.[34] In each of these cases, the property belonging to each population group had been ceded to the government, which handled all compensation on a state-to-state basis. In no case had individual compensation been made to the owners. Israel argued that it was in a similar position *vis-à-vis* the Jewish refugees from Arab countries and that what had taken place with the Palestinians was in fact no more than an exchange of populations. This argument has never been accepted, either by the Arabs or by the international community.

The Israeli Custodian had broad and extensive powers. He could take over most Arab property simply by producing its owner "absentee", and he could not be questioned as to how he had decided that this was the case.[35] Under Israeli regulations, every Palestinian who had left his place of residence in Palestine after the date of the United Nations Partition Resolution of 29 November 1947 could be classified as an absentee. This included people who had travelled only a few miles to a nearby town or village. In many such cases, and even in places where some people stayed behind, the entire population of the village was pronounced "absentee" and the returning villagers were required to pay rent to the Custodian for the use of their land. Elsewhere, as in Acre and Shafa Amr, Arab farmers were not allowed to cultivate their lands, which were taken over by the Custodian for Jewish use.[36] In this way, the new state absorbed 15 million *dunums* of Palestinian land which was declared not to be individually owned, as well as 3 million *dunums* of land belonging to individual Palestinians. Subsequently, and through a variety of mechanisms, this land was transferred first to a development authority and later, in 1960, to the Israel Lands Authority. The latter body administers all Israeli land, regarded as the inalienable property of the Jewish people and under no circumstances to be transferred to non-Jews.[37] Thus, the refugees' land had been permanently put beyond their reach.

The legal basis for Palestinian compensation has another aspect. The resolution which admitted Israel to UN membership required that Israel abide by the obligations of the international body's previous resolutions. These included the repatriation of refugees and payment of compensation. The resolution states that "no expropriation of land owned by an Arab in the Jewish state shall be allowed except for public purposes . . . in all cases of expropriation, full compensation as fixed by the Supreme Court shall be paid previous to dispossession".[38] Furthermore, Israel was repeatedly asked to respect the inalienable rights of the civilian population as prescribed by the 1949 Geneva Convention.

Resolution 194 clearly designated that the parties who should make compensation were the government of Israel or "authorities responsible". The latter presumably referred to the Jewish organisations active in Palestine before the State of Israel had been founded, such as the Jewish Agency, the Jewish National Fund and terrorist groups like the Stern and Irgun gangs. The same resolution went on to establish the Conciliation Commission for Palestine, whose task was to implement its provisions. In a subsequent General Assembly resolution passed in December 1959, the Commission was instructed to "make such arrangements as it may consider necessary for the assessment and payment of compensation in pursuance of . . . Resolution 194 . . . and to take measures for the protection of the rights, property and interests of the refugees". Unfortunately, the Commission failed in its duty, excepting in the matter of the frozen bank accounts already mentioned, and a proposal was eventually put forward in 1961 to appoint a custodian of Arab property.[39] Such an appointment would have helped protect the property rights of the refugees pending a final resolution, and would have enabled them to derive income from their use. But, thanks to US opposition, the proposal failed to get the two-thirds majority in the General Assembly, and it was defeated each time it was brought to the UN subsequently.

The Assessment of Palestinian Losses

The task of assessing the extent of Palestinian losses for the purposes of drawing up claims for compensation is obviously quite complex by now, and even at the time, there was no agreed final figure. This was not least in part due to the fact that the Israeli government kept details of the Arab land and property it had appropriated secret. Throughout the early years of Israel's statehood, the UN had considerable difficulty in obtaining accurate information about Israel's disposition of Arab property, despite numerous requests to this effect from the CCP. The latter therefore had to come up with an estimated figure derived from indirect sources, which in 1951 it put at 16,324,000 *dunums* lost, worth P£100,383,784.[40] Thus, more than 80 per cent of Israel's total area was land belonging to the refugees, although only a quarter of this was said to be cultivatable.[41] Of the 370 new Jewish settlements set up between 1948 and 1953, 350 were built on absentee land. The CCP detailed the number of properties, shops and businesses left by Arabs and which fell into Jewish hands: everything in the cities of Jaffa, Acre, Lydda, Ramleh, Beisan and Majdal; large parts of 94 other cities and towns; and 388 villages and 10,000 shops and businesses. Most of the Arab citrus groves were taken over by the Custodian of Absentee Property, as were the olive groves. In 1951, the fruit produce of former Arab groves provided 10 per cent of Israel's foreign currency earnings and olives were its third-largest export. In addition, a third of Israel's stone production was obtained from 52 Arab quarries which had also been appropriated by the Custodian.

These estimates did not take into account the refugees' moveable property, much of which was destroyed or looted during the events of 1948. However, according to a *Haaretz* report of 15 June 1951, four million P£'s worth of such property was in the hands of the Custodian. The CCP estimated the value of moveable property – defined as motor vehicles, household effects, livestock, agricultural and industrial equipment – to be P£20 million, although admitting that this was unlikely to be accurate. To overcome these difficulties of estimation, the CCP proposed setting up sub-committees which would determine property ownership and evaluate damage. The Arab participants agreed, but Israel did not. So the CCP was left with its global estimate of P£120,000 as the total sum of Palestinian property losses for the time being. In 1953, an attempt was made to assess the extent of Palestinian losses more accurately. The UN Refugee Office began a thorough identification of all Palestinian property as of May 1948. It used the land ownership registers of the government of Palestine, some of which had been turned over to Israel and some to the Jordanian authorities. Many records were also held on microfilm in London and yet others had been handed to the UN.[42] Tax records were also used to assist in drawing up more accurate figures for the value of the land. The task proves difficult and many records were illegible or incomplete. By 1964, the Refugee Office had identified 453,000 plots of refugee-owned or leased land totalling 7,069,091 *dunums*, which is less than half the amount previously estimated by the CCP.

It is clear that the difficulties of defining exactly how much Palestinian property was lost in 1948, and therefore how much compensation is needed, are immense. However, it has also been pointed out that compensating the Palestinians for what happened in 1948 (and by extension in 1967) will entail more than an assessment of property values. Hadawi and Kubursi – whose excellent work on this subject remains the best source we have – have listed the components which should form the content of Palestinian compensation claims.[43] They have used the Jewish postwar restitution claims against Germany as a model, and have come up with a classification involving the following categories: immoveable property, that is land and buildings, privately and collectively owned, and public places such as railways, schools, churches and mosques; moveable property, ranging from appliances to furniture to tools and implements, and also including human skills and education; what they call "lost opportunities", that is income lost from jobs and careers; and finally, psychological damage, that is the denial of security, identity and development of potential and hence the loss of equilibrium and happiness.

At the end of the day, of course, the loss of a homeland and all that that entailed for the Palestinians in loss of life as well as material loss can never be compensated for. But even then, it would seem that the estimate of Palestinian losses drawn up by the Conciliation Commission for Palestine in 1951 was very low. Hadawi considered that it was set at P£120 million because it used only a small sub-set of these losses which excluded many of the categories outlined in the paragraph above. It also excluded Jerusalem and all non-cultivatable land from the calculation. A second, much higher estimate of P£1,933 million was provided by the Arab Higher Committee in Cairo in 1955. This figure included moveable property and took account of lost agricultural and other income. But it still failed to include the full range of losses and used lower than market rates for land and property prices. A third assessment was made in 1956 by the expert committee of the League of Arab States.[44] This adopted a methodology of assessing land lost with regard to its type of use, scarcity value and revenue it generated. It also included monies blocked in banks and insurance companies' funds. The result which the Arab League came up with was the same as that provided by the Arab Higher Committee and again, in Hadawi's view, it failed on several counts. The figures for land size and use were not detailed enough, not well related to their tax categories, and the revenue and rent income values were arbitrarily calculated.

The fourth estimate came in 1966 from the well-known Palestinian economist, Yusef Sayegh.[45] His stance was that the loss of Palestine was primarily a moral one whose costs far exceeded those of land and property. Nevertheless, he presented a different methodology for assessing the claim for Palestinian compensation. He classified the losses into what he called "personal property", that is houses, hotels, shops, bank deposits, land, livestock and furniture; "share of public property", meaning government buildings, roads, railways and ports, as well as schools, hospitals, water networks, forests and public land; "income opportunities", such as loss of employment and skills and professional expertise; and factories, warehouses and commercial buildings. He added two other interesting categories: "transitional costs", meaning the economic effects of the repercussions of the refugee exodus on the West Bank and Gaza; and "separation costs", that is the costs borne by neighbouring Arab countries with the burden of absorbing the refugees and the economic loss to these countries resulting from the removal of the Palestinian market. He estimated the total losses as categorised in this way to be P£756.7 million, which is a figure somewhere in between those of the CCP and the Arab League.

Kubursi, who reviewed and critically analysed all previous assessments of Palestinian losses, presented his own estimate.[46] This is carefully worked out in considerable detail and with great precision and takes account of all the variables mentioned above. He puts all "non-human losses" (excluding land) incurred under the heading of capital ownership, which includes industrial and agricultural capital, commercial capital and stocks, hotels and restaurants, personal wealth, infrastructure and natural resources. In assessing the value of land lost to the refugees, he uses UN records relating to 1946 and 1947 which identify urban and rural land areas by a number of variables. He also uses data which have been neglected in previous evaluations, that is government of Palestine property sales for 1946 and 1947. Overall, more than 4,000 recorded sales were identified in this way with details of their location, type of ownership and sale price. He found that the value of land and property losses incurred by the refugees in 1948 was P£743 million which, he asserts, is still an underestimate of the true cost.[47] When human capital losses are added, meaning the loss of skills and potential due to refugee unemployment or low-wage work in the host countries, the figure rises to P£1,182.2 million.

Kubursi converts these sums to 1984 rates in dollars, making allowance for inflation, and gets a figure of $147,000 million for the total losses and $92,000 million for physical property losses alone. The same sums converted to pounds Sterling, and allowing for British inflation rates between 1948 and 1984, yield £79,500 million. It must be stressed again, however, that all such figures exclude the psychological and human suffering of the people of Palestine consequent on the loss of their homeland, to which it would be difficult to assign a monetary value.

Conclusion

The above discussion should have illustrated the complexities of arriving at a true figure for the value of Palestinian losses incurred in 1948. The task will be no less difficult for the losses to Palestinians thereafter in the war of 1967 and in the continuing expropriation of Palestinian assets in the occupied territories. However, this should not preclude the work of making these assessments, and indeed it could be said that the Palestinians themselves – with a few notable exceptions – have been remiss in not doing so. This is in part due to the Palestinian anxiety about the right of return. The fear amongst Palestinians for decades was that if they accepted compensation from Israel – had it even been forthcoming – they would have renounced their right to return to their homeland. This was based partly on a misunderstanding of UN Resolution 194, which was thought to enjoin return *or* compensation, but also on distrust and fear of Israel. Thus, it was only in 1982 that the PLO obtained copies of the CCP's records of Palestinian property from the UN and also of the British registers, although nothing seems to have been done with them. They are said to be currently housed in the PLO's office in Damascus, to which access is difficult.[48] Jordan also has copies of the UNCCP's records and itself possesses a variety of other Palestinian land records, dating from both before and after 1948. Following discussions between the Palestine Authority and the Jordanian government, it was reported that the latter agreed in 1997 to release copies of land records and maps relating to the West Bank and also Mandate records relating to Gaza.[49] There is no indication as yet as to whether these documents will be incorporated with the rest of the archives in Damascus.

Recently, non-official bodies and individuals have begun to collect data on Palestinian ownership of property in preparation for seeking restitution and compensation from Israel. In particular, interest has focused on Palestinian-owned land in West Jerusalem before 1948. Undoubtedly, this process has been boosted by the 1993 Oslo agreement between Israel and the PLO. By including the refugee issue as one of the subjects for negotiations between the two sides, this has laid the groundwork for defining the questions of restitution and compensation. However, neither the PLO nor the Palestine Authority has yet come out with a clear policy on this issue, nor indeed on the right of return. What is needed now is an official Palestinian comprehensive register of land, property and all other losses which can form an authoritative basis for compensation claims. This should include the losses incurred after 1948 and take account of non-material losses as well.

Persuading Israel, which has successfully evaded making any meaningful reparations to the Palestinians for 50 years, to do so now will not be easy. It is important to understand that if this issue comes up for discussion, the Israeli negotiators will bring with them an unequivocal denial of responsibility for all aspects of the refugee problem.[50] The official Israeli position on the right of the refugees to return and on their compensation has been frozen since the 1950s – namely that Israel bears no responsibility for the flight of the Palestinians and hence none for their compensation. Officially, Israel acknowledges no responsibility for the War of 1948 which created the refugee exodus and sees this war as one instituted by the Arab states against Israel. Forced to defend itself, it could not be blamed for the consequences as they related to the Palestinians. In response to the argument that, irrespective of how the Palestinians fled, Israel benefited immeasurably from their property and belongings at the time and that it should make recompense, the Israelis make the point that they were obliged to house the Jews who came from Arab countries. This meant that Israel's resources were stretched beyond any capability of offering help to the Palestinians, and, in addition, there was the fact that Israel received no compensation from the Arabs to settle its own refugees.

In recent years, an unspoken consensus appears to have grown in the US and Europe over how the refugee issue should be resolved. This has implicitly accepted Israel's rejection of return for the 1948 refugees and now looks to ways of resettling them elsewhere with the help of an international aid fund. The US would seem to be in support of this position, as has been expounded in a recent authoritative book on the subject.[51] Negotiations have already taken place between US, Israeli and Jordanian representatives over resolving the refugee issue by way of resettling them in the countries of their present residence.[52] The compensation envisaged in Resolution 194 would then be payable, not to the refugees, but to the countries which are meant to house them – including some which are outside the Arab world. Even so, there is an awareness that Israel itself might need to make some gesture towards the refugees in recognition of the bitterness which this issue has engendered. Gazit, writing in 1995 from a more left-wing position than that of the present government, put forward the idea of an Israeli "declaration of moral compensation" to the Palestinians.[53] This would require them to formally renounce their right of return and Israel would then make a statement which recognised the sufferings of the Palestinians. Even then, he stresses the danger of appearing to accept blame or responsibility for the Palestinian problem which Israel might run by making such a statement. At the same time, Israel should offer a financial contribution to the Palestinian refugees, on condition that it was limited in scope and part of a rehabilitation fund set up by the wealthy Arab states and the industrialised world. On no account must the offer of compensation imply any acceptance of responsibility on Israel's part for the refugee problem.

It is fair to assume that this remains in essence the Israeli position today and for the foreseeable future. A number of factors have conspired to enable Israel to shirk its legal and moral responsibilities towards the displaced Palestinians. Not least has been the unconditional support provided to Israel by the US and Europe, the impotence of the UN to enforce its resolutions on Israel and the acquiescence of the international community. But the Palestinians themselves must also bear part of the blame. Throughout the last 50 years, they have been remarkably passive about their right to restitution and compensation, and their case has scarcely been heard. Studies of the subject are few and far between and there exists no formal Palestinian machinery to provide ready documentation and information on this important issue or to enable individuals to make claims for their losses. Not a single publicity campaign has been set up to expose what can only be described as a legal and moral scandal. Even in 1997, when the question of Jewish claims for Nazi gold was so widely debated throughout the Western world, nothing was heard about the Palestinian claims.

The point is not that the Jews should not seek further compensation for wrongs committed against them, but that these Jews, and Israel in particular, also bear a huge moral and material debt to their own victims, the Palestinians. The case for Palestinian compensation is compelling and needs to be clearly heard.

NOTES

1 *The Jewish Chronicle*, 7 February 1998.
2 *The Independent*, 18 February 1997; *The Guardian*, 5 December 1997.
3 *The Jewish Chronicle*, 7 February 1997.
4 Quoted in *The Independent*, 8 February 1997.
5 Quoted in *The Jewish Chronicle*, 28 November 1997.
6 G. Lavy, *Germany and Israel: Moral Debt and National Interest* (London: Frank Cass, 1996), p. 1.
7 Ibid., p. 11.
8 Sami Hadawi, *Palestinian Rights and Losses in 1948* (London: Saqi Books, 1988), pp. 139–41.
9 Ibid., pp. 48–59.
10 Hadawi, *Palestinian Rights*, p. 142.
11 Don Peretz, *Israel and the Palestinian Arabs* (Washington DC: The Middle East Institute, 1958), p. 217.
12 Shlomo Gazit, *The Palestinian Refugee Problem* (Tel Aviv: Tel Aviv University, Jaffee Center for Strategic Studies, 1995), p. 21.
13 Several excellent accounts of the 1948 exodus are now available which dispel these myths. For example, Ilan Pappe, *The Making of the Arab–Israeli Conflict,*

1947–1951 (London: I.B. Tauris, 1994); Benny Morris, *The Birth of the Palestinian Refugee Problem, 1947–1949* (Cambridge University Press, 1987); and Nur Masalha, *Expulsion of the Palestinians* (Washington DC: Institute for Palestine Studies, 1992), and *idem, A Land Without a People* (London: Faber and Faber, 1997).

14 J. B. Schechtman, *The Arab Refugee Problem* (New York: The Philosophical Library, 1952), pp. 109–11.
15 Peretz, *Israel*, p. 183.
16 E. H. Buehrig, *The UN and the Palestinian Refugees* (Bloomington, Ind.: Indiana University Press, 1971), p. 23.
17 Ibid., pp. 23–4.
18 Peretz, *Israel*, p. 218.
19 Gazit, *The Palestinian Refugee Problem*, p. 22.
20 Hadawi, *Palestinian Rights*, pp. 130–1.
21 Peretz, *Israel*, p. 223.
22 Ibid., pp. 226–7.
23 Ibid, p. 236.
24 Hadawi, *Palestinian Rights*, p. 102.
25 M. R. Fischbach, "Settling Historical Land Claims in the Wake of the Arab-Israeli Peace", *Journal of Palestine Studies*, XXVII, 1997, pp. 38–50.
26 *Haaretz*, 21 February 1997.
27 Gideon Levy, *Haaretz*, 21 December 1997.
28 G. H. Falah, "Recent Jewish Colonisation in Hebron" in D. Newman (ed.), *The Impact of Gush Emunim* (London: Croom Helm, 1985), pp. 245–60.
29 Hadawi, *Palestinian Rights*, pp. 214–15.
30 Ibid., pp. 218–20.
31 UN Document A/AC. 25W. 81/Rev.2, 1949, reproduced in ibid., pp. 209–13 and also pp. 90–1.
32 Cited in ibid., p. 88.
33 Schechtman, *Arab Refugee Problem*, pp. 98–101.
34 Ibid., pp. 105–7.
35 Peretz, *Israel*, pp. 149 ff.
36 Ibid., pp. 152–3.
37 Fischbach, "Settling Historical Land Claims", p. 39.
38 Cited in Hadawi, *Palestinian Rights*, p. 86.
39 Ibid., p. 97.
40 Fischbach, "Settling Historical Land Claims", pp. 39–40.
41 Peretz, *Israel*, pp. 143 ff.
42 Ibid., pp. 211–12; Fischbach, "Settling Historical Land Claims", p. 40.
43 Hadawi, *Palestinian Rights*, p. 121.
44 Ibid., pp. 128, 137.
45 Ibid., pp. 132–6.
46 Ibid., p. 147 ff.
47 Ibid., p. 183.
48 Fischbach, "Settling Historical Land Claims", p. 40.
49 Reported in the *Jerusalem Post International*, 17 May 1997 and cited in Fischbach, "Settling Historical Land Claims", p. 42.

50 Shlomo Gazit's study of the refugee problem, from which the remarks in this section are drawn, is a particularly illuminating source for understanding Israel's likely negotiating position in the final status talks.

51 Donna E. Arzt, *Refugees into Citizens: Palestinians and the End of the Arab–Israeli Conflict* (New York: The Council on Foreign Relations, 1997).

52 *Al-Quds al-Arabi*, 3 November 1997.

53 Gazit, *Palestinian Refugee Problem*, pp. 19–22.

9

Truth, Justice and Reconciliation: Elements of a Solution to the Palestinian Refugee Issue

Rashid Khalidi

Many difficult and complex issues must be resolved in order to achieve a just, comprehensive and final settlement of the question of Palestine and of the Arab–Israeli conflict. The most basic among them is undoubtedly the problem of the more than 700,000 Palestinians who became refugees during the fighting of 1947–9 – half of the Arab population of Palestine at that time. It will probably also be the most intractable issue to resolve, more so even than the formidably difficult question of Jerusalem. This is true because the massive demographic transformation which produced the refugee problem was a crucial turning point in the struggle over Palestine between the Zionist movement and the Palestinian people. Since its inception over 100 years ago, this struggle has always focused primarily on matters of population and land. This demographic transformation, hailed as "miraculous" by Chaim Weizmann, the first President of Israel,[1] had profound historical, social and moral consequences which continue to resonate until the present day.

The Palestinian refugee issue is central to the conflict between Arabs and Israelis. For some, including many Palestinians, it is *the* basic issue of the conflict from which all else has flowed over the past half-century. Nevertheless, its treatment in Arab–Israeli negotiations thus far reflects the unremitting pressure from the Israeli side for more than 50 years to ignore, diminish and ideally to bury the whole question of the Palestinians made refugees in 1948. Notwithstanding this constant pressure, the refugee issue must be forthrightly addressed if there is to be a just and lasting peace, for two eminently practical reasons. Firstly, for over three million Palestinians who live outside

Palestine, who constitute more than half of the Palestinian people, of whom most are refugees and descendants of refugees, it is a crucial issue which will largely determine their attitude towards a comprehensive peace, and therefore whether such a peace will be lasting. Secondly, its resolution on a satisfactory basis is vital to a number of host countries, notably Lebanon and Jordan, but also to several states in the Gulf region.

Many proposals have been made for solving the problem of Palestinian refugees over the past 50 years. Some involved full or partial return of the refugees to their homes and compensation for their losses; others were based on resettlement of the refugees in Arab countries; still others involved combinations of these and other proposed elements of a solution. One element missing from most of these proposals, however, is a recognition that the key to the resolution of this issue lies in Israel's, finally, after 50 years, accepting that it bears the primary responsibility for the creation of the Palestinian refugee problem. As with similarly emotionally fraught and complex issues, such as those involving Japanese actions in East Asia during the Second World War, or Switzerland and "Nazi gold", the key requirement for a solution is not so much compensation (important though that is), as acceptance of responsibility and some form of moral atonement. Gross injustice has been done to the Palestinians. It may be difficult for the Israelis to accept that this was in large measure Israel's doing, for such an admission would require substantial revisions in their self-image and in their national narrative. Moreover, many Israelis feel – probably correctly – that their state could not have come into being without a demographic transformation of Palestine such as occurred in 1948, and that it benefited immeasurably from this transformation and its consequences in terms of acquisitions of land and property, whether Israel was responsible for what happened or not.

A recent New York Council on Foreign Relations report suggested the establishment of an "international fund to settle the outstanding claims of refugees displaced by the Arab-Israeli conflict".[2] However, the creation of such an anonymous body, useful though it may be as part of a larger solution embodying several different elements, is utterly insufficient by itself to achieve a solution. Property *is* important, of course, as is compensation for harm done. But acknowledgement that a wrong has been done by those who did it, or their successors, is perhaps more important to a lasting political solution. This is particularly true if, for whatever reason, it is impossible to achieve full justice and the satisfaction of all claims. A British prime minister has recently admitted his country's share of the responsibility for the Irish famine for the first time after nearly 160 years. And in South Africa, the Truth and Reconciliation Commission has operated on the same principle of recognising a wrong done, even if absolute justice is unattainable.

Vital though they are, acceptance of responsibility and atonement are only the first step towards achieving a resolution of the problem. The Palestinian refugees have an internationally sanctioned right of return or compensation, laid down in United Nations General Assembly Resolution 194 of 1948[3] (which the United States supported and presumably still supports). If, as Secretary of State Albright rightly pointed out during a recent trip to Bosnia, victims of the Bosnian conflict have the right to return to their homes a few years after they were forced to leave them, then surely the same principle should apply to the Palestinians after 50 years.

Whether and to what extent this is practicable today, 50 years after the events; where and when this return could take place; what numbers would be allowed to return and to where; whether compensation would be acceptable in lieu of return, and how much compensation; to which mixture of individuals and public and private bodies would compensation be directed; and how property issues are to be dealt with — all are difficult problems which must be negotiated. Nevertheless, if a final, comprehensive and just resolution of the Arab–Israeli conflict is the goal, it is essential that all aspects of the refugee issue, which has been ignored for so long, be placed at the centre of negotiations between the Palestinians and Israel, and that it is treated with the seriousness which it fully deserves.

This issue is so painful for both sides because it cuts very close to the bone: the events of 1947–9 (and those of 1967, which produced further Palestinian refugees, known under the rubric of "displaced persons") are central to the national narratives of both the Palestinian and Israeli peoples, and were crucial turning points in their respective histories. Since the circumstances surrounding the emergence of the Palestinian refugee issue are so seminal in the self-view of both peoples, it simply cannot be dealt with as most other issues have been in the Israeli–Palestinian negotiations thus far. Put bluntly, in this case, history cannot be declared irrelevant and set aside in the interests of an expedient solution which corresponds to the unequal balance of forces between Palestinians and Israelis. Dealing with the issue of Palestinian refugees in a just and comprehensive manner will require squarely facing history, not ignoring it. It will also require accepting that the two parties involved, the Palestinian and Israeli peoples, are affected deeply and quite differently by the way in which the tragic genesis of the Palestine refugee question shaped their respective pasts. For Israelis, the events of 1947 and 1948 – partition, and what the Israelis call the "War of Independence" – are seen as a national rebirth after the Holocaust and are a cause for national celebration; for Palestinians, the same events are seen as an unmitigated disaster and are the focus of national mourning, with the 1948 War known as *al-Nakba*, "the catastrophe".

The past 15 years have witnessed the development of a whole genre of serious historical scholarship which has established the general outline and many of the specifics of the course of events in the creation of the refugee problem. It builds upon and confirms the conclusions of a few pioneering researchers who, many years earlier, began to establish a narrative which explained how and why nearly three quarters of a million Palestinians left their homes. Much of this new work is by Israeli writers such as Benny Morris, Avi Shlaim, Anita Shapira, Ilan Pappe, Gershon Shafor, Tom Segev and Simha Flapan. Many of them are so-called "revisionists" or "new historians" because they have challenged aspects of the traditional Zionist-Israeli interpretation of events in 1948.[4] Their work, and that of Palestinian scholars such as Walid Khalidi, Nur Masalha, Issa Khalaf and Elie Sanbar,[5] and of others like Erskine Childers, Norman Finkelstein, Michael Palumbo, Janet Abu Lughod and Mary Wilson,[6] have made abundantly clear the causes and course of the process which turned between 700,000 and 750,000 Palestinians into refugees during the fighting of 1947–9.[7]

Needless to say, there is no unanimity among these authors. Some of them were among the first to examine newly opened Israeli, United Nations, Western and Arab archives for the period, archives which still require further careful examination and some of which are not yet accessible to researchers. There are, moreover, significant differences between some of the works cited above over major issues. For example,

Norman Finkelstein is highly critical of Benny Morris for substituting a new myth for the one he helped to demolish.[8] Some authors argue for Arab factionalism and weakness contrasted with the unity and ruthlessness of the Zionist movement and its leadership as crucial factors in what happened. Others stress the continuity of the concept of "transfer" of the Arab population outside Palestine in Zionist thinking as central to explaining what occurred in 1947–9. There remains also a lingering unwillingness on the part of some Israelis and many of their sympathisers to accept any element of this new approach.[9] Nevertheless, there exists today a credible and documented historical picture far more complete than ever before of why the Palestinians left, and of the significance of Israel's role in this process.

But it is not only because many of the facts are becoming known and can no longer be denied by serious scholars that history must be an element in the solution. Rather, it is because the national self-view of the Palestinian people was in such large measure shaped by these traumatic events that any approach which tries to sweep history under the rug will be futile. Very simply, any settlement which in effect denies that gross injustice was done to their entire people in 1948 would require the Palestinians to deny core elements in their own national narrative. With all the allowances necessary when making comparisons between situations which are inherently dissimilar, one might as well ask Israelis to deny the Holocaust, or Americans to deny Pearl Harbor, as to ask Palestinians to deny what they know as *al-Nakba* (the catastrophe).

Thus, whenever this issue is finally addressed, it will be crucial that the outcome involves an acceptance by Israel of its share of responsibility for these events. Such an acceptance should involve some form of official recognition that the deliberate actions of Israel's founding fathers turned more than half of the Palestinian people into refugees between 1947 and 1949, and led to the loss of nearly all of their property. This will not be easy to do, particularly given the fact that, as we have seen, the 1948 War, in which some 6,000 Israelis died, is heroically inscribed in the Israeli national narrative as the War of Independence. It is a seminal event in Israeli history which many older Israelis remember and all have learned about in a sanitised, bowdlerised and falsified nationalist version. For most Israelis, these events, whatever Israel's responsibility for them, were necessary to the creation of a

Jewish state, and by this calculus, the end justifies the means. Acceptance of such responsibility, moreover, flies in the face of decades of strenuous efforts at denial of any responsibility by the Israeli state. These efforts go all the way back to 1948, have powerfully shaped the Israeli national consciousness on this issue and have had a significant impact on Western opinion.[10]

There are two further reasons why it is important that a different approach be followed with the refugee issue than has been taken thus far in the Palestinian–Israeli negotiation process which began at Madrid in 1991. The first is that in any intractable conflict such as this one, real reconciliation can only begin when there has been acceptance of the weight of history. History has been almost totally ignored in the efforts to achieve a Palestinian–Israeli settlement thus far. This is surely part of the reason that reconciliation between the two peoples has not yet started in any meaningful way. Indeed, given the powerful emotional impact of the dispossession and suffering of the Palestinian refugees on Arab public opinion over the past half-century, the absence of an honest effort among Palestinians and Israelis to confront the painful facts of history has seriously hindered reconciliation between Israel and the eight Arab countries with which it is at peace or has commercial or diplomatic relations.

We need only look at other situations where there has been a significant effort to accept the weight of history – whether in the German–Jewish relationship, in Korean–Japanese relations, or in South Africa, for example – to see how important such an initiative is. It is not the German reparations to Israel, nor the compensation to the Koreans, not the awarding of sums of money to victims in South Africa – important though these steps have been – which have made possible the building of bridges over chasms many thought would never be crossed. It is rather that in these cases a beginning has been made to face the truth and confront history – particularly by the side which bears primary responsibility for the outcome. In regard to the most important issue which divides Palestinians and Israelis, that of refugees, such a process has yet to begin.

Flying out of Ben-Gurion Airport a few years ago, just before Yom Kippur (the Day of Atonement) on a Lufthansa flight bound for Frankfurt full of cheerful Israelis, I witnessed a scene which would have been inconceivable immediately after the Holocaust. It represented an example in the most mundane terms of at least the beginnings of a real reconciliation. Although the crimes committed by the Nazis against the Jews were unforgivable and although commerce and travel do not by themselves signify reconciliation – after all, some Palestinians today fly El Al – there was a normality to the scene aboard that Lufthansa flight which indicated the distance which Jews and Germans have come since 1945.

The Holocaust and *al-Nakba* are of course not comparable in any way – if only because of the far greater number of lives affected by the Holocaust, the utterly evil intentionality which drove it, and the sheer monumental scale of the genocide which it encompassed: six million people killed and almost the entirety of European Jewry displaced and dispossessed. While about 750,000 people, half of the Arab population of Palestine, were displaced and dispossessed as a result of the events of 1947–9, most of them survived this ordeal: a total of 13,000 Palestinians died during this conflict, most of them civilians.[11]

But the Holocaust remains our benchmark for man's inhumanity to man, and if it has any universal relevance, it teaches that we should not be allowed to forget or forgive wrongs committed against a whole people. Whatever the possible justifications and the circumstances, in 1948 a wrong was done to the entire Palestinian people. We are still very far from a Palestinian–Israeli reconciliation similar to that between Germans and Jews, or between white and black South Africans, which is based on confronting history and on atonement for this wrong.

The second reason why this approach is necessary in regard to the refugee question is quite a different one: there exists a clear mandate, sanctioned by an international consensus regarding the Palestinian refugees of 1948, which goes back to the earliest phase of the problem. It would be a serious mistake to simply ignore this mandate, as so many other relevant international resolutions (such as those relating to Jerusalem, to Israeli settlements in occupied territories, and even the principle of land for peace embodied in Security Council Resolution 242 of 22 November 1967) have been ignored, either in principle or in practice, in the negotiations thus far between Palestinians and Israelis. As has already been mentioned, the relevant mandate is embodied in General Assembly Resolution 194 (III) of 11 December

1948, which sets forth a clear basis for the settlement of this question. In summary, it calls for permitting those refugees "wishing to return to their homes and live at peace with their neighbors" to do so, while compensation should be paid for the property of those choosing not to return, and for loss of or damage to property" of all refugees.[12] This is a simple formula, and one which was reiterated annually by the General Assembly after 1948.

The implementation of this 50-year-old resolution will not be so simple, partly because Israel has for many decades absolutely rejected this formula. It is worth noting, however, that during the deliberations of the Palestine Conciliation Commission at Lausanne in 1949, Israel did in practice accept negotiations on the basis of this resolution. At one stage, Israel accepted a proposal for the return of the nearly 250,000 Palestinians in the Gaza Strip as part of a territorial exchange, and at another, Israel itself proposed the return of as many as 100,000 refugees.[13] It is clear, nevertheless, that Israel's acceptance of such proposals was no more than tactical: according to Benny Morris, Israeli Foreign Minister Moshe Sharrett put the latter proposal forward on the assumption that "the Lausanne talks would collapse, in which even the '100,000 offer' would never have to be implemented".[14] Although they were initially willing to consider it, in the end both the United States and the Arab states considered this figure far too low. The Arabs ultimately rejected the proposal which, as Sharrett expected, died with the collapse of the Lausanne conference in September 1949.

Among the other reasons why it will be difficult to implement the formula embodied in General Assembly Resolution 194 is that since the Madrid process began, the United States has allowed this and other resolutions to fall into oblivion. It has done so with the blanket declaration that rather than UN resolutions being applicable, questions at issue between Palestinians and Israelis are subject to negotiation between the parties. This is not just a convenient device for the abandonment of long-standing American commitments. It also allows a balance of forces which is overwhelmingly favourable to Israel to play the major role in determining outcomes, rather than international law or the international consensus embodied in UN resolutions. It is imperative that this not be allowed to happen in this case, both because it is essential that the rule of law be upheld and that United Nations resolutions are respected, and because this resolution embodies a modicum of justice. On this issue above all others, justice must be the basis of a settlement if it is to have a chance of being a lasting one.

There are overwhelming practical difficulties in the way of implementing this resolution as well. In most cases, the homes and villages of those who became refugees in 1948 no longer exist, having been either destroyed during and after the fighting of 1947–9, or taken over and absorbed into Israeli population centres. The most comprehensive study of this process, the impressive collective work *All that Remains*, lists a total of 418 Arab villages occupied and depopulated during the 1948 War. Most of them have since been destroyed, with a few repopulated by Israelis.[15] In urban areas not treated in this work, there exists a dwindling stock of formerly Arab housing, much of it now dilapidated, but in virtually every case this has been occupied since 1948 by new Israeli residents – some of them Arabs.

There are therefore practically no empty homes left to which Palestinian refugees could return. As regards those homes located in villages in rural areas where the great majority of Palestinian refugees originated, the eloquent photographs and the village-by-village surveys presented in *All that Remains* show that virtually nothing habitable remains standing today. In that sense, the specific language of Resolution 194 ("refugees wishing to return to their homes") simply cannot be implemented. In any case, these refugees and their descendants today number several times the nearly 750,000 people who were driven from their homes in 1948, and it is therefore impossible even to contemplate their "return" in strictly literal terms.

Moreover, in practical political terms, the return of three million Palestinians to the areas of what is now Israel where they (or their forebears) originally lived would overturn the demographic transformation which made possible the establishment of Israel as a state within a substantial Jewish majority in 1948. It is highly unlikely – some would say completely inconceivable – that this would be acceptable to any Israeli government under any circumstances which can be envisioned. While in moral terms this may not be a powerful argument (it hinges on a highly subjective calculation of what value attaches to the existence of a Jewish state in Palestine, as against the cost which the existence of such a state imposes on the Palestinians), in practical political terms, it certainly is. For where is the political will to come from to persuade a large majority of citizens of a powerful country like Israel to accept something to which they are deeply opposed? It is highly doubtful that the will to do this exists today or that it is likely to exist in the future, amongst the international community.

Even if such a return were acceptable in whole or in part, would Palestinian returnees accept the only possible interpretation of the qualifying language of the same paragraph of this resolution calling them to "live at peace with their neighbors", which is that these returnees accept to live as minority Arab citizens of the Jewish state of Israel and in accordance with its laws? Would not the availability and levels of compensation offered affect directly the numbers of those refugees and their descendants "choosing not to return"? It is clear from these questions that even if the *principles* embodied in Resolution 194 are accepted, there will remain many practical and political difficulties in the way of its implementation.

Why then is it so important that this resolution be the basis for a settlement of this issue? Beyond the importance of upholding the principle of a right to return which has been the bedrock of the international consensus on this issue for several decades, it is important because it constitutes a recognition *in principle* of the wrong done not only to individual Palestinians, but also to the entire Palestinian people five decades ago. Given the great practical and political difficulties just noted in the way of implementation of the provisions relating to return in General Assembly Resolution 194 (III), such a recognition in principle is all the more important.

This recognition must come from Israel, but it should also come from the world community. The Palestinian people became refugees and "lost" their country as a result of many factors. In the first place, these include the actions of their Israeli opponents. But they include as well the actions of other states, and their own massive political failures in the decades preceding 1948. The latter is a topic many Palestinians have been reluctant to discuss in the past, both because of the still-painful wounds which it opens up and because it appears to weaken the argument for Israel's sole responsibility for the events of 1948.[16]

But these things also happened in some measure because of the collective decisions and actions of the international community. These included the extension of a League of Nations Mandate for Palestine to Britain in 1922, which called explicitly (the text of the Balfour Declaration was repeated almost verbatim in the text of the Mandate for

Palestine) for the establishment of a Jewish national home in a country with a 90 per cent Arab majority. How this was to be done without violence to the rights of the Palestinians was never satisfactorily explained by the League of Nations, the British, the Zionists, or anyone else.[17]

Twenty-five years later, in Resolution 181, the United Nations General Assembly called for the partition of Palestine. At this point the country had a 66 per cent Arab majority, while Jews owned only seven per cent of its land. The partition plan called for dividing Palestine into an Arab and a Jewish state, with the latter comprising 56 per cent of the country, including nearly all its fertile land. These fateful actions taken by the international community from 1922 until 1947 guaranteed decades of bitter and unremitting conflict in Palestine, conflict which has not yet ended. As a result, the international community shares in some degree the responsibility for the predictable outcome of its own actions. It should therefore shoulder part of the moral and material obligations which must be assumed if there is to be a final resolution of this problem.

That responsibility could finally be discharged as part of a permanent, just and comprehensive resolution of the question of Palestine if the solution to the refugee problem embodies recognition of a wrong done, both to individual Palestinians and to the Palestinians as a people, via acceptance of the principle of return or compensation of all those who became refugees in 1948 and their descendants. It is worth noting that the Palestine Liberation Organisation has accepted the limitation of what it formerly claimed as an unrestricted right of return for all refugees to the principle of return *or* compensation, in accordance with relevant United Nations resolutions.[18]

Such a permanent resolution of the refugee problem should include – as a separate item – the unrestricted return to the West Bank and Gaza Strip of all those persons displaced after the 1967 War. This process should already have been well under way, according to the Oslo Accords of 1993, but it has been obstructed by Israel for the past five years. This separate but related problem should in principle be solvable with a minimum of disruption or obstacle, since both Israel and the Palestinians agreed on the principle of the return "of persons displaced from the West Bank and Gaza Strip in 1967" in Article XII of the Oslo Accords, signed in Washington in September 1993.[19]

As we have seen, there will be many practical difficulties in the way of the return of 1948 refugees. Clearly refugees cannot return to homes which no longer exist; nor can they return at all unless Israeli opposition is overcome. There is also the possibility that some may no longer desire to do so, or may prefer to obtain restitution for their losses. But as many 1948 refugees and their descendants as possible should have the option of return; all deserve recognition of the suffering they have undergone as a result of their being made refugees and all deserve restitution for their material losses and compensation for their suffering, whether or not they choose, or are able, to return.

In conclusion, what is the best outcome that those made refugees in 1948 and their descendants can look forward to today, 50 years after their dispossession? The following are five elements of a solution which, while not fully or absolutely just, embodies an attempt to weigh justice for those who have been victims of injustice for half a century against the formidable practical and political difficulties sketched out above, and the potential for doing injustice to others.

1. The first element is that there must be a formal recognition of Israel's primary responsibility for the creation of the Palestinian refugee problem in 1948. This might come about in the context of the conclusions of a truth and justice commission or a truth and reconciliation commission which, if convened in time, might still be able to collect testimony from a few of the refugees themselves and some of those who contributed to making them refugees. The South African example, and several from Latin America, show what a powerful cathartic effect such testimony can have.

Establishment of such a commission could not and would not be the impartial act of some neutral body, or one carried out by an international agency; rather it would have to be the result of a joint Palestinian–Israeli decision. Taking such a decision would necessarily involve a willingness on the part of Israeli leaders to accept responsibility for the fact that Israel was in some measure built on the ruins of Arab Palestine in 1948. This will be extremely difficult for any Israeli politician to do, even at such a temporal remove from the events. It is nevertheless essential if the page of 1948 is to be turned by the Palestinians and their grievance finally put to rest.

Moreover, for the actions of such a commission to be effective, this recognition must ultimately go well beyond statements by Israeli politicians and the deliberations of a truth commission. It must also extend to the powerful means of socialisation under the direct control of the Israeli state. These include history text books, museums, the identification and preservation of historical sites all over the country,[20] and indoctrination within the military. They also include Israel's powerful international propaganda apparatus, which, over the past half-century, has convinced so many abroad of Israel's complete innocence as regards the creation of the Palestinian refugee problem.

2. Secondly, it must be accepted that all Palestinian refugees and their descendants have a right to return to their homes *in principle*, although the modalities of such a return are necessarily subject to negotiation. *In practice*, many of them will be unable to exercise this right, whether as a result of Israel's refusal to allow all of them to do so, or of the disappearance of their homes and villages, or because of the sheer number of people involved. However, it should be accepted in principle that as many refugees as possible should be allowed to return to what is now Israel.

Given that such a return would take place within the context of a final, comprehensive, mutually agreeable resolution of the Palestinian–Israeli conflict and, hopefully, the comprehensive resolution of all aspects of the Arab–Israeli conflict, the pretext that such returnees would form a potential fifth column in a situation of war would at least be significantly undermined. It cannot be stressed strongly enough that there is a dialectical process at work here: resolution of the refugee issue through Israel taking a generous stand on refugee return would go a long way towards alleviating negative attitudes towards Israel in the Arab world, and make a comprehensive and lasting peace more likely. At the same time, the return of any Palestinians to homes inside Israel would only be conceivable in a situation of comprehensive Arab–Israeli peace, to which such a return would contribute measurably.

There remains one more obstacle: the continuing desire of many, perhaps most, Israelis for Israel to be as purely Jewish as possible. The revisionist histories of 1948 show that this desire was perhaps the primary factor in causing Israel's leaders to advocate, and in many areas to instigate, the departure of the largest possible number of

Palestinians in the first place. While such attitudes survive and indeed thrive among the Israeli public, Israel has existed for 50 years with a large Palestinian minority – now numbering about a million – which in fact has been remarkably well integrated, particularly considering the systematic discrimination to which it was subjected. The return of more Palestinians – at least in the numbers which are likely to be acceptable to Israel – would only marginally increase the size of this minority. It is true, however, that it might nevertheless exacerbate ongoing debates about the nature of the Israeli polity.

Should the principle of the return of a number of Palestinian refugees be accepted, some might be able to do so via a process of family reunification for those Palestinians whose home villages still exist inside Israel (about 100 such Arab villages still exist), who have family living there and who are willing to become law-abiding citizens of the State of Israel. It should be possible under these circumstances to secure the regulated entry of tens of thousands of people per year over several years.

In 1949, a small and fragile Israeli state offered to accept family reunification for up to 100,000 Palestinian refugees, or about 15 per cent of the total. There is no reason why today an Israel at peace with its neighbours and bestriding the region like an economic and strategic colossus could not make a similar gesture. It could do this, for example, by accepting the return of 15 per cent of the approximately three million refugees and their descendants, some 450,000 people. It is particularly galling for Palestinians suffering persecution and statelessness within sight of their ancestral homes to accept that none of them can ever return to Palestine, while unlimited numbers of Jewish victims of persecution from much farther afield are welcome. Such a proposal would address directly these feelings of resentment.

3. A third element of a lasting resolution of this issue is the provision of reparations for all those who choose not to return or are not allowed to do so, and compensation for all those who lost property in 1948. Property losses alone, according to a detailed estimation by Atef Kubrusi, range from $92 billion to $147 billion at 1984 prices, when the study was done.[21] Using an entirely different approach to calculate reparations, $30,000 per person for an arbitrarily chosen figure of three million eligible refugees and their descendants yields a figure of $90 billion. Lest this seem like a great deal of money, we

should recall that $90 billion amounts to less than seven years' worth of US transfers to Israel in the form of grants, loans and guarantees.[22]

It must be added that if compensation for property lost is the basis for part of this restitution, as is indicated by General Assembly Resolution 194, and as it was for part of the German reparations to Israel, then Jews who left or were forced to leave Arab countries during or after the 1947–9 War also have a legitimate claim. In spite of the many important dissimilarities in the two situations (the Palestinians had nothing to do with the departure of Jews from Arab countries; Jews coming to Israel were "returning" to their ancestral homeland, and did so voluntarily, according to the Zionist understanding of these events; and several Arab countries, such as Morocco, have accepted the principle of the return of any Jews who desire to do so), these property claims are valid, and should certainly also be dealt with as part of such a comprehensive Arab-Israeli settlement.

It is important to stress that although the two matters are necessarily connected, the question of reparations for property of Jewish citizens who left the Arab countries is exclusively a matter for the Arab states and Israel to resolve bilaterally or multilaterally, rather than for Palestinian–Israeli negotiations. Moreover, these Jewish populations came to Israel under quite different circumstances from a number of Arab countries (Morocco, Algeria, Tunisia, Libya, Egypt, Syria, Lebanon, Yemen and Iraq), all of which have to be involved in such a negotiation, while many Arab Jews did not end up in Israel.

4. A fourth element is the right to live in the Palestinian state-to-be and to carry its passport. This right was already putatively extended to all Palestinians by the 1988 Palestinian Declaration of Independence, which stated that the state of Palestine was the state of all the Palestinians. The right to live in this state – the collective right of return to Palestine, as it were – should not be subject to negotiation with Israel or any other power: it would be a sovereign right of any independent Palestinian state, whenever such a state is established. However, this "right" will in practice necessarily be restricted by the new country's absorptive capacity, which would be limited, but which could be increased by determined efforts by the Palestinian public and private sectors and by international donors.

Whether efforts to expand the economic capacity of the country will in fact be exerted will be one of the great tests of the Palestinian

Authority. This should be a primary concern of all Palestinians in holding this Authority to account for its actions. However, we should not be subjected to ahistorical comparisons with the remarkable achievement of Israel, which nearly doubled its Jewish population within little more than two years of its establishment by taking in approximately 600,000 Jewish refugees.[23] It must be remembered that in 1948–9, Israel had the benefit of the huge stock of housing, and of agricultural, industrial and other forms of capital, seized from more than 700,000 Palestinians whom the Israeli state had just made refugees. The Palestinian Authority, by way of contrast, starts its life with an economy drained of capital by 30 years of occupation.

Recalling the major differences between these two dissimilar situations should not cause us to refrain from harsh criticism of the Palestinian Authority, should it fail to make the necessary efforts to build up the economic absorptive capacity of Palestine as it has failed to do during its brief existence thus far. Recalling these differences, however, should spare us undeserved comparisons based on ignoring the historical realities between the Israeli situation in 1948 and that of the Palestinians today.

The Palestinian leadership today can certainly be faulted for lacking utterly the single-minded drive to "ingather the exiles" exhibited by the Israeli state-builders of the early years of Israel's existence. Nevertheless, the fundamental differences between the capabilities of a sovereign Israeli state backed by the US and USSR from its inception, and a Palestinian Authority without sovereignty, and indeed with little land and very little authority, should never be lost sight of.

5. Finally, there remain two groups whose situation requires special attention. These are the Palestinian refugees in Jordan and those in Lebanon – a few points relating to those in Lebanon apply to those in Syria as well. Each group has special requirements if this problem is to be resolved in terms of attainable justice.

Palestinians in Jordan, beyond any of those who choose to return to the areas under the control of the Palestinian Authority today, or the Palestinian state tomorrow, and beyond any reparations they may receive, require a final and equitable resolution of their legal and national status as both Palestinians and Jordanians. This can only come about as a result of a constitutional arrangement freely arrived at between democratically elected governments in Jordan and Palestine.

One solution which might be envisaged in Jordan would involve offering Palestinians who choose to remain in that country a choice of either full rights of citizenship as Jordanians, or alternatively somewhat more limited rights as citizens of the Palestinian component of a Jordanian–Palestinian confederation. Such an arrangement, or another acceptable to a majority of both Palestinians and Jordanians, will hopefully be possible in the not too distant future. As with the Palestinian right of return to the Palestinian state, this question involves exclusively Palestinian (and Jordanian) sovereign rights, which are exclusively a matter for bilateral consideration and which should not be the subject of negotiations with Israel or any other third party.

As far as Lebanon is concerned, a resolution of the status of Palestinians is extremely urgent, both because of the precarious economic, social and political situation of the Palestinian population there, and its direct impact on the internal Lebanese equilibrium, which is an urgent item on the country's political agenda. In Lebanon there is no option for a constitutional arrangement such as might be envisaged in Jordan, since there is no likelihood of Lebanon granting most Palestinians full rights of citizenship, which is an option unacceptable to all of the country's major political forces and probably to most Palestinians.

If the provisions mentioned under 1 to 5 above come into force, some Palestinians in Lebanon (as well as others in Syria) may leave for the Palestinian state with their newly acquired rights and their reparations; some may be allowed to choose to return to their original home villages in Galilee as Israeli citizens or otherwise to return to Israel; and many will use their new Palestinian passports to travel abroad in search of work. Nevertheless, many in both Lebanon and Syria will choose to stay where they are, or will have no choice but to do so. The status of those who remain in Lebanon is therefore in urgent need of revision, which will at the very least involve their receiving Palestinian passports and nationality,[24] and being granted permanent resident status and the right to work, together with other special rights in Lebanon although not including rights of citizenship. This will involve long and difficult Palestinian–Lebanese negotiations.

Of all the Palestinian refugee communities, the plight of those in Lebanon is the cruellest of all. These people have suffered prodigiously for the Palestinian cause since the 1960s, living in harsh conditions between 1948 and 1968 and again since 1982. They do not have the extensive options for economic and social integration into the host society enjoyed by Palestinians in Jordan and Syria. While important aspects of this problem will have to be resolved in negotiations with Israel, and via Israel's accepting some share of its responsibility for a solution, in part this is a problem for Palestinians and Lebanese to solve amongst themselves. It will be yet another test of the performance of the Palestinian Authority and of the PLO. In particular, it will be a test of whether the latter is willing and able to shoulder its responsibility to represent *all* the Palestinian people, and to begin a serious negotiation of this matter with the Lebanese government, or whether instead it will be reduced to being the bargaining agent only for the Palestinians living in the West Bank and Gaza Strip.

We have seen from the unsatisfactory results of the Madrid–Washington–Oslo negotiating process over more than six years just how fragile is a framework erected on a weak foundation. Without grounding itself in history, without confronting the truth, without reference to international legitimacy and the most elementary principles of justice, such a framework cannot survive for long. Unfortunately, this description characterises the entire Palestinian–Israeli negotiating process as it has unfolded so far. This has been due to a combination of factors, including the callous pragmatism of US policy-makers, a balance of forces massively favourable to Israel (whose leaders would prefer to ignore both history and international legitimacy) and profound weaknesses in Palestinian negotiating performance from Oslo onwards.

The resolution of the Palestinian refugee issue must avoid all of these pitfalls and at the same time be grounded in the difficult process of the acceptance of the truth about the past and the present. This includes both the truth about what happened in 1948 and the truth about what is attainable 50 years later. The latter is essential because, the facts of power being what they are, it is highly unlikely that complete or absolute justice will be done in this case in the near future. Perhaps it can never be done.

Working from the South African model, it is clear that we need truth, but we also need justice and, finally, reconciliation. We need truth so that the harm done in 1948 can be acknowledged by all concerned, which means facing history honestly, acceptance of responsibility by those responsible or their successors, and solemn atonement for what was done 50 years ago. We need truth also in order to clarify the limits of what can be done to right that injustice without causing further harm. Once these limits have been established, it should be possible to work towards attainable justice and therefore towards reconciliation. This is essential, because our ultimate objective should be to end this conflict for good, which can only occur via true reconciliation, based on truth and justice.

NOTES

1 Cited in Rona Gabbay, *A Political Study of the Arab–Jewish Conflict: The Arab Refugee Problem* (Geneva: Droz, 1959), p. 110.
2 *US Middle East Policy and the Peace Process: Report of an Independent Task Force* (New York: Council on Foreign Relations, 1997), p. 4.
3 This is Resolution No. 194 (III) of 11 December 1948. The key operative paragraph is 11. George Tomeh (ed.), *United Nations Resolutions on Palestine and the Arab–Israeli Conflict*, vol. 1, 1947–1974 (Washington DC: Institute for Palestine Studies, 1988), pp. 15–17.
4 Tom Segev, *1949: The First Israelis* (New York: Free Press, 1986); Simha Flapan, *The Birth of Israel: Myth and Reality* (New York: Pantheon, 1987); Benny Morris, *The Birth of the Palestinian Refugee Problem, 1947–1949* (Cambridge: Cambridge University Press, 1988) and *1949 and After: Israel and the Palestinians* (Oxford: Clarendon Press, 1990); Avi Shlaim, *Collusion across the Jordan: King Abdullah, the Zionist Movement and the Partition of Palestine* (New York: Columbia University Press, 1988); Gershon Shafir, *Land, Labor and the Origins of the Israeli–Palestinian Conflict 1882–1914* (Cambridge: Cambridge University Press, 1989); Anita Shapira, *Land and Power: The Zionist Resort to Force, 1881–1948* (Oxford: Oxford University Press, 1992); Ilan Pappe, *The Making of the Arab–Israeli Conflict, 1947–1951*, rev. edn (London: I. B. Tauris, 1994).
5 Walid Khalidi (ed.), *All that Remains: The Palestinian Villages Occupied and Depopulated by Israel in 1948* (Washington DC: Institute for Palestine Studies, 1992); "The Arab Perspective" in W. R. Louis and R. Stookey (eds.), *The End of the Palestine Mandate* (Austin: University of Texas Press, 1986), pp. 104–36; " 'Plan Dalet': The Zionist Master Plan for the Conquest of Palestine", *Middle East Forum*, 37, 9 (November 1961), pp. 22–8; "The Fall of Haifa", *Middle East Forum*, 35, 10 (December 1959), pp. 22–32; "Why Did the Palestinians Leave?", *Middle East Forum*, 34, 6 (July 1959), pp. 21–4; Nur Masalha, *Expulsion of the Palestinians: The Concept of "Transfer" in Zionist Political Thought, 1882–1948* (Washington DC: Institute for Palestine Studies, 1992); Issa Khalaf, *Politics in Palestine: Arab Factionalism and Social Disintegration, 1939–1948* (Albany: State University of New York Press, 1991); Elias Sanbar, *Palestine, 1948: L'expulsion* (Paris: Livres de la Revue d'Etudes Palestiniennes, 1984).

6 Erskine Childers, "The Other Exodus", *The Spectator*, no. 6933 (12 May, 1961), 672–5, and "The Wordless Wish: From Citizens to Refugees" in Ibrahim Abu-Lughod (ed.), *The Transformation of Palestine* (Evanston, Ill.: Northwestern University Press, 1971), pp. 165–202; Norman Finkelstein, *Image and Reality of the Israel–Palestine Conflict* (London: Verso, 1995), pp. 51–87; Michael Palumbo, *The Palestinian Catastrophe: The 1948 Expulsion of a People from their Homeland* (London: Faber and Faber, 1987); Janet Abu-Lughod, "The Demographic Transformation of Palestine" in I. Abu-Lughod, *Transformation of Palestine*, pp. 139–64; Mary Wilson, *King Abdullah, Britain and the Making of Jordan* (Cambridge: Cambridge University Press, 1987).

7 There is no accurate count of the number of Palestinians who became refugees in 1947–9. The Technical Committee on Refugees of the Palestine Conciliation Commission, meeting in Lausanne in August 1949, reported that they totalled 711,000 (Benny Morris, *The Birth of the Palestinian Refugee Problem*, p. 284). Nur Masalha, *Expulsion of the Palestinians*, pp. 175, 207, gives figures of 750,000 and 730,000. Using perhaps the most careful methodology, the compilers of *All that Remains*, Appendix III, p. 582, estimate the number "conservatively" at between 714,150 and 744,150.

8 Chapter 3 of Finkelstein, *Image and Reality*, pp. 51–87, is devoted to a meticulous examination of how the evidence which Morris has marshalled justifies conclusions far more sweeping than those he reaches, and does not support some of his arguments.

9 The most notable work presenting this unreconstructed view is Ephraim Karsh, *The Fabricating of Israeli History: The "New Historians"* (London: Frank Cass, 1997). For a devastating critique of this book, see Ian Lustick's review essay, "Israeli History: Who is Fabricating What?" in *Survival*, September 1997, pp. 156–66. Another prominent defender of the traditional position is Shabatai Teveth, the semi-official biographer (some would say hagiographer) of David Ben-Gurion. See his *Ben Gurion and the Palestinian Arabs: From Peace to War* (Oxford: Oxford University Press, 1985) for a statement of his views which have changed little in spite of the partial opening of the Israeli archives and the large number of new publications on the subject over the past decade and a half.

10 The key element in this web of falsehood and denial was the "their leaders told them to leave" myth, assiduously propagated by Israeli diplomacy from the very beginning, and thereafter picked up and propagated by Israeli sympathisers in the West. The first to dispute this powerful canard were Walid Khalidi and Erskine Childers in the articles in *Middle East Forum* and *The Spectator* published from 1959 to 1961 cited in notes 6 and 7 above. Childers' article sparked a lengthy exchange in the columns of *The Spectator* from May to August 1961. This entire myth has now been totally discredited.

11 These figures are the result of the research of 'Arif al-'Arif, *al-Nakba* (6 vols., Beirut and Sidon: al-Maktaba al-'Asriyya, 1956–60), vol. 5, pp. 1047–53.

12 Tomeh (ed.), *United Nations Resolutions*, pp. 15–17.

13 Morris, *The Birth of the Palestinian Refugee Problem*, pp. 266–85.

14 Ibid., p. 282.

15 Khalidi, *All that Remains*, p. xx.

16 In recent years there has been less reluctance on the part of Palestinians to broach the theme of Palestinian failure, bespeaking the growing maturity of Palestinian historiography. Works reflecting this new frankness include Issa Khalaf, *Politics in Palestine: Arab Factionalism and Social Disruption, 1939–1948* (New York: State University of Albany Press, 1991) which examines various causes of Palestinian failure; Philip Mattar, *The Mufti of Jerusalem: Al-Hajj Amin al-Husayni and the Palestinian National Movement* (New York: Columbia University Press, 1988), who calls the Mufti's policies "a failure" which "contributed to the dispossession of the Palestinian people"; and R. Khalidi, *Palestinian Identity: The Construction of Modern National Consciousness* (New York: Columbia University Press, 1997), whose final chapter devotes its concluding section (pp. 186–209) to the Palestinian proclivity for the "portrayal of failure as triumph".

17 For an insight into the cynical mentality which governed British thinking at this time, see the memo on Syria, Palestine and Mesopotamia by Foreign Secretary Arthur James Balfour, dated 11 August 1919, reproduced in J. C. Hurewitz (ed.), *The Middle East and North Africa: A Documentary Record*, 2nd edn (New Haven: Yale University Press, 1979), vol. 2, pp. 184–91, especially pp. 188–9 dealing with Palestine.

18 For details on the evolution of the PLO position on the right of return, see R. Khalidi, "Observations on the Right of Return", *Journal of Palestine Studies*, XXI, 2 (Winter 1992), pp. 29–40, especially pp. 32–6.

19 For details, see Salim Tamari, *Palestinian Refugee Negotiations: From Madrid to Oslo II*, Institute for Palestine Studies Final Status Issues Paper (Washington: Institute for Palestine Studies, 1996).

20 Examples would include the sites of Deir Yassin and Qastal, the former the scene of a massacre in which 254 Palestinian civilians perished, and the latter the focus of a decisive battle in which the Palestinian regional commander, 'Abd al-Qadir al-Husayni, died in battle. These two events took place within days of one another in April 1948, and played decisive roles in the exodus of Palestinians from villages in the area west of Jerusalem.

21 Atef Kubursi, "An Economic Assessment of Total Palestinian Losses" in Sami Hadawi, *Palestinian Rights and Losses in 1948: A Comprehensive Assessment* (London: Saqi Books, 1988), pp. 115–89.

22 US Ambassador to Israel Martin Indyk has stated that the total of "US loans, grants and loan guarantees" to Israel came to $13 billion annually, *Wall Street Journal*, National Edition, 6 July 1997, p. 5A.

23 This is well described in Segev, *1949: The First Israelis*, pp. 95 ff.

24 In late 1997 there were unconfirmed press reports that Syria had begun to recognise passports issued by the Palestinian Authority (although it was not clear whether Palestinians with Syrian refugee identity documents would be allowed to hold such passports). If confirmed, this would mean that one element of this problem might be on the way to resolution for Palestinians in Syria, and possibly in Lebanon.

Concluding Vision:
A Return to Israel/Palestine?

Ghada Karmi

As the foregoing papers demonstrate, there is an impasse at the heart of the Palestinian refugee problem which, on present evidence, will make it insuperably difficult to resolve. Very simply, this impasse lies in the utter incompatibility in the positions of the two protagonists. On the one hand, the Palestinians abide by the rights of their case in international law and basic justice and demand a return to their homeland and full compensation for their losses; and on the other, Israel is adamant in rejecting outright both these propositions. Since Israel is by far the stronger party, its wishes have hitherto taken precedence over the Palestinian claims. Clearly, however, there can be no resolution to the problem unless this impasse is addressed.

It is currently envisaged that the solution to the refugee issue will come through final status negotiations in the Oslo process. At the same time, European and American initiatives have appeared aiming at assisting this process by putting forward ideas on a refugee "return" to a future Palestinian state; and since the state will not be able to accommodate all the refugees, there are plans to settle them in the Arab countries of their present residence and also outside the Arab region. Compensation would be provided through an international fund to assist the host countries in this task. It is not clear at the moment if any other form of compensation for individual or collective Palestinian losses is envisaged.

A solution of this kind is based on certain premises: that a Palestinian state capable of absorbing the refugees will indeed come into being; and that the refugees themselves and the Palestinians at large will be satisfied with such an outcome after 50 years of displacement, suffering and adherence to their cause. It seems to me that neither of these assumptions can be taken for granted and they will need careful examination.

If we take the first premise, that of the creation of a Palestinian state at the termination of the Oslo agreement, we see that there are considerable obstacles in the way of such an outcome. In the first place, the Oslo agreement nowhere provided for such a result; indeed, one of the striking aspects of this agreement is that it proposes no end result at all beyond the negotiation of troop redeployments and the obligation to discuss other issues. And in the second place, there must now be considerable doubts about its survival. It is clear that, irrespective of whether one supported it or not, the agreement has run into serious difficulties and may no longer be viable. A number of its provisions, as agreed between the Palestinians and the previous Israeli government, have not yet been fulfilled by the present government. The most important of these is the delay to the permanent status negotiations and the changes taking place in the Palestinian territories ahead of these negotiations.

It will be recalled that the Oslo agreement had been structured on the basis of two stages, a so-called interim or transitional period of five years, leading to a final phase when a permanent settlement would be drawn up between the parties.[1] The agreement had stipulated that final status talks (in which the refugee issue is to be discussed) would start no later than the beginning of the third year after it was signed, that is by January 1997. Not only have the talks not started, but Israel's Prime Minister has put forward an alternative proposal – side-stepping the interim terms altogether and proceeding directly to the permanent settlement, to be decided in a six- to nine-month phase of intensive negotiations between the two sides.[2]

Meanwhile, the timetable on troop development from Palestinian territory has been delayed. The Oslo agreement had stated that the final settlement would be based on Security Council Resolutions 242 and 338. These resolutions stress the obligation of Israel to withdraw from territories occupied in the war of 1967, including the West Bank and Gaza. In accordance with this idea, a timetable for the redeployment of Israeli forces from these areas was drawn up with the last Israeli government and also with the present one under the Hebron agreement. However, after the partial Israeli withdrawal from

Hebron in January 1997, no further redeployment of troops has taken place. On this evidence it may be said that the Oslo agreement as it was drawn up in 1993, and in subsequent agreements before the election of the present Israeli government in May 1996, is now suspended, if not defunct.

Despite this, the idea of a separate Palestinian state, existing "alongside Israel", continues to be envisaged, and not just by Palestinians. According to some commentators there is widespread, if tacit, acceptance of the idea even in Israel.[3] Although there has never been any official Israeli endorsement of a Palestine state, there is a feeling of resignation towards this as a probable outcome. The hardline Israeli Foreign Minister Ariel Sharon, was quoted on 25 November 1997 as saying that he recognised "with deep regret" that giving the Palestinians an entity of their own would lead inevitably to the establishment of a Palestinian state.

Of course the Palestinian state idea preceded Oslo by two decades. But it has never enjoyed such credence since it was first raised in 1974, when the Palestine National Council (PNC) voted at its 12th meeting to establish a Palestinian "authority" on any liberated part of the Palestinian homeland. In the later 1970s this decision was defined to further mean that a state should be set up on the liberated lands. Ever since then, the Palestinian leadership has consistently aimed for an independent state, to be set up in the West Bank and Gaza with East Jerusalem as its capital.

After the Oslo Accords were signed in 1993, this position was crystallised and found support, both tacit and overt, from the Arab world and the international community – with the exception of Israel and the US. Although the exact boundaries of the proposed state have not been defined, even by the Palestinians, and international support has not expressed itself in terms of square metres of land which might constitute the new state, the idea of such an entity "alongside Israel" has taken firm hold. And, according to some commentators, there is widespread if tacit acceptance of the idea, even in Israel.[4]

Today, the idea of two states so dominates discourse about the final outcome of the peace process as to exclude all other possibilities. The unspoken assumption is that it is this potential state which will repatriate at least a proportion of the refugees and thus play the major role in solving the problem. Yet it is by no means certain that a

Palestinian state will come into being. There are considerable logistical obstacles in the way of setting up a Palestinian state, which a glance at the latest map of the occupied territories can illustrate. This shows a West Bank pock-marked by Jewish settlements encircling Palestinian towns and separating them from each other, criss-crossed by so-called "by-pass" roads built for the exclusive use of Israelis and breaking up Palestinian territory even more. Sharing the territory of the West Bank and Gaza with the Palestinians are 160,000 Jews living in over 14 urban and 82 rural settlements. In addition to these are 11 settlements in and around East Jerusalem, giving this part of the city a Jewish population of 200,000. When the latest settlement at Jabal Abu Ghoneim (Har Homa) is built to the south of Jerusalem, the separation between Jerusalem and the West Bank will be complete. The map thus shows no territorial continuity between the Palestinian areas in the West Bank, which are cut off from each other, from Gaza, and from Jerusalem.

If the settlements remain, then any projected Palestinian state would have no meaningful territory on which to become established. The problem is further complicated by the lack of natural resources from which the Palestinian areas currently suffer. One of the effects of 30 years of Israeli occupation has been a transfer of resources from the Palestinian inhabitants to the settlers. Thus, Meron Benvenisti, the ex-Deputy Mayor of Jerusalem and an expert on the West Bank, calculated in 1989 that 90 per cent of its cultivable land and 75 per cent of its water had been switched to the settlers and beyond them to Israel.[5] Since the Palestinian economy is heavily dependent on agriculture (in 1991 it accounted for 35 per cent of the West Bank Gaza's GDP, as compared with 2 per cent for Israel), this depletion of land and water is extremely serious. To make matters worse, there has been a significant lack of investment in the infrastructure of the West Bank and Gaza during the years of Israeli occupation. Sara Roy, who undertook a detailed study of Gaza's economy in 1995, has described the impact of Israel's occupation of the Strip as a deliberate process of "de-development".[6]

Unskilled labour in Israel consequently became a major economic activity for Palestinians from Gaza and the rest of the occupied territories. In 1990, nearly 35 per cent of the Palestinian labour force was working in Israel. Due to these factors, the already weakened

Palestinian economy became heavily dependent on Israel. Since 1993, the economic situation in the Palestinian territories has deteriorated further as a result of the Israeli policy of sealing off Gaza and the West Bank and the importation of foreign labour into Israel. The Palestinian areas are thus disadvantaged by high unemployment (at least 50 per cent in Gaza, 20 per cent in the West Bank), imposed trade restrictions, an undeveloped industrial base and poor natural resources. Any Palestinian state set up on this basis is obviously not viable and could only survive with the infusion of billions of dollars' worth of aid.

A different approach would be needed in order to change this situation – for example, the lifting of border closures and a willingness to share resources equitably – but there is little in the current Israeli government's plans which is encouraging in this regard. It has instituted a vigorous programme of settlement expansion with a target to settle 500,000 Jews in the Palestinian territories by the turn of the century, and Palestinian land is still being expropriated for this purpose. The closures are still in place, as are widespread restrictions on the movement of goods from and between the Palestinian towns and villages. Such a situation makes meaningful financial investment and effective trade in the Palestinian areas virtually impossible and further retards the chances of improving the Palestinian economy.

Palestinian hopes of independence from Israel suffered a further blow when at the end of May 1997, Israel's Prime Minister Binyamin Netanyahu set out his vision for the final settlement, as revealed in a leaked report to the Israeli press.[7] According to this, Israel would keep most of the land and control all the resources. East Jerusalem would remain part of Israel's "united capital" for ever. All Israeli settlements and their connecting roads would remain, leaving about 40 per cent of the West Bank and 60 per cent of Gaza for the Palestinians. In the West Bank, there would be three main Palestinian cantons, around Nablus, Hebron and Jericho, not connected with each other or with Gaza. The Jordan Valley would remain under Israeli control. Other plans speak of Israel retaining 75 per cent of the West Bank and giving its Palestinian inhabitants the choice of staying under Israeli sovereignty or moving to the Palestinian areas.[8]

At the same time, there is an alternative plan, known as the Beilin–Abu Mazen plan, so called because it was drawn up secretly by the previous Labour Foreign Minister, Yossi Beilin, and the Palestinian leader Abu Mazen (Mahmoud Abbas) in 1995.[9] Under this plan, about 90 per cent of the West Bank, including the Jordan Valley, would be returned to the Palestinians and Israel would annex the areas around Jerusalem which include the largest settlements. The Palestinian state which results from this plan will be demilitarised and divided into non-contiguous areas. Palestinian refugees may return to this state, but not elsewhere in former Palestine. The existence of a Beilin–Abu Mazen plan has been denied by the Palestinian Authority, but no one seriously doubts that there were such discussions.

Although the plan cedes more land to the Palestinians, it shares with Netanyahu's proposal the same fundamental problem, which is that they both make the idea of a Palestinian state untenable. That is, without a total removal of the settlements and an Israeli withdrawal from East Jerusalem, the formula hitherto put forward – for a Palestinian state to be set up in the whole of the West Bank and Gaza up to the 1967 borders, with East Jerusalem as its capital – simply cannot occur. In order to realise the aim of the two states, one would have to postulate either an Israeli renunciation of the settlements and East Jerusalem, or an external force willing to pressurise Israel into doing so. Neither of these options is currently on offer – and indeed they were not on offer under the previous Israeli government. In fact, the practical difficulties of evacuating all the settlers and disengaging from the West Bank, in terms of security, water and infrastructure, would be so formidable as to make an Israeli government of any persuasion unwilling to do it.

For these reasons, a Palestinian state as envisaged is not feasible, and the situation on the ground makes even a physical separation of the two peoples hard to achieve. Netanyahu himself has recognised this situation and has concluded that an independent Palestinian state is untenable for that reason alone.[10] Given these circumstances, it seems reasonable to seek a solution other than the two-state idea.

If it is not possible to have two states in that area, then the option of one state containing both peoples would seem the obvious alternative. There is nothing novel about this suggestion; on the Palestinian side the advocacy of a single-state solution goes back nearly 30 years. The proposal to create what was then called a secular democratic state in Palestine was first propounded in 1969 by the left-wing PLO faction, the Popular Democratic Front for the Liberation of Palestine (PDFLP) and formally adopted in the modified version of a "democratic state of Palestine" by the 6th PNC meeting in the same year.[11] This was described as a state in all of historic Palestine wherein Muslims, Christians and Jews would enjoy the same rights, free from religious and sectarian discrimination, with Hebrew and Arabic as the official languages. The intention at the time was not only to offer liberation for the Palestinians, but for the Jews as well, whom the PLO saw as condemned by Zionism to live in the perpetual insecurity of a Jewish state.[12]

With a few exceptions, this proposal met with rejection on both sides. The Israelis considered it quite simply a recipe for their destruction, and most Palestinians thought it an unacceptable concession to the enemy, worrying that in such a state, the more technologically advanced Jews would dominate. After the mid-1970s the idea was never followed through by either side and it was quietly dropped after 1974, as the option of a West Bank state began to unfold. In recent times, and faced by the current political impasse, the idea of one state for the two peoples has begun to resurface among a small number of left-wing Israelis and Palestinians, albeit from varying perspectives and for different motives.[13] The debate centres on what form this state should take, whether bi-national or secular or democratic.

Bi-nationalism is the preferred solution amongst the Israelis. This is not a new idea in Israeli thinking. During the 1930s and 1940s, European intellectual Zionists like Martin Buber, Judah Magnes and Arthur Ruppin, were much interested in creating a bi-national state in Palestine in which both communities could live together. A number of small Jewish groups based on this idea grew up in Palestine during the 1920s and 1930s, the best known of which was Brit Shalom.[14] A few Palestinians agreed with the bi-national idea because they thought it could be a way of halting Zionist ambitions towards creating a Jewish state in Palestine.[15] But the vast majority were opposed to bi-nationalism in any form, since it would have given a foreign minority who had no rights to the country an equal share of Palestine and would have enabled them to pursue their Zionist aim of domination. On the Jewish side, the advocates of bi-nationalism remained a small, ineffective minority, and their ideas were superseded in 1948, when Israel was set up as a Jewish state.

The discourse on this theme then went into abeyance, but it has now resurfaced. Modern day, left-wing Zionists such as Meron Benvenisti, the ex-Deputy Mayor of Jerusalem, and the Israeli journalist Haim Baram, are today concerned with bi-nationalism once again. They point to the fact that separation, given the present pattern of Jewish settlement and contiguity of the two peoples in the Palestinian territories, is not realistic. And it is also not ethically acceptable, because any form of Palestinian self-rule or state in the present imbalance of power between the two sides will lead to nothing less than a collection of bantustans.

In a bi-national state, Jews and Palestinians would coexist separately in a federal arrangement. Each community would run its own affairs autonomously and be guaranteed the legal right to use its own language, religion and traditions. Both would participate in government in a single parliament which would be concerned with matters of supra-communal importance, defence, resources, the economy, and so on. Such a state would form the homeland of both communities and could be modelled on the cantonal structure of Switzerland or the Belgian arrangement between Flemings and Walloons, with two regional and one central government.[16]

The democratic secular state, on the other hand, envisions a one-man, one-vote polity without reference to ethnicity or creed. It would aim to create an equitable pluralist society on the western democratic model and is opposed to an arrangement of separate communities. This idea has far fewer adherents and these, outside the tiny ranks of anti-Zionist Jews, are mostly Palestinian. But irrespective of which system is chosen, the one-state solution is unlikely to find acceptance amongst the mass of Palestinians or Israelis. And, for bi-nationalism to be equitable and not just a rehash of the present formula of Israeli hegemony, critics have stressed the need to include the right of return for Palestinian refugees to the state and for restitution of the land and resources which were stolen from them.[17]

Of course, this discussion is somewhat academic in the light of current Israeli public opinion, where bi-nationalism in any form attracts only minimal support. The secular state idea can be expected to fare even worse, for it would effectively spell the end of Zionism and force Israelis to share equitably with non-Jews the land they view as exclusively Jewish. It is scarcely more desirable for the Palestinians, for whom it means the end of the dream of a sovereign Palestinian state which had become familiar and seemed – until recently – so attainable. The prospect of life with the enemy, after decades of hatred, would seem highly unpalatable, and with the obstruction over the peace process, the closures and economic hardship, the mood in the occupied territories has reached a point of desperation. The Palestinians aim fervently for an end to the occupation, not a new relationship with the Israelis.

Yet, the one-state solution is the only feasible option which could not only repatriate all the refugees, but also offer the "just and comprehensive solution" which has become such a cliché in the peace discourse. Ironically enough, it is the Israeli government's annexation policies in the occupied territories which have destroyed the two-state option. In fragmenting the West Bank so effectively, they have ensured that no separate state can exist there and thus opened the door to the one-state alternative. As a result, the option of a Palestinian state is no longer feasible. Nor, from a Palestinian viewpoint, is it even desirable. A two-state solution, had it ever happened, would have been unstable and ultimately unacceptable to the Palestinians for the following reasons: it would have given them at best a truncated entity, certainly demilitarised and economically dependent, on a fifth of their original homeland – even were they offered the whole of the West Bank, Gaza and East Jerusalem, these would form only 23 per cent of Mandate Palestine; and it would have been unable to absorb the four million displaced Palestinians and would end any hope of their right to return to their homes.

The Palestinian sense of injustice – which derives fundamentally from the loss of their homeland and the denial of their right to return – will not be redressed by an unequal arrangement of two states. And if the injustice is left unresolved, it will remain a source of instability and a cause of "terrorism" in the region. As Meron Benvenisti recently put it, in the Hebrew press: "Separation can't solve a thing . . . because even if Arafat accepts it today because of his inferior power, it provides a basis which future generations of Palestinians will rise against. Such asymmetry is bound to explode."

No one denies that there will be massive obstacles in the way of implementing a one-state solution in Israel/Palestine. The past cannot be reversed, but a solution, even at this late stage, which permits the equitable sharing of the whole land between the two peoples and repatriates the refugees will help lay the foundations for a stable future. A single homeland to include both peoples will not be easy to achieve and may indeed seem utopian now, but anything less cannot fully address the fundamental issue of the displaced Palestinians which lies at the heart of the conflict.

NOTES

1 Institute for Palestine Studies, *The Palestinian–Israeli Peace Agreement* (Washington DC: IPS, 1994), pp. 117 ff.
2 *Haaretz*, 9 November 1997.
3 Orlit Azulay-Katz, "The Palestinian State: Everyone is for it Except Barak", *Yediot Ahoronot*, 27 December 1996.
4 Ibid.
5 Quoted in *The New York Times*, 22 October 1989.
6 Sara Roy, *The Gaza Strip: The Political Economy of De-Development* (Washington DC: Institute for Palestine Studies, 1995).
7 *Haaretz*, 29 May 1997.
8 Hagi Hoberman, *Hatsofeh*, 4 December 1997.
9 Nahum Barnea, *Yediot Ahoronot*, 2 February 1997.
10 Jeff Halper, "Resolving the Conflict: The Nation-State and Nation in Israel/Palestine", *Palestine–Israel Journal*, 4, 1997, p. 71.
11 Aryeh Yodafat and Yuval Arnon-Channa, *PLO Strategy and Tactics* (London: Croom Helm, 1981), pp. 55–7.
12 David Hirst, *The Gun and the Olive Branch* (London: Faber and Faber, 1977), p. 292.
13 See for instance, Yair Sheleg, *Kol Ha'ir*, 31 January 1997.
14 Susan Lee Hattis, *The Binational Idea in Palestine during Mandate Times* (Haifa: Shikmona Publishing Co., 1970), p. 38 ff.
15 For example, Ahmad al-Khalidi and Musa Alami.
16 Jenab Tutunji, Kamal Khalidi, "A Binational State in Palestine: The Rational and Moral Choice", *International Affairs*, 73, 1997, pp. 31–59.
17 Tikva Honig-Parnass, "Binationalism versus the Secular Democratic State", *News From Within*, vol. 3, March 1997, pp. 26–9.

Select Bibliography

Abu-Lughod, Janet, "The Demographic Transformation of Palestine" in Ibrahim Abu-Lughod (ed.), *Transformation of Palestine* (Evanston, Ill.: Northwestern University Press, 1971), pp. 139–63.

Abu-Sitta, S. H., "The Right of Return, Sacred, Legal and Possible" [in Arabic], *Al-Mustaqbal al-Arabi*, Beirut, vol. 9, no. 208, June 1996, pp. 4–38.

Aharoni, Yair, *The Israeli Economy: Dreams and Realities* (London: Routledge, 1991).

Arzt, Donna E., *Refugees into Citizens: Palestinians and the End of the Arab-Israeli Conflict* (New York: The Council on Foreign Relations, 1997).

Berry, J., "Acculturation and Psychological Adaptation: A Conceptual Overview" in J. C. Berry and R. C. Annis (eds.), *Ethnic Psychology: Research and Practice with Immigrants, Refugees, Native Peoples, Ethnic Groups and Sojourners*, Selected Papers from a North American Regional Conference of the International Association for Cross-Cultural Psychology held in Kingston, Canada, 16–21 August 1987 (Amsterdam: Swets and Zeitlinger, 1988).

Dabbagh, T. and A. B. Faraj, "The Importance of Developing Desalination Technology and its Impact on Water Scarcity in the Arab World" [in Arabic], The Second Seminar on Water Resources and Uses in the Arab World (The Arab Fund for Economic and Social Development, Kuwait, 8–10 March 1997).

Davis, Uri, Antonia Max, John Richardson, "Israel's Water Policy", *Journal of Palestine Studies*, vol. 9, no. 2, 1980.

Efrat, Elisha, *Geography and Politics in Israel since 1967* (London: Frank Cass, 1988).

Eisa, Naguib (ed.), "Water Problems in the Middle East" [in Arabic], *Strategic Studies, Research and Documentation Centre*, Beirut, vol. 1, 1994.

Elmadad, Khadija, "Appropriate Solutions for the Palestinian Refugees", Paper presented to the IGCC Conference on "Promoting Regional Cooperation in the Middle East", Vouliagmeni (Greece), November 1994 (via IGCC). (Internet on gopher://gopher-igcc.ucsd.edu: 70/OF-1%3A78291%3AElmadad-Refugees).

Elmusa, Sharif S., "Dividing the Common Palestinian–Israeli Waters", *Journal of Palestine Studies*, vol. XXII, no. 3, Spring 1993.

Falah, Ghazi, "The 1948 Israeli–Palestinian War and its Aftermath: The Transformation and De-Signification of Palestine's Cultural Landscape", *Annals of the Association of American Geographers*, 86(2), 1996, pp. 256–85.

Finkelstein, Norman G., *Image and Reality of the Israeli–Palestinian Conflict* (London: Verso, 1995).

Flapan, Simha, *The Birth of Israel: Myths and Realities* (London: Croom Helm, 1987).

Giant, J., "A Proposal for a Permanent Settlement Plan for the Palestinian Refugees", Paper presented to the IGCC Conference on "Promoting Regional Cooperation in the Middle East", Vouliagmeni (Greece), November 1994 (via IGCC). (Internet on gopher://gopher-igcc.ucsd.edu:70/OF-1%3A78291%3AGiant-Refugees).

Hadawi, Sami, *Palestinian Rights and Losses in 1948* (London: Saqi Books, 1988).

Hathaway, J., *The Law of Refugee Status* (Toronto: Butterworth, 1991).

Heller, Mark A., *A Palestinian State: The Implications for Israel* (Cambridge, Mass.: Harvard University Press, 1983).

Hillel, Daniel, *Rivers of Eden: The Struggle for Water and the Quest for Peace in the Middle East* (Oxford University Press, 1994).

Jackson, I. C., "The 1951 Convention relating to the Status of Refugees", *International Journal of Refugee Law*, vol. 3, no. 3, 1991.

Kahhala, Subhi, *Water Problems in Israel and their Impact on the Arab–Israel Conflict* [in Arabic], Paper no. 9 (Beirut: Institute of Palestine Studies, 1980).

Khalidi, W., "Plan Dalet: Master Plan for the Conquest of Palestine", *Journal of Palestine Studies*, vol. 18, no. 1, Autumn 1988, pp. 4–20.

—*From Haven to Conquest* (Washington DC: Institute of Palestine Studies, reprint 1987).

—*All that Remains: the Palestinian Villages Occupied and Depopulated by Israel in 1948* (Washington DC: Institute for Palestine Studies, 1992).

Al-Khazen, F., "Palestinian Settlement in Lebanon: A Recipe for Conflict", *Journal of Refugee Studies*, vol. 10, no. 3 (1997).

Kuhlman, T., *Asylum or Aid? The Economic Integration of Ethiopian and Eritrean Refugees in the Sudan* (Leiden: African Studies Centre, 1994).

League of Arab States, Resolution 5093, 1991.

Lehn, Walter and Uri Davis, *The Jewish National Fund* (London: Kegan Paul International, 1988).

Locke, R. and A. Stewart, *Bantustan Gaza* (London: CAABU/Zed Press, 1985).

Lowi, Miriam R., *Water and Power: The Politics of a Scarce Resource in the Jordan River Basin* (Cambridge University Press, 1993).

Masalha, Nur, *Expulsion of the Palestinians: The Concept of Transfer in Zionist Political Thought, 1882–1948* (Washington DC: Institute of Palestine Studies, 1992).

—*A Land Without a People: Israel, Transfer and the Palestinians* (London: Faber and Faber, 1997).

Masri, George, *Israeli Interests in Arab Waters* [translated into Arabic], (Paris: Centre d'Etudes Euro-Arabe, 1996).

Morris, Benny, *The Birth of the Palestinian Refugee Problem 1947–1949* (Cambridge: Cambridge University Press, 1987).

—*1948 and After: Israel and the Palestinians* (Oxford: Clarendon Press, 1990).

Al-Natour, S., "The Legal Status of Palestinian Refugees in Lebanon", *Journal of Refugee Studies*, vol. 10, no. 3 (1997).

Palumbo, Michael, *The Palestinian Catastrophe* (London: Quartet Books, 1987).

Pappe, Ilan, *The Making of the Arab–Israeli Conflict, 1947–1951* (London and New York: I. B. Tauris, 1992).

Peretz, Don, *Palestinians, Refugees and the Middle East Peace Process* (Washington DC: US Institute of Peace Press, 1993).

Perron, Marc, *The Refugee Working Group: One Year Later*. Notes for Remarks by Marc Perron, Assistant Deputy Minister (Africa & Middle East) Department of Foreign Affairs and International Trade to the Institute for Social and Economic Policy in the Middle

East, John F. Kennedy School of Government, Harvard University, 24 February 1995. (Internet address: http://www.arts.mcgill.ca/MEPP/PRRN/docs/peronharvard95.html).

Rogers, Peter and Peter Lydon (eds.), *Water in the Arab World: Perspectives and Prognoses* (Boston, Mass.: Harvard University Press, 1994).

Sanbar, Elias, Interview in *Al-Hayat*, Daily, London, 18 and 19 December 1996, p. 18.

Schiff, B., *Refugees unto the Third Generation: UN Aid to the Palestinians* (New York: Syracuse University Press, 1995).

Segev, Tom, *The First Israelis – 1949* [Arabic trans.], (Washington DC: Institute for Palestine Studies, 1986).

Sofer, Arnon, "Geography and Demography in Eretz-Israel 2000" [Arabic trans.], *Journal of Palestine Studies*, no. 1, Winter 1990, pp. 117–35.

Takkenberg, L., "The Protection of Palestinian Refugees", *International Journal of Refugee Law*, vol. 3, no. 3, 1991.

Tamari, Salim, *Return, Settlement, Repatriation: The Future of Palestinian Refugees in the Peace Negotiations Final Status Strategic Studies* (Institute for Palestine Studies February 1996, Section VIII. (Internet on http://www.arts.mcgill.ca/MEPP/PRRN/PAPERS/TAMARI2.HTML.).

Thicknesse, Sybilla Gratiana, *Arab Refugees: A Survey of Resettlement Possibilities* (London and New York: Royal Institute of International Affairs, 1949), vol. viii, p. 68.

United Nations, General Assembly Official Record 1948 3rd Session Part 1, 1st Committee, 201st Meeting, 1948.

UN Report, *Water Resources of the Occupied Palestinian Territory*, UNA/AC.183 (02) W21 (New York: United Nations, 1992).

Zureik, Elia, *Palestinian Refugees and the Peace Process* (Washington DC: Institute for Palestine Studies, 1996).

Index

A

'Abd al-Qadir al-Husayni   43
Abkhazia (in former Soviet Georgia)
    152, 161
Abu Gosh   42
Abu Hassan   91
Abu Lughod, Janet   224
Abu Mazen (Mahmoud Abbas)   247–8
Abu-Sitta, Salman, as contributor
    171–92
Acre   185, 209
Adams, Michael   99
Afghan refugees   29
African National Congress (ANC)   12
agriculture   246
    refugees' right of return and   186–7
Albak, Shmuel   95
Albright, Madeleine   223
Allon, Yigal   76, 100
Alterman, Natan   70, 71
Amman   18
'Aqbat Jabir camp   94–6
Arab Higher Committee   45
Arab League (League of Arab States)   13,
    39, 44, 200, 213
Arafat, Yasser   xiv, xvi, 55, 58, 251
Armenians, Turkish compensation to
    206–7
Arzt, Donna E.   180
Ashdod   183

atrocities   49, 51–2, 97, 99, 128, 173
Avi-Yonah, Michael   83
Avidan, Meir   76, 77
'Ayn Sultan camp   94–6
Azzam Pasha   44

B

Balad al-Shaykh   42
Balfour Declaration   xv, 66, 231
Barak, Judge   113
Barakat, Halim   63, 96
Baram, Haim   250
Barclays Bank   203
Bayt Awa   89, 90
Bayt Marsam   89, 90
Bayt Nuba   87, 88, 89, 97
Beer Sheba   181, 183
Begin, Menahem   77
Beilin, Yossi   248
Beilin–Abu Mazen plan   247–8
Beirut   19
Beit-Hallahmi, Benjamin   89
Ben-Amotz, Dan   66
Ben-Gurion, David   39, 43, 44, 50, 53,
    59, 71, 72, 82, 101, 102
Ben-Moshe, Eytan   82
Benvenisti, Meron   80–1, 246, 250, 251
Benziman, Uzi   81, 82, 84, 85
Bernadotte, Count Folke   133, 140, 153
bi-nationalism solution   249–52

Bosnia   124, 142, 152, 160, 223
Bristol Report   28
Brit Shalom   249
Britain *see* United Kingdom
B'Tselem   115
Buber, Martin   59, 249
Bulgaria   209
Bureir   176
al-Burj   89, 90

C
Cairo Interim Agreement   3
Canada Park   89
Carmel, Moshe   77
Casablanca Protocol (1965)   13, 14
Centre of Islamic and Middle Eastern
    Law   1
Childers, Erskine   44, 45, 224
China   xiv, 158
Clinton, Bill   xv, xvi
compensation and reparations   197–217
    Palestinians   200–17, 234–5
        assessment of losses   210–14
        legal basis for   206–10
    for victims of Holocaust   197–200,
        206, 226
Conciliation Commission in Palestine
    (PCC)   10, 13, 30, 135, 140, 153,
    164, 191, 202, 203, 211, 214–15, 228
conflicts *see* wars and conflicts
Continuing Committee   3
Cook, Robin   198
Council of Europe   155
Council on Foreign Relations   222
Crimean Tatars   155, 160
Croatia   152, 160, 161
Curzon, Lord   xv
Cyprus   152

D
Damascus   21
Danin, Ezra   53, 79
Davar (newspaper)   69, 71, 72, 76, 78,
    79, 81
Davidi, Aharon   70
Dawamiyya   52, 173
Dayan, Moshe   xii, 70, 75–6, 77, 81, 82,
    84, 90, 92, 98, 100, 101, 102, 114

Deir Qaddis   100
Deir Yassin   44, 128, 173, 178
diaspora *see* Palestinian exodus
Dimona   183
Dodd, Peter   63, 96
domino effect theory   39, 43
Dulles, John Foster   202

E
Eban, Abba   76
Economic Survey Mission   30
economy of Palestinian areas   xiii, 246–7
Ein el-Tal camp   21
Eisenhower, Dwight   xv
Eitan, Raphael   70
Elat   183
Emmaus (Imwas)   87, 89, 97, 179
Eshkol, Levi   84
Ethridge, Mark   165–6
European Union   28, 56, 124
exodus *see* Palestinian exodus

F
family unification   118-19
Fanon, Franz   55
Faraa camp   27
Fatah   55
Finkelstein, Norman   47, 224, 225
Flapan, Simha   224

G
Gaza   183
    agriculture in   186, 246
    economic backwardness of   xiii, 246,
        247
    occupation of   56
    Palestinians exiled from   xiii, 18, 63,
        91, 97, 98–9, 100
    Palestinians in   14–15, 24–7
Gazit, Shlomo   180, 200, 216
Geneva Conventions   xix, 11, 118,
    129–32, 141, 142
Germany, compensation for victims
    of Holocaust   198–200, 206, 226
Ghabisiya   138–9
Ginat, J.   33–4
Golan, Arnon   40
Golan Heights, refugees from   96, 97

Goldstein, Dov 70
Goren, Shlomo 86
Guardian, The 95, 99
Guardian Weekly 76
Guatemala 157
guerrilla warfare and terrorism 56
Gulf War xiv, 58, 116, 137
Gush Etzion 40

H
Ha'am, Ahad xii
Haaretz (newspaper) 71, 73, 81, 86, 98, 205
Habla 90
Hadawi, Sami 212, 213
Hagana movement 41, 72
Haifa 40, 43, 48, 185
Hajdenberg, Henri 198
Hallaj, Mohammed 28
Hama 21
Hamahteret Hayehudit 86–7
HaMoked 115
Ha'olam Hazeh (magazine) 99
Har Homa 246
Har-Tzion, Meir 69–70
Harris, William 63, 96–7
Hazaz, Haim 70, 71–2
Hebron 97, 100, 206, 244–5, 247
Heller, Mark 174
Henaikin camp 16
Hertzog, Haim 76, 81, 82, 91–3, 95
Hertzog, Yaacov 76
Herut party (later Likud) 64
Herzl, Theodor 49, 65
Hitler, Adolf xiii
Holocaust 49, 227
compensation for victims 197–200, 206, 226
Homs 21
Hungary 207
Hussein, King of Jordan 162
Hussein, Saddam xiv

I
Ikrit 139
'Ilabun 51
Imwas (Emmaus) 87, 89, 97, 179
India 207, 208

Indyk, Martin xvi
International Campaign for Jerusalem (ICJ) 1
International Convention on the Elimination of All Forms of Racial Discrimination 136, 156
International Covenant on Civil and Political Rights 113–14, 128, 136, 156
Intifada 57, 205
Iraq 137
Jews from 202, 203
Ireland 223
Israel
agriculture in 186–7, 246
citizenship and residency rights in
Jews 127–8, 132, 155–6
Palestinians 112–14, 116, 127, 136–9
compensation for victims of Holocaust and 199–200
courts in 137–9
education in 66
foundation of xi, 55, 172, 225–6
historical debate in 37–59
land policies xiii, xvi, 33, 52, 64, 202, 204, 208–9
Palestinian exodus from *see* Palestinian exodus
politics of 38, 64
population in 181–5
treaties with Jordan 16
United States of America and
monetary subsidies xiii, xvi, 202
partition of 1948 44–5, 48, 56
political links xv–xvi
support in UN for 137, 157, 228
water resources 187–9
see also wars and conflicts; Zionism
Israeli Defence Forces (IDF) 39–40
activities against Palestinians after 1967 war 80–94

J
Jabal Abu Ghoneim 246
Jabaliya camp 183
Jaffa 40, 48
Jenin 98

Jerash camp   18
Jericho   247
    refugee camps   94–6
Jerusalem   40, 68, 246
    clearing of former Jewish quarter
        85–6
    destruction of al-Magharbeh quarter
        80–5, 97
    holy places   112
        Muslim   86–7
        Wailing Wall   81, 82, 83
    Israeli annexation of   112
    Palestinians   247, 248
        expulsions   xvi, xix, 80–6, 97,
            111–20, 136–7
        legal status of   111–14
        status of city   111, 116–19
"Jerusalem of Gold" (song)   68, 69
Jewish Agency   48, 49, 50, 51
Jiftlik   89, 90
Jordan   58, 215
    Palestinians in   xiii, 13, 16–18, 162,
        163, 236–7

K

Karmi, Ghada, as contributor   197–217,
    243–52
Karsh, Ephraim   39, 41
Katznelson, Berl   71, 79
Kawkab al-Hawa   69
Kenan, Amos   88
Kfar Qassim   xiii
Khalaf, Issa   224
Khalidi, Ahmed   180
Khalidi, Rashid   xiv, xvi
    as contributor   221–39
Khalidi, Walid   47–9, 52, 224
al-Khatib, Anwar   92, 93
kibbutzim   186, 191
Kissinger, Henry   xvi
Kol Ha'ir (newspaper)   94
Kollek, Teddy   82, 83, 85
Korea   226
Kubursi, Atif   212, 213–14, 234

L

Labour Party (Israel)   38, 56, 64, 205
Lahat, Shlomo   81, 82, 83, 84, 85, 92, 95

Lajnat al-Tawjih   56
Latakia camp   21
Latrun area   87–9, 97, 98
League of Arab States (Arab League)   13,
    39, 44, 200, 213
League of Nations, British Mandate
    in Palestine   xv, 53, 230–1
Lebanon
    civil war in   18
    Israel's destabilisation of   58
    Palestinians in   8, 12, 13, 14, 18–21,
        31, 236, 237–8
Lifschitz, Zalman   79
Likud Party (Israel)   38, 64, 205
Livneh, Eli'ezer   72–5
London, Treaty of (1839)   206
Lorch, Netanel   39–40
Luxembourg Agreement   199
Lydda   100

M

Maariv (newspaper)   70, 71, 72
Madaba camp   16
Madrid peace process   56, 57, 67, 116,
    226
al-Magharbeh quarter, destruction of
    80–5, 97
Magnes, Judah   249
al-Ma'in   177
Majdal-Ashqelon   183
al-Malik al-Afdal   81
Mao Tse-tung   55
Mapai party   71, 72
Marie-Thérèse, Sister   85, 89, 90, 93
Marka camp   18
Marxism   46
Masalha, Nur   xii, 46, 48, 49–50, 52, 174,
    224
    as contributor   63–102
massacres and atrocities   49, 51–2, 97, 99,
    128, 173
Meir, Golda   171
Melman, Yossi   76, 81
Mikunis, Shmuel   97–8
Milstein, Uri   95
Mishmar Ha-Yarden   40
Morris, Benny   45-6, 47, 49, 52, 53, 100,
    224, 225, 228

Mossad   76
Mossenson, Yigal   70
Mozambique   29
Mufti of Jerusalem   39, 44
Multilateral Working Group on Refugees
    27–8

N
Nablus   247
Namibia   152
Narkiss, Uzi   77, 81, 82, 83, 84, 86, 87,
    89, 90, 92–3, 95, 99
Nazareth   185
Negev desert   186
Netanyahu, Binyamin   xiv, xvi, 67, 247,
    248
New York Times   90, 98
Nu'aymah camp   94–6

O
Observer, The   98–9
L'Orient   90
Oslo Accords/agreement   xv, xx, 1, 3, 14,
    57, 142–5, 159, 204, 215, 231–2, 238,
    243–5
Ottoman Bank   203
Oz, Amos   67–9, 75

P
Pa'il, Meir   87, 95
Pakistan   29, 207, 208
Palestine
    British Mandate   xv, 53, 230–1
    economy of Palestinian areas   xiii,
        246–7
    exodus from *see* Palestinian exodus
    partition of (1947)   10, 41, 44-5, 51,
        53, 56, 127, 231
    re-formation of   235–6, 243–52
Palestine Conciliation Commission (PCC)
    10, 13, 30, 135, 140, 153, 164, 191,
    202, 203, 211, 214–15, 228
Palestine Liberation Organisation (PLO)
    14, 38, 119
    activities of   56, 57
    Charter of   52, 54, 55
    diplomacy   56, 57–8, 231
    Intifada   57, 205

Palestine National Authority (PNA)
    119–20, 145, 183, 203, 215, 236
Palestine National Council (PNC)
    56–7, 162, 245, 249
Palestinian exodus   xi–xvii, xix–xxi, 1–4
    compensation and reparations for
        200–17, 234–5
        assessment of losses   210–14
        legal basis for   206–10
    diversity within Palestinian Diaspora
        15–27
    expulsions from Jerusalem   xvi, xix,
        80–6, 97, 111–20, 136–7
    family unification   118–19
    from Gaza   xiii, 18, 63, 91, 97, 98–9,
        100
    in Gaza   14–15, 24–7
    history and historiography of   37–59
    host countries
        insecurity of status in   13–15
        integration in (*tawteen*)   13–14, 30–4
    in Jordan   xiii, 13, 16–18, 162, 163,
        236–7
    in Lebanon   8, 12, 13, 14, 18–21, 31,
        236, 237–8
    legal, geographical and statistical aspects
        7–34
    massacres and atrocities   49, 51–2, 97,
        99, 128, 173
    Palestinian elite and   43, 50–1, 53
    peace process and   27–30
    as refugees   8–15, 27–30
        from 1948 conflict   37–59, 132–5,
            151, 153, 172–4, 224, 225, 232
        from 1967 conflict   63–102, 136
        from Jerusalem   xvi, xix, 80–6, 97,
            111–20, 136–7
        historiographic debate on   37–59
    right of return   132–45, 151, 153,
        155–60, 162–3, 231–2, 233–4
        agriculture and   186–7
        change of sovereignty and   154–6
        changed character of home area and
            159–61
        duration of   161–3
        feasibility of   171–92
        Geneva Conventions and   129–32,
            141, 142

individual's   156–9
Israeli courts and   137–9
Oslo agreement and   142–5, 159
plan for   180–92
practicalities   190–1
remedies   137–45
resettlement as alternative to
    163–4, 174, 180, 202
UN High Commissioner for Refugees
    and   139–40
United Nations and   124, 133–7,
    139–42, 152–9, 163–6
Universal Declaration of Human
    Rights and   125–9, 201
    water resources and   187–9
solutions of problem of   221–39,
    243–52
in West Bank   8, 14–15, 21, 23–4
from West Bank   63, 87–102
Palestinian Legislative Council   116–17
Palestinian Resistance Movement   19
Palumbo, Michael   224
Pan-Africanist Congress (PAC)   12
Pappe, Ilan   xi, xiv, 224
    as contributor   37–59
Peace Now movement   38
Peres, Shimon   205
Peretz, Don   174
Plan D   41–2, 47–50, 53
Popular Democratic Front for the Liberation
    of Palestine (PDFLP)   249
property rights   190–1
Puerto Rico   156

Q
Qalqilyah   90, 98
Al-Qasem, Anis, as contributor   123–45
Qibya   97
Qiryat Gat   183
Quigley, John, as contributor   151–66

R
Rabin, Yitzhak   xiii, 42, 205
Ramleh   100, 175
Raviv, Dan   76, 81
Reddaway, John   90
refugees
    Jewish   40, 41

Palestinian people see Palestinian exodus
refugee documentation (RD)   14
see also right of return
Relief and Works Agency for Palestinian
    Refugees (UNRWA)   9–12, 16,
    19, 21, 27, 31, 74, 137, 140, 191, 202
reparations see compensation and
    reparations
right of return   123–45, 151–66, 231–2,
    233–4
agriculture and   186–7
change of sovereignty and   154–6
changed character of home area
    and   159–61
duration of   161–3
feasibility of   171–92
Geneva Conventions and   129–32,
    141, 142
individual's   156–9
Israeli courts and   137–9
Israeli Law of Return   132
Oslo agreement and   142–5, 159
plan for   180–92
practicalities   190–1
remedies   137–45
resettlement as alternative to   163–4,
    174, 180, 202
UN High Commissioner for Refugees
    and   139–40
United Nations and   124, 133–7,
    139–42, 152–9, 163–6
Universal Declaration of Human Rights
    and   125–9, 201
water resources and   187–9
Robinson, Mary   159
Romania   207, 209
Roy, Sara   xiii
Ruppin, Arthur   66, 249
Rwanda   124, 142, 161

S
Sabra camp   19
Sadat, Anwar   xvi
Safad   40, 48
Safsaf   52
Salman, Yaacov   83
Sanbar, Elie   224
Sapir, Pinhas   76, 93

Sa'sa'a   51
Sayegh, Yusef   213
Scharansky, Nathan   89
Scharansky Hope Forest   89
Segev, Tom   224
Sèvres, Treaty of   206–7
Shafa Amr   185, 209
Shafor, Gershon   224
Shaftesbury, Lord   66
Shahak, Israel   xvi
Shaham, Zeev   90
Shamir, Moshe   70
Shamir, Yitzhak   67
Shapira, Anita   224
Shapira, Yaacov Shimshon   82
Sharett, Moshe   49, 50, 180, 201, 228
Sharon, Ariel   58, 70, 245
Sharon, Aryeh   83
Shatila camp   19
Sheikh Radwan housing scheme   33
Shemer, Na'omi   68, 69–70
Shlaim, Avi   224
Sidon   18
Sinai   73
  refugees from   97
Smith, Terence   90
South Africa   xvi, 152, 223, 226
South West Africa People's Organisation
  (SWAPO)   12
Soviet Union   57, 71, 155
  partition of 1948 and   48, 56
Steiner, George   xii
Stern Gang   133
Suknah camp   16
Switzerland, compensation for victims of
  Holocaust   197–8
Syria, Palestinians in   8, 13, 21, 22, 237

T
Tamari, Salim   28–9
Tanai, Dan   83
terrorism   56
Teveth, Shabtai   42–4
Thicknesse, Sybilla Gratiana   174
Tiberias   40, 48, 185
Tibet   12
Times, The   95–6
Tripoli   19

Truman, Harry S.   48, 180
Tsemel, Leah   xii, xvi
  as contributor   111–20
Tubi, Tawfiq   98
Tulkarm   98
Turkey   152, 209
  compensation to Armenians   206–7
Twain, Mark   67
Tyre   18

U
U Thant   158
Ukraine, Crimean Tatars in   155, 160
Unit 101   70
United Kingdom   223
  British Mandate in Palestine   xv, 53,
    230–1
  UN and   157, 158
United Nations   44, 206, 209–10
  Declaration of Human Rights   xix,
    113, 125–9, 156, 201
  Development Programme (UNDP)
    191
  High Commissioner for Refugees
    (UNHCR)   11, 12, 129, 139–40,
    152, 154
  International Convention on the
    Elimination of All Forms of Racial
    Discrimination   136, 156
  International Covenant on Civil and
    Political Rights   113–14, 128, 136,
    156
  Palestine Conciliation Commission
    (PCC)   10, 13, 30, 135, 140, 153,
    164, 191, 202, 203, 211, 214–15, 228
  refugees' right of return and   124,
    133–7, 139–42, 152–9, 163–6
  Relief and Works Agency for Palestinian
    Refugees (UNRWA)   9–12, 16,
    19, 21, 27, 31, 74, 137, 140, 191, 202
  Resolution 181   127, 231
  Resolution 194   xix, 14, 31, 38, 134–5,
    137, 140–1, 145, 153, 157–9, 163–4,
    207, 214, 223, 227–8, 229, 235
  Resolution 237   136
  Resolution 242   141, 164–6, 227, 244
  Resolution 338   244
  Resolution 513   141

Resolution 2452A   136
Resolution 2452B   140–1
right of return and   124, 133–7,
    139–42
Security Council   141–2, 152
UNICEF   18
United States of America
    Bosnia and   124
    citizenship and residency rights   156
    Indians in   xii–xiii
    Israel and
        monetary subsidies   xiii, xvi, 202
        partition of 1948   44–5, 48, 56
        political links   xv–xvi
        support in UN for   137, 157, 228
    Palestinians and   57, 58, 158, 216
    UN Resolutions against Iraq and   137
Universal Declaration of Human Rights
    xix, 113, 125–9, 156, 201
Ussishkin, Menahem   79

V
Vidal, Gore   xv
Vilner, Meir   97–8
Volcani, Yitzhak   79

W
Wailing Wall   81, 82, 83
wars and conflicts
    1948   xi, 8, 39–42, 45, 48–55, 128,
        172–3, 224, 225
    1956   xiii

1967   xiii, xix, 54–5, 56, 59, 63, 80
Gulf War (1991)   xiv, 58, 116, 137
Washington Post, The   76
water resources   187–9
Wavell camp   19
Weighill, Marie-Louise, as contributor
    7–34
Weitz, Yossef   42, 51, 52, 78–80
Weizmann, Chaim   xi, xv, 65–6, 198, 221
West Bank
    economy of   246–7
    exodus from   63, 87–102
    occupation of   56
    Palestinians in   8, 14–15, 21, 23–4
Wilson, Mary   224

Y
Yadjur   42
Yalu   87, 89, 97
Yannai, Yaacov   82, 83
Yarmouk camp   21

Z
Zangwill, Israel   xi–xii, 65
Zionism   xi–xii
    agriculture and   186
    expulsion of Palestinians and   46–50,
        52–3, 54, 64–75, 174
    historiography of   37, 38
Zureik, Elia   180
Zurief   52